Roman Life *was prepared under the supervision of Eleanore H. Cooper, Directing Editor of the Scott-Foresman Latin Program*

ROMAN LIFE

Successor to Private Life of the Romans

MARY JOHNSTON

SCOTT, FORESMAN AND COMPANY

Chicago   Atlanta   Dallas   Palo Alto   Fair Lawn, N.J.

To

H.W.J., E.H.S., H.B.J.

CONTENTS

Terra Mater

Chariot racing

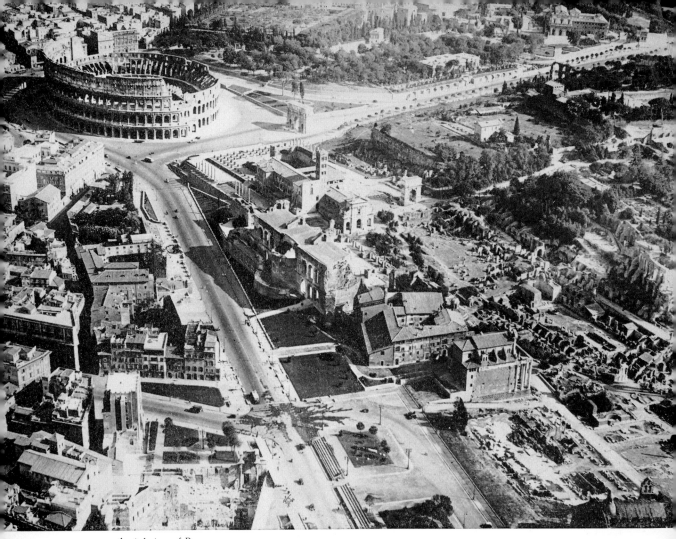

Aerial view of Rome

GIFTS OF
ARCHAEOLOGY

A Roman garden—painting from the Villa of Livia

PURPOSE OF ARCHAEOLOGY

How buildings and whole cities fell into ruin, how some vanished from sight and were rediscovered, is part of history. Archaeology, the study of ancient things, interprets what is found and explains, or even rewrites, history. From the places where the Romans lived, worked, worshiped, and amused themselves—from their burial places, too—from their art, their inscriptions, and their literature, we build up a picture of the Roman way of life, and people the past with living figures—not merely with stately statues.

Archaeology deals with the discovery and interpretation of ancient sites and ancient objects of art or use. These are

Portrait statue of Emperor Trajan

Air view of Roman fields at Zara, Dalmatia

Excavations at Cosa, Italy

sometimes found by accident—remains of Roman London reappeared when sections of the modern city were bombed in the Second World War. Such finds are often made in Rome when space is cleared for a new building. Many edifices in the Roman World—from Asia to Spain, from Britain to Africa—have remained at least partly in sight, but modern methods have made their history and purpose clearer.

REMAINS EVERYWHERE

It is almost impossible to take a casual walk across fields in Italy without finding fragments of brick, terra cotta, and pottery on the surface of the ground. Not only throughout Italy, but everywhere the ancient Romans lived, evidences of their way of life are being uncovered. In parts of France and Britain it is said that anywhere, if one digs deep enough, some fragment of Roman work will inevitably be found. The Near East has yielded wonderful pottery and glass now in museums; the shifting sands of North Africa have uncovered and revealed whole cities of the past. One of the largest Roman amphitheaters that has been found is in the great city—now a waste—of Thugga, North Africa.

The most famous Roman remains in the world are in the ancient cities of Pompeii, Herculaneum, and Ostia. The ruins of Pompeii, buried by the eruption of Vesuvius in A.D. 79, have shown us a middle-class Italian town with paved streets and sidewalks, public buildings, houses whose decorations—and sometimes furnishings—have been preserved, shops with equipment where businesses were carried on.

Herculaneum, buried by the same disaster, is being cleared. A large part of Ostia, seaport of Rome, abandoned for

Air view of the excavated Roman town of Leptis Magna, on the coast of North Africa—with ruins of the bath in the foreground

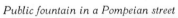

Public fountain in a Pompeian street

A street in Ostia today

Garden of a house in Herculaneum, with modern planting

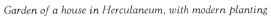

centuries, has been uncovered and reveals houses and apartments, shops and public buildings.

The more common an article is, the less likely it is to be described in literature. In the Latin colony of Cosa, on the sea ninety miles above Rome, American excavators since 1948 have uncovered many humble objects like scale weights, counters for games, *stili* of bone for writing, *fibulae* (safety pins), table and kitchen utensils. In other parts of Italy excavators frequently find ancient bits.

Thus archaeology fills in gaps left in our reading. Histories that were written on the basis of literary evidence are being revised and amplified in the light of the constantly increasing body of this concrete evidence.

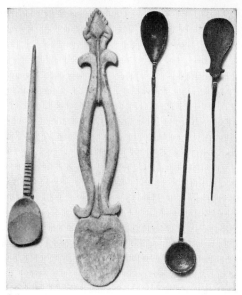

Silver spoons

During excavation in Herculaneum, rails were used to remove cars of debris

Forum of Pompeii, with Vesuvius in the background

Garden in the House of the Vettii

MODERN METHODS

There was a time when excavations were carried on like treasure hunts—chiefly in search of objects of art, and whatever seemed uninteresting was swept aside. Now archaeologists recognize that the commonest things are important, and if the history of the site is to be understood and the stones are to be properly read, the precise level at which an object is found must be recorded.

So in modern scientific archaeology even the smallest handful of earth or ashes is carefully sifted to find and preserve not merely tiny objects, but fragments from which articles may be reconstructed. Whenever possible—if they are not so valuable or so perishable that they must be put in museums for safekeeping—articles are left where they are found.

One of the most useful tools of modern archaeology, developed within the last twenty years, is the air photograph. In a dry season pictures taken of a site from

At Herculaneum every spoonful of earth was sifted before being hauled away in the little cars

In Winchester, England, citizens help uncover a Roman pavement

the air in an oblique light will show crop marks revealing the disturbance of the soil in ancient times for ditches or foundations. Such sites, localized on a map, can save much hit-or-miss digging. Air photography, especially during and since the Second World War, has revealed much about Roman town-planning and has shown outlines of fields and roadways that are now invisible at the ground level.

DIFFERENT EXCAVATIONS

Conditions of excavation vary greatly. Pompeii is easily cleared of the volcanic pumice stone and ash which Vesuvius showered over the city. The work at Herculaneum—buried at the same time— is slow and difficult. Here stone and ashes, mixed with water, flowed over everything and hardened into stone. When Ostia was

Air view of Pompeii

Ruins of Timgad, Africa

abandoned, silt from the Tiber and sand from the seashore gradually covered streets and buildings. Excavation here is easy—as it is in Roman cities in Africa, where the sands of the desert blew over abandoned settlements.

SOURCES OF INFORMATION

Our sources of information on the life of the Romans, then, are three: their literature, so far as it has survived; inscriptions great and small, formal or informal; material objects built, made, or used by the Romans for any purpose—from a great building or highway to kitchen

A triumph, from Leptis Magna

A mosaic being restored in England after the bombardment of World War II

Roman Forum from the west

In this model of ancient Rome. the Tiber is on the right; the Colosseum, at upper left; the Capitolium, left of center; the Circus Maximus, upper right; the Theater of Pompey, lower left; above it, the Circus Flaminius; the Theater of Marcellus near the Tiber

utensils or bits of jewelry. In painting, mosaic, or sculpture, Roman art sometimes gives us representations of objects in actual use and their users that help our understanding of Roman ways of living. All that is found from any source is carefully studied and compared, and from this information, there is built up a picture of the Romans—rich and poor— and the way they lived.

In this famous cameo, the Gemma Augustea, the feet of Augustus and Roma rest on weapons of conquered peoples, while Orbis Romana, symbol of civilization, crowns the emperor with laurel, and Oceanus and Terra Mater look on. At the left, behind Tiberius as he steps from his chariot, is Victoria; and Germanicus, his aide, is beside him. In the lower panel are Roman soldiers and prisoners

DAYS IN
ANCIENT ROME

CITY STREETS

Two thousand years ago Rome was a great and crowded city. It was busy and noisy, smoky and dusty. There were beautiful temples and public buildings. The rich had begun to build large and handsome residences. There were many apartment buildings and shabby tenements. Narrow streets mounted the seven hills and wound between them.

Through the streets came dignified senators and other prosperous Romans. Some walked, some were carried in litters—covered and curtained couches on poles borne by sturdy slaves. Each Roman gentleman was attended by servants and followed by groups of poor citizens, who were eager to be seen with a great man.

Romans still told proudly of early days, when great men had lived as simply as poor ones; but the traditional simple way of life for all alike was gone forever. The rich were living richly and the poor were living poorly. But even for the poor, life in the great city was not drab. There was always something to see, to tell, and to hear. There were the great State festivals and processions, shows in the theater, races, and fights in the arena—spectacles that all might enjoy.

HOURS OF THE DAY

The Roman day was divided into twelve hours; the hours of night were not counted. Since each hour was one-twelfth of the time between sunrise and sunset, its length varied with the season of the year. On March 20 and September 23, when darkness and light were equal, Roman hours were equivalent to ours. On December 22 the day was less than nine of our hours long, and each hour not quite forty-five minutes; while on June 21 a Roman day

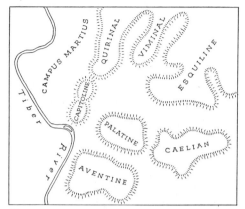

The seven hills of Rome

Arch of Titus

was over fifteen hours long, and each hour about seventy-five minutes. For ordinary purposes we may use an old rhyme.

> The English hour you may fix.
> If to the Latin you add six.

When a Latin hour is above six, it is more convenient to subtract six than to add.

COSTUME

A citizen of Rome was known at once by the heavily draped white woolen toga which only a Roman citizen might wear. For convenience and economy, workmen wore belted tunics of dark wool. Soldiers strode along in shining armor and heavy hobnailed boots. Varied costumes showed people from all the countries around the Mediterranean Sea. Sometimes a toga covered a naturalized citizen of foreign birth or descent—easily distinguished from the stiff-backed Romans, who resented these newcomers, especially if they were of Greek or Oriental origin. Many languages were heard on the streets, as well as every shade of Latin—the cultured language of the educated gentleman—the accents of different provinces, the careless speech of the ignorant.

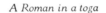

Corinthian columns in the Forum of Julius Caesar

A Roman in a toga

The Curia, or Senate-House, today

SHOPS

On the ground floor of many buildings small shops lined the streets. These were wide open above the counters during the business day, but closed at night and during the daily siesta. Wares from all the known world were shown in Rome, some cheap, some rare and expensive.

Many articles were made by a craftsman in a little shop where he worked and sold his goods, and where sometimes he lived. Markets supplied foods, which were often brought into the city before daylight in farm carts—as they still are in Italy. Some shops served hot food to be eaten where the customer stood or to be carried home. People wandered along the shopping streets, inspecting or buying.

AQUEDUCTS

Great aqueducts brought water from the mountains. There were many fountains, large or small, along the streets, from which the poor carried water for household use. Women filled their jars, set them on their heads and stepped gracefully away—as one sometimes sees them still doing in Italian towns. Rich men had water piped into their houses.

GOVERNMENT

Down in the Forum from early morning until noon, courts were in session and the Senate met. Court decisions and votes in the Senate often affected the lives of people far away—and in time perhaps even our own history. Unless the press of business was so heavy that afternoon sessions were necessary, courts and Senate adjourned for lunch, which was usually followed by rest, exercise, and bath.

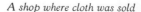
A shop where cloth was sold

EARLY RISING

But before business in the Forum began, the city was awake. Even before daylight, boys were on their way to school, often escorted by elderly slaves. Outside the houses of the rich and powerful, clients were waiting for the doors to open. A gentleman of the upper class—the man of whom we read most often in Roman literature—began his day before sunrise. After a simple breakfast he worked at home on his private affairs, looking over accounts, consulting with his managers, giving directions, and dictating letters to a secretary.

Cicero and Pliny found these early hours best for their literary work. Horace tells of lawyers giving free advice at three in the morning. When his private business was finished, the master of the house took his place in the *atrium*—the great reception room of the house—and the doors were opened for *salutatio* (the calling hour). Waiting clients were admitted and paid their respects, or asked for the help and advice that it was the master's duty to give.

All this business of the early morning might be set aside if the gentleman was invited to a wedding, to the naming of a child, or to the coming of age of a friend's son. Such functions took place early in the day. But in any case the Roman later went down to the Forum. Whether he walked or was carried in a litter, he was attended by his clients. At his elbow was his *nomenclator* (slave who whispered the names of those who spoke to him), since politeness required a person of lower rank to speak first, without waiting for recognition.

This mosaic floor shows the labors of Hercules

In this decoration above the right entrance of the Arch of Constantine, the medallions show the emperor hunting and offering sacrifice, while the panel portrays a court

BUSINESS

Business in the courts and the Senate began about the third hour of the day—about nine o'clock, as we reckon time—and might go on until the ninth or tenth hour.

Except on extraordinary occasions, a Roman citizen's morning business was over by eleven, the usual time for lunch. Then came the midday rest, which lasted for an hour or more, and was so general that streets were not merely quiet but as deserted as at midnight. One Roman writer chose this period as the proper time for a ghost story.

If necessary, business was taken up again in the afternoon, and might continue until three or four o'clock. Since there was no adequate lighting in public places, sessions of the Senate had to be concluded before dark.

ENTERTAINMENTS

On public holidays—as many as 132 days a year in the time of Augustus—there were no sessions of the court nor meetings of the Senate. Time usually given to business might be spent at the theater, the circus, or the games. Some Romans of the upper classes avoided these shows unless they were officially connected with them, and used the time to get away to their country places.

RELAXATION

On ordinary days in the city, after the siesta, a Roman was ready for his daily visit to one of the public bathing establishments, or for exercise on the Campus Martius and a swim in the Tiber. In the great public baths there was space to rest, or to stroll about, meeting friends, hearing the news, consulting business associates, or talking over any of the matters that men now discuss at their clubs.

Augustus

Token entitling the holder to a loaf of bread

After this, in the middle of the afternoon, came dinner at home or at the house of a friend. This was followed by conversation or entertainment in the dining room until the guests left for home and bed. In the country this program was not greatly changed, and a Roman took with him to the provinces, so far as he could, the customs of his life in Rome.

POOR ROMANS

Much depended on a man's social position and business, the routine varying with individuals, the time of year, and the day. The poor, whether idle or industrious, have left no records in literature of their business or personal affairs. Our knowledge of their working places, homes, and tools is based on what archaeologists have found and the representations in sculpture, mosaic, or fresco of workers at some trades.

The homes of poor people were unheated, badly lighted tenements, without water on the upper floors, jerry-built, scantily furnished, and unsanitary. Poor men, too, used the early hours, rested at midday, and saw the same public shows that the great and wealthy enjoyed.

Statuettes of comic actors

Procession of girls

THE ROMAN
WAY OF LIFE

View on the Palatine

Altar on the Palatine to an "unknown god," dating from about 100 B.C.—copy of a much earlier one

Denarius of Octavian, showing a curule chair

THE EARLY ROMANS

Farmers and shepherds, the Romans believed, had settled on the Palatine Hill in prehistoric times. There they built huts, and thus founded the city of Rome. They were plain and hard-working people, but their sense of law and order, the solidarity of their family life, their belief in the gods that they worshiped with simple and regular rites, their readiness to unite against their enemies, were qualities that they handed down to make the strength of Rome. They left no written records, but for a long time their way of life was the Roman way.

Legend tells us that seven kings in succession first ruled Rome, which was founded in 753 B.C. by Romulus—the earliest of them. It was the custom of the king to call together, for advice and consultation, the heads of families—the fathers (*patres*). This assembly of older citizens (*senes*, old men) was named the senate. The members of families of patres —patricians—made up the greater part of the citizen body. They were the Roman people—*populus Romanus*.

When the monarchy ended—traditionally with the expulsion of the last king— the government became a republic, with annually elected officers. The senate was then made up of descendants of patrician families, men who had held the high governmental offices entitling them to the famous curule chair. They were called *nobiles* (nobles). Thus the nobility and the senatorial families were practically the same.

When the Republic was established, patricians were the only citizens with full rights, but there was a constantly increasing body of freeborn men who were not full citizens because they were not of patrician descent. As these commoners—plebeians—became more numerous, more prosperous, and more insistent on their rights, they were slowly and reluctantly granted full citizenship. After they finally achieved public office, they identified their interests with those of the patricians, and thus kept the Roman Republic conservative.

CLASS DIVISIONS IN ROMAN SOCIETY

Under the Republic Romans were divided into three great classes—nobles, knights, and commons. The noblemen formed a kind of political aristocracy. The knights (*equites*) were the businessmen of Rome—bankers, financiers, speculators. In early days citizens of their rank—the equestrian order—were men who could afford the equipment needed to serve in the cavalry. For a long time no hard and fast line was drawn between nobles and knights. A Roman nobleman might class himself with the knights if he had the four hundred thousand sesterces (about $20,000) required for this rank.

After the plebeians had won the political rights once held only by patricians, any freeborn citizen might become a candidate for high office. However, Emperor Augustus (27 B.C.–A.D. 14), by limiting eligibility for curule offices to men whose ancestors had held such positions, formed a hereditary nobility, to which each succeeding emperor made additions. The lists of knights were also revised by the emperor, who thus controlled admission to the equestrian order.

OCCUPATIONS AND CAREERS OF NOBLES

From the old patricians, Roman nobles inherited certain aristocratic standards of conduct, which limited their business activities.

Men of the noble class were believed to be above any kind of work for the sake of gain, but agriculture was always considered an honorable occupation, even for senators, as were certain industries for which the raw material came from the land—quarrying, brickmaking, and the like.

It was in the government and the army that noblemen found their careers, but even there they served without pay. This was well enough in early times when every Roman citizen was a farmer whose small fields yielded enough for his simple wants, and who left his farm only to serve his country—as did the famous dictator Cincinnatus when he was called from his plowing to head the State in an emergency (458 B.C.).

NOBLEMEN IN AGRICULTURE

After the nobles grew wealthy from the spoils of foreign conquests, they were no longer content to cultivate a few acres and live simply. Instead, they acquired land until they owned great estates. The devastations of war and competition with slave labor caused many independent farmers to lose their small farms, which came into the possession of rich men. Many noblemen also acquired estates in the provinces; the revenues from these helped them live in luxury at Rome.

The traditional farm life that Cicero described and praised in *Cato Major*, his "Essay on Old Age" (44 B.C.), would hardly have been recognized by Cato himself, though even in his time (235–149 B.C.) few farmers were working their own land. Aims and methods of farming had wholly changed. Grain—once an important crop—could be imported by sea more cheaply than it could be grown at home. The rich landowner's income came from his cattle and sheep, his vineyards and olive groves—sources of the profitable commodities wine and oil. Sallust (84–34 B.C.) and Horace (65–8 B.C.) complained that land for crops was lost by the extension of great private parks.

Model of a ship that carried grain from Rome to Britain

POLITICS AS A CAREER

During the Republic politics must have been profitable only for those who played the game to the end. This meant holding in succession the offices of quaestor, aedile or tribune, praetor, and consul. Quaestors were attached to the treasury; some served in Rome and some in Italy; one quaestor was sent out with each general or provincial governor as treasurer or paymaster.

The aediles supervised markets, food supplies, streets, and public buildings in Rome, and had charge of some great

Aedile giving the signal for a chariot race to begin

public spectacles. Tribunes were the representatives of the plebeians. Praetors were judges, and two consuls headed the government. After a term of office at Rome each praetor and consul was sent for at least a year to govern one of the provinces.

Each office was held for one year, and the minimum age for candidates was fixed by law. No salary was attached to any public office, and the indirect profits from a lower office would hardly pay campaign expenses for the next higher. Candidates often spent great amounts of money on public entertainments, in order to win popularity and votes. Even after the right to vote was taken from the common people in the time of the Empire, such expenditure continued to be a heavy obligation.

C. Julius Caesar, consul in 59 B.C.

The political influence of noblemen and senatorial families was so strong that it was difficult for an outsider (*novus homo*) to be elected to office. Since there were no organized political parties to nominate a man and work for his election, a Roman candidate had to present himself to the voters and conduct his own campaign. Cicero was proud because, without powerful family backing, he was elected to the highest offices.

PROFITS FROM POLITICS

Profits came from positions in the provinces, where honest men might find good investments. A community might ask an honest official to become its patron and look after its interests at Rome. For this help valuable presents were often given. Cicero's justice and moderation as quaestor in Sicily were rewarded when the Sicilians made it possible for him, as aedile, in charge of the grain supply at Rome, to import their grain at low prices.

On the other hand, the provinces were gold mines for corrupt officials. Every kind of graft, robbery, and extortion was practiced, and a governor was expected to enrich not only himself but also his staff. The poet Catullus complained bitterly of the selfishness of Memmius, who prevented his staff from plundering the poor province of Bithynia. The most notorious profiteer was Verres, governor of Sicily, who cruelly looted that province of its treasures. This story is told in detail in Cicero's orations against Verres. Unlike many corrupt governors, Verres paid the penalty for his crimes; he was prosecuted and went into exile. Although the emperors did much to reform provincial administration, the salaries paid the governors did not always save the provincials from official extortion.

LAW AS A CAREER

In Roman times, just as today, the practice of law often led to a successful political career. For men like Cicero, with no family influence, the law was the only way to political advancement. There were no requirements for practicing in the courts. There were no public prosecutors and a Roman could bring suit against another on any charge. Sometimes a young politician brought a suit solely for publicity, even though there were no grounds for the charges.

Lawyers were forbidden by statute to accept fees. In early times a dependent went to his patron for legal advice and protection, which the patron was obligated to give. In theory lawyers of later times were at the service of all who sought their advice. Men of high character made it a point of honor to give their legal knowledge freely to fellow citizens, but grateful clients could not be prevented from making valuable presents, and generous legacies were often left to successful lawyers.

Cicero had no other way of adding to his private income, so far as we know, although he states that he observed the law about taking fees. Yet he owned a house at Rome on the Palatine Hill, a wealthy quarter in his time, as well as eight country places. Although never considered a rich man, he lived well and spent money freely on books and works of art.

How easily and to what extent the laws against fee-taking were evaded is shown by the fact that the Emperor Claudius (A.D. 41–54) limited the amounts that might be asked. Judges as well as lawyers were of course subject to corruption, but Latin writers say more about bribing of juries. With the profits from a province before him, a praetor did not need to stoop to taking bribes.

Roman knights, headed by musicians, proceeding to a temple for sacrificial rites

THE ARMY AS A CAREER

Military commands and office-holding were closely connected. A young man of good family might begin his public career by serving on the staff of some general. After returning to Rome, at the proper age (thirty in Cicero's time) he could run for the quaestorship. He might thus increase his military experience, since a quaestor was sent out with each general. As such, he might serve as treasurer and paymaster in the army. Later, as governor of a province, he would be in command of troops stationed there and might often be called on to defend boundaries or quell uprisings. He might even engage in wars of conquest.

There were a number of legitimate ways, according to the usage of the times, in which a profit might be made in the army—plunder from cities taken, ransoms from cities spared, and returns from the sale of thousands of captives.

THE ARMY AS A GOLD MINE

In theory the spoils of war went to the treasury in Rome, but in fact they first passed through the hands of the commanding general—who too often kept what he pleased for himself, his staff, and his soldiers and then sent the rest to Rome. Entirely illegitimate were profits made in furnishing supplies to the army at outrageous prices or in diverting supplies to private use. Cicero praised Pompey for his honesty in such matters. Reconstruction of conquered territory frequently brought rich returns; probably the Haedui paid Caesar a large sum for securing their supremacy in central Gaul after he had defeated the Helvetians.

The civil wars (87–82 B.C.) that cost the best blood of Italy made the victors immensely rich. Besides looting the State treasury, the conquerors confiscated the estates of their opponents and sold them to the highest bidder. Nominally, the proceeds went to the treasury, but the amounts actually sent there were small in comparison with the personal profits to the victors.

While Sulla was dictator in Rome (82–79 B.C.), names of friends and foes alike were put on the proscription lists. Only the most powerful influence could save the lives and fortunes of proscribed persons. Because no one dared bid against a favorite of the dictator, a freedman of Sulla bought the estate of Roscius of Ameria, valued at three hundred thousand dollars, for one hundred dollars.

Settling demobilized soldiers on grants of land made good business for the commissioners who directed the distribution of land taken from the enemy. The grants were of farm land, and bribes came both from soldiers and from the former owners of the land.

KNIGHTS AND THEIR CAREERS

Long before the time of Cicero the name *eques* (knight) had lost its original military significance, and Romans of the equestrian order had become capitalists. They found in business the excitement and profits that nobles found in politics and war. From early times their corporations financed and carried on great public works, bidding for contracts let by government officials. Under the Empire certain important administrative positions were opened to knights, many of whom made a regular career of office-holding. But on the whole the equestrian order remained the class engaged in "big business." The immense scale of their operations relieved them from the reproach of working for money.

Though big business never had the

power at Rome that has sometimes been attributed to it, still, in the later years of the Republic, knights, as a class, had considerable political influence. They held the balance of power between the senatorial and popular parties. Generally they used this power only to get legislation favorable to them as a class and to secure as provincial governors men that would not examine too closely their transactions in the provinces. Knights, as well as noblemen, found in the provinces a source of wealth. Their chief business there was collecting revenues on a contract basis. For this purpose corporations were formed, which paid into the public treasury a lump sum fixed by the senate. This sum was collected—and profits were made—by squeezing money from the unhappy provincials. So hateful was the system that the very word *publicanus* (tax collector) became a synonym for "sinner."

Knights also financed provinces and allied states, advancing money to meet various expenses. Sulla once levied a contribution of twenty thousand talents (about \$20,000,000) in Asia. The money was advanced by a corporation of Roman capitalists, who collected the amount six times over. Then Sulla intervened, lest there should be nothing left for him in case of future need. More than one pretender was set on a puppet throne in the East to secure the payment of heavy loans made him by Roman capitalists.

As individuals, knights also carried on extensive and profitable operations. Grain in the provinces, wool, ores, and manufactured articles could be moved only with the money they advanced. They also engaged in commercial enterprises abroad, from which they were barred at home, buying and selling as well as advancing money to individuals. The usual rate of interest was 12 per cent, but often this rate was exceeded. When Cicero went to Cilicia as governor in 51 B.C., Marcus Brutus was lending money in the province at 48 per cent and trying to collect compound interest on it. Brutus expected the governor to enforce payment of loans made at this high rate of interest.

Treasury, center of Rome's financial activities

COMMERCE AND INDUSTRY

Roman commerce covered all known lands and seas, although Italy itself had little export trade. Pliny the Elder (A.D. 23–79) states that trade with India and China took from Rome more than five million dollars yearly. The West—Gaul, Spain, and Britain—sent more raw materials to Italy than did the East, but fewer finished articles.

Few traces of a factory system can be discovered, although something of the sort seems to have been developed in iron at Puteoli, in fine copper and bronze work and perhaps also in silverware and glass at Capua, in pottery at Arretium, and in brick and tile at Rome. Spinning and weaving were probably done at home by women who sent their work to dealers —perhaps fullers, since cloth went to them for finishing.

Wholesale business was largely in the hands of capitalists, while retail business was carried on by freedmen and foreigners. Furnishing food for Rome employed thousands, but as a rule, suppliers seem to have dealt directly with retailers, and there were few middlemen.

Bankers united money-changing with money-lending. Money-changing was necessary in a city to which came coins from all parts of the world. Although money-lending was not considered a respectable occupation for a Roman, it could be carried on discreetly in the name of a freedman. Bankers took deposits, paid interest, and made payments on written orders. They helped clients with investments and through their foreign connections supplied travelers with what we call letters of credit.

Building was done on an immense scale and at great cost. Public buildings and many private buildings were erected by contract. Those standing now, and ruins, too, show that though letting contracts for public buildings was profitable for the

Pottery bowl

Silver dish

Over such a banker's counter passed coins from all parts of the Empire

officials in charge, the construction was well done. Crassus (112–53 B.C.) did an unusual sort of salvage business. Whenever he heard that a building seemed certain to be destroyed by fire, he himself, or an agent, rushed there and bought the property from the lamenting owner— naturally at a low price. Then gangs of trained slaves fought the flames and saved the building. Afterwards, other slaves, acting as architects and builders, repaired the damage.

THE COMMON PEOPLE

Freeborn citizens of Rome below the nobles and the knights may be roughly divided into two classes, soldiers and very poor men. In addition to idle, worthless men drawn to Rome by the dole of free grain and the excitement of city life, many thrifty, industrious citizens were forced into cities by war and failure to find employment elsewhere. The civil wars drove many small landowners away from their farms or unfitted them in various ways for the labors of farming. Pride of race or the competition of slave labor closed other occupations to them. No close estimate of the number of the displaced and unemployed men can be given, but before Caesar's time it is known to have been more than 300,000.

The unemployed were occasionally helped by being moved to newly established colonies on the frontiers. During his short administration of affairs at Rome (48–44 B.C.), Caesar gave as many as 80,000 men this opportunity of making a living. But only those with some pride and ambition were willing to emigrate, so that the undesirable element was left behind.

Aside from beggary and petty crimes, the only way such idle men could get money was by selling their votes. This made them a real menace in the days of the Republic, but under the Empire their political influence was lost. In addition to a regular dole of food, the government found it necessary to distribute money occasionally to relieve want. Some poor men played client to the upstart rich, but most were content to be fed by the State and amused by free shows and games.

COMMON MEN IN THE ARMY

About 104 B.C. Marius reorganized the army, doing away with the property qualification for a soldier. From that time on, the most enterprising young men of the common people turned to the army. They enlisted for a term of twenty years at stated pay, and received certain privileges after an honorable discharge. In the rare times of peace they were employed on public works. The pay was small, perhaps forty or fifty dollars a year in Caesar's time, about as much as a laborer could earn by heavy work. But a soldier had, instead of the stigma of humble labor, the exciting prospect of war, as well as hope of presents from his general and loot from plunder.

Many inscriptions have been found describing the life and service of individual soldiers and listing promotions and decorations. After he finished his service, a soldier might, if he chose, return home, but many veterans formed connections where they were stationed and lived there on free grants from the government. These settlers helped greatly in spreading Roman civilization and the use of Latin.

FREEDMEN

The practice of manumission of slaves greatly increased the number of free workmen, while the prospect of freedom made slaves ambitious and industrious. In some respects the effects on society were good. On the other hand, since slaves came from all parts of the world, a constantly increasing cosmopolitan population was added to the native citizen body, which had been impoverished and weakened by the civil wars. The Greeks and Orientals were clever and industrious, easily adapting themselves to slavery and also to freedom. This large infiltration from the East changed the character of the free population for the worse, since these new citizens did not have the political traditions of the native Italians and neither understood nor cared to understand Roman institutions.

By the end of the Republic the practice of manumission had grown general enough to cause alarm, and Augustus limited it by legislation. Freedmen filled many trades and professions, especially those despised by freeborn Romans. Some were highly trained and educated, while others were masters of a craft or trade learned in slavery. Many became wealthy and were generous and useful citizens. Freedmen attained their greatest wealth and power as officials in the imperial household in the first century A.D., when they held important administrative offices that were transferred later to the knights. But neither a freedman nor his son could attain true social equality with freeborn citizens.

A self-made man who was also vulgar and ostentatious was a favorite target of satirists. Petronius, who died in Nero's reign (A.D. 54–68), has left in "Trimalchio's Dinner" a brilliant sketch of a wealthy and vulgar freedman.

SMALL TRADESMEN

From excavations at Pompeii we have some idea of the shops of the time and the business of small tradesmen. These little stores were usually the street-side rooms of private residences; ordinarily they had no connection with the house itself. Often such a shop was just a small room with a counter across the front, closed with heavy shutters at night but open to the street in the daytime. A shopkeeper often slept in the room where he worked.

Some houses (e.g., the House of Pansa) had shops of several rooms. The bakery had six rooms, four of which opened on the street. In one of them were found several mills for grinding grain. In some cases a stairway led to a room or two on the floor above, where the shopkeeper's family lived.

Goods sold over the counter might be made directly behind it. There the shoemaker had his bench and case of lasts, and made, sold, and repaired shoes. In some shops there were masonry counters with holes where hot food was kept for sale. In one Pompeian shop change was found scattered on the counter, where it had been dropped as the terrified customer and shopkeeper fled when Vesuvius erupted. Locksmiths, goldsmiths, and other craftsmen had their own tools and sold their own goods. There were also shops where men sold goods made elsewhere on a larger scale—red-glazed pottery from Arretium, ironwork from Puteoli, and copper and bronze utensils from Capua.

Shoppers drifted along the streets from counter to counter, buying, bargaining, or "just looking." The poet Martial (first century A.D.) describes a dandy going from one shop to another in the fashionable shopping district of Rome. He demands that the covers be taken off expensive table tops and that their ivory legs be submitted to his inspection; he criticizes objects of art and has some laid aside; leaving at last for luncheon, he buys two cups for a penny and carries them home himself!

Festival of a guild of boys

ROMAN GUILDS

In very early times, guilds of various trades were organized at Rome for perfecting and handing down the technique of their crafts. Most of what we know about the guilds comes from inscriptions of the imperial age. Roman guilds differed from both medieval guilds and modern trade unions; there was no system of apprenticeship and members did not use their organization to demand higher wages or better working conditions. Competition with slave labor made strikes useless. Workmen were not compelled to join the guilds, and there were no patents or special privileges in the way of work.

Eight of the ancient guilds—tanners, cobblers, carpenters, goldsmiths, coppersmiths, potters, dyers, and, oddly enough, flutists—traced their organization to Numa, second king of Rome. The shops of workmen in the same craft seem to have been located in the same neighborhood, just as in our cities similar businesses

are sometimes grouped together. Cicero speaks of the street of the scythemakers. As knowledge of the arts advanced and as labor was further divided, other guilds were formed. For example, the ancient guild of shoemakers was supplemented by other guilds, each concerned with a special kind of shoe.

In the later Republic the use of the guilds by unscrupulous politicians for political purposes led to the suppression of most of them, and from that time the formation of new ones was carefully limited. There seems to have been no restriction on the formation of burial societies, also called guilds. Even when not so organized, a guild often maintained its own common burial ground.

SOCIAL LIFE IN GUILDS

Guilds provided workingmen with some opportunity for social life, since they gave freedmen—and occasionally slaves—the right to hold office and manage affairs,

Magistrates in a procession

for they had their magistrates and councilmen, in addition to the regular body of members known as *plebs*. When there was a distribution of money, members shared in proportion to their rank in the guild.

Each guild had one or more patrons, chosen for wealth and reputation for generosity, and its own patron deity and religious rites. Members had a regular time and place for business and social meetings; and if they were prosperous, or had a generous patron, they might own their own hall. Treasuries were kept up by initiation fees, dues, and fines. On important holidays guild members proudly marched in processions with banners flying.

GOVERNMENT OFFICE WORKERS

Employees in the offices of various magistrates were mostly freedmen. They were paid by the State, and though appointed nominally for one year, apparently held their jobs during good behavior. They owed their long tenure largely to the fact that regular magistrates served short terms and were rarely reëlected. Magistrates who had no experience in conducting their offices needed trained and experienced assistants.

The highest ranking men in civil service were the *scribae*, whose name gives no idea of the extent and importance of their duties. Work now done by cabinet officers, secretaries, department heads, bureau chiefs, auditors, comptrollers, recorders, accountants, private secretaries, and stenographers was done by scribae. The poet Horace is said to have taken a position as scriba in the treasury department when he returned to Rome after the Battle of Philippi (42 B.C.). These positions were always in great demand. Below them were others almost as necessary but not equally respected, including those of lictors and messengers. Civil servants were given special places at theaters and circuses.

PROFESSIONS AND TRADES

In the last years of the Republic, professions and trades—between which no distinction was made—were largely given over to freedmen and foreigners.

Architecture was considered respectable, and Cicero put it on a level with medicine. But some occupations were thought undignified; undertakers and auctioneers were disqualified for office by Caesar. Teachers were poorly paid and usually regarded with contempt. Emperor Vespasian (A.D. 69–79) was the first to endow professorships in liberal arts.

Letter-writing was carried on as a business by men who collected news and gossip of the city and had copies made by slaves. Persons away from the city who were not receiving personal letters from Rome and were able and willing to pay for this service subscribed to these newsletters. In a way, these letters were the forerunners of newspapers.

PHYSICIANS AND SURGEONS

For a long period the treatment of the sick, apart from religious rites to gods of health or disease, must have been limited to household remedies and charms such as Cato describes in his work on farming.

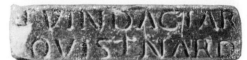

Oculist's stamp

Physician examining a patient

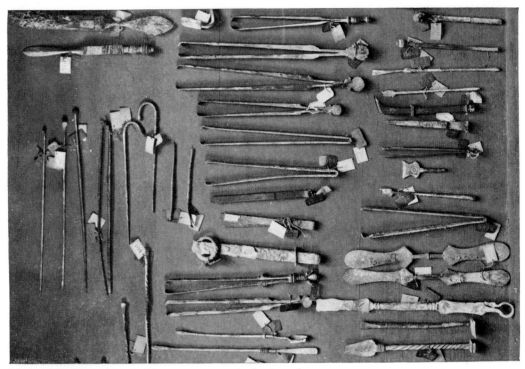

Many of the Romans' surgical instruments were similar to modern ones

Surgery seems to have developed in early times in connection with the treatment of soldiers' wounds.

Physicians and surgeons were sometimes slaves; more often, freedmen or foreigners, especially Greeks. The first foreign surgeon in Rome was a Greek (219 B.C.). Eventually Caesar gave citizenship to Greek physicians who settled in Rome, while Augustus granted them certain privileges. Numerous medical terms in use today bear witness to the Greek influence in the history of medicine.

In knowledge and skill, both in medicine and surgery, practitioners at Rome were not far behind those of only two centuries ago. We can judge their medical and surgical methods from such books as those of Celsus, a Roman who wrote in the first century of our era, and Galen, the great Greek physician, who came to Rome about A.D. 164. Surgical instruments found at Pompeii are easily identified.

Galen wrote that by his time surgery and medicine had been carefully distinguished from each other. There were also oculists, dentists, and other specialists, and occasionally women physicians. In the second century A.D., many cities had salaried medical officers for the treatment of the poor and provided rooms for their offices. By the time of Emperor Trajan (A.D. 98–117), doctors were regularly attached to the legions.

There were no medical schools, but physicians took pupils, who accompanied them on their rounds. The poet Martial complains of the many cold hands that felt his pulse when a doctor called with his train of pupils.

During the imperial period, physicians in attendance at great houses seem to have been well paid, judging by the estates of those attached to the court. Two doctors left a joint estate of a million dollars, while another received from Emperor Claudius a yearly salary of $25,000.

LIFE OF FREE WORKMEN

In spite of a continual increase in slave labor, there continued to be free workmen—some of them freed slaves—who worked at many trades and at heavy labor in cities and even on farms. Writers tell us little about these workmen, but inscriptions, especially those dealing with the guilds, give some information. Free workmen were not always as well off as some slaves or freedmen, for they had to depend on their own efforts to find work without any patron to help them.

The wages of independent workmen cannot have been high, but free distribution of grain helped to lower living expenses, and vegetables, fruit, and cheese were cheap. Workmen could seldom afford meat, but probably they managed to buy some cheap wine, which they mixed with water. If a man was married, his wife might increase the family income by spinning or weaving. Workers lived in cheap tenements, and in the mild climate there was no fuel problem. They wore coarse woolen tunics and wooden shoes or sandals. Games gave them free amusement on holidays, and public baths were cheap and often free. The guilds afforded social life, and membership in a guild or burial society guaranteed decent burial.

Carpenters' tools—hammer, square, triangle, plummets, and saws

Pont du Gard, a Roman aqueduct which for centuries brought water to Nîmes, France

LIFE IN ROMAN TOWNS

ROMAN TOWNS

In the countries bordering on the Mediterranean and in England there are many towns and cities that were once Roman. In some of them signs of Roman life remain—ruined temples, amphitheaters, baths, aqueducts, or perhaps ancient structures still in use, as the amphitheater at Arles, France, and the famous Pantheon in Rome. Such evidences of the past are still being found. In 1954 workmen digging in London uncovered the foundations of a second-century Roman temple on the site of a bombed office building. Archaeologists found that the temple was dedicated to Mithras, god of light, whom many—especially soldiers—worshiped.

When Rome ruled the western world, all these Roman towns and cities were full of bustling activity. People were occupied with family and business concerns, just as we are. Citizens were also busy with civic affairs, for most towns in Italy and the provinces were self-governing and had charters of their own, some of which have been found.

TOWN OFFICIALS

Magistrates were elected by popular vote. There was no party system, but election notices painted on walls at Pompeii show that all classes took a lively interest in elections. The spirit of municipalities was not democratic; classes were divided by clearly drawn lines. Candidates for office had to be eligible for membership in the town council (for which there was a property qualification), of good reputation, and not engaged in any disreputable business.

An official received no salary. Each magistrate was expected to pay a fee on election and to make substantial gifts for

Fire burned behind this image of Mithras, to show that he was god of light

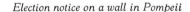

Election notice on a wall in Pompeii

the benefit of the citizens and the beautifying of the town. These gifts were usually commemorated by inscriptions, many of which have been preserved. During his year of office each city official, like the great magistrates at Rome, wore a purple-bordered toga, sat in a curule chair with its purple cushion, was attended by lictors, and had a special seat at all public shows.

Tombstone of centurion stationed in Britain; the vine stick shows his rank

TOWN COUNCILS

A *curia* (town council) usually consisted of one hundred members (*decuriones*), including ex-magistrates. These men had to be at least twenty-five years old, freeborn, and owners of a stipulated amount of property. They were entitled to the best seats at the games; and at any public distribution of money, they received a larger share than common people. They also seem to have used city water free of charge. On admission to the curia each member probably paid a fee and made a generous gift to the city.

KNIGHTS

Members of the equestrian order made up the aristocracy of the towns, as the nobles composed the upper class at Rome. Conspicuous among them were former army officers—occasionally tribunes, but more often centurions, who were sometimes retired with equestrian rank, especially chief centurions of the legions. Although some soldiers settled in the provinces where they had served, others came back from the army and became important citizens in their home towns (*patriae*). Inscriptions survive which give the war records of retired officers, and show their benefactions to towns.

AUGUSTALES

Below the equites and apart from them were rated the wealthy freedmen. Though they were ineligible for office or council, a special distinction and an opportunity for service was given them under the Empire as members of the *Augustales*, a college of priests in charge of the worship of Augustus and succeeding emperors. Annually the decurions selected a board of six (*seviri*) to act for that year. At the

Air view of Arles, where a Roman theater and amphitheater are still in use

ceremonies of which they took charge, the Augustales were entitled to wear bordered togas and knights' gold rings. These priests paid a fee on election and provided the required sacrifices. Many inscriptions show that they proudly rivaled the decurions in gifts to the community.

PLEBS AND POOR FREEDMEN

Below these classes were the plebs— citizens who were not entitled to serve in the council—and still lower were the poor freedmen. These were the men who kept small shops or worked in them; they belonged to the many guilds of which we find traces at Pompeii. Although these people worked hard and ate plain food, their lives were not all drudgery. The

magistrates usually saw to it that bread and oil, the two great necessities of life, were abundant and cheap, and that there were free shows in amphitheater and theater, and occasionally free public banquets. Even small towns had their public baths, where fees, always low, were sometimes remitted through the generosity of a wealthy citizen.

PUBLIC BUILDINGS AND PRIVATE BENEFACTORS

In the construction of baths, theaters, amphitheaters, forums, streets, bridges, aqueducts, arches, and statues, many towns were modeled on Rome. Though the architecture of private houses varied with the region, public buildings and public works throughout the Empire were distinctively Roman. Striking examples are found in Africa, where in the imperial age the Romans maintained thriving towns in regions that are now deserts of drifting sand.

Strong civic pride and rivalry with neighboring towns often caused the construction of handsome buildings and public works. It has been said that never in the world were there so many impressive towns as in the Roman Empire during the third century of our era. Yet municipal taxation was not heavy, and revenues from lands and other city property could not possibly pay for all these magnificent works and buildings. Much was expected from the generosity of the official class; much was received. Others, too—women as well as men— gave liberally. Inscriptions regularly commemorated these gifts. Sometimes in appreciation of his generosity, the curia voted a citizen a statue of honor—and frequently the honored man paid for the statue, too!

The amphitheater at Pompeii was donated by two men who had held high office in the city, and an amphitheater and a temple at Casinum were given by a lively and distinguished old lady, Ummidia Quadratilla. Among the gifts of Pliny the Younger to his native town of Comum was a library, with funds for its maintenance. The dedication of such a building was often celebrated by the giver himself with a banquet for the community, in which the citizens shared according to rank.

SCHOOLS

Roman towns did not boast large and conspicuous school buildings such as we have. There were no school taxes, and until a very late period, education usually remained a private matter. Wealthy citizens occasionally made endowments for educational purposes, but there were not so many gifts for schools as for other charitable foundations.

With the spread of Roman influence elementary schools must have been started throughout Italy and the provinces. When Agricola was governor of Britain in the first century of our era, he found the establishment of schools a useful aid in strengthening the Roman hold on the conquered territory. There were more advanced schools in the larger towns and cities. At the beginning of the second century, Pliny the Younger tells of contributing generously to a fund for opening a school in his native town of Comum, so that boys might not have to go to Mediolanum (Milan). The arguments he uses for educating boys at home are much like those frequently advanced today for establishing junior colleges.

Some boys were sent to Rome, where naturally there were better schools and more famous teachers than country towns could afford. Horace's father, though not a rich man, took his son from his native Venusia to Rome.

TOWN LIFE VERSUS CITY LIFE

At all times the man who was Roman-born looked down on country towns and people. Satirists contrasted the quiet simplicity of a town with the turmoil and vice of cosmopolitan Rome; but then, as now, many preferred the exciting life of a great city with all its drawbacks to the more comfortable, quiet living that their incomes might permit them to have in a town.

Property was cheaper and rents were lower in small towns. There one could live in a comfortable house on an income which would provide only a cramped lodging in a city apartment house (*insula*).

Tunic and sandals could be worn with propriety instead of the expensive toga and high shoes that etiquette demanded in Rome. The range of interests in a small town was narrower and often intensely local, but an active and generous citizen might find an outlet for his energies in civic activity and generosity which would never be open to him in Rome. That such outlets were welcome is shown by the keen competition for local honors until a late period of the Empire.

GREAT MEN OF THE TOWNS

Every town was proud of its own great men who had become important in the outside world. When a famous man came home, callers poured in to renew his acquaintance. Such a man might be chosen as their patron at Rome, to look after the interests of the town. Much generosity was expected from a patron. Pliny the Younger, who was chosen patron of the small town of Tifernum Tiberinum when he was a young man, later acknowledged the compliment by building a temple there. Of course he attended the dedication and paid for the customary banquet. Cicero was patron of the Sabine town of Reate, and when consul in 63 B.C., he called on some of its young men to help arrest the Catilinarian conspirators at the Mulvian Bridge, just north of Rome. The Italian hill-town of Arpino still remembers with pride that Marius the general and Cicero the orator were both born there.

Though most of the great Latin writers came from the municipalities of Italy or the provinces, they tell us little about life in the country towns. Much of what we know has been learned from ruins and excavations of cities in Italy—especially Pompeii and Ostia—and others scattered throughout the Roman world. Most of these remains belonged to the imperial period. Besides streets and buildings, inscriptions are of great importance, for they tell us much about the lives and careers of citizens whom literature never mentions.

Citizens following a plowed furrow which marks the circumference of the town they will build

In this mosaic picture of a country estate in North Africa, farm work and hunting are shown, including birds being driven into a net

LIFE IN THE COUNTRY

Cart and oxen

AGRICULTURE

Farming was the chief industry of early Italy. One proof of its importance is the great number of rural festivals in the Roman calendar. At all times the leading interests of the Romans were agricultural rather than commercial. Agriculture was the proper occupation of the senatorial class. Writers of all periods looked back with pride to the days when a Roman citizen-farmer tilled his own land with the help of his sons and perhaps a slave or two, and when a dictator was summoned from the plow.

In addition to casual references in literature, our sources of information about Roman farming include writings by the Elder Cato in the second century B.C., by Varro and Vergil at the beginning of our era, by Columella and Pliny the Elder in the first century A.D., and by Palladius in the fourth. Farm implements and activities are shown in some works of art, and hundreds of metal parts of tools have been found in excavations in different parts of the Roman world.

GEOGRAPHIC AND CLIMATIC CONDITIONS

The geographic and climatic conditions of Italy made possible varied production. In the valley of the Po the soil was alluvial—rich and deep. The volcanic ash forming the plain of Latium gave a subsoil rich in potash and phosphate, though the surface soil was thin and easily exhausted. Once there had been great forests here, but cutting timber on the hills had caused erosion and rendered much land unproductive—a thing which has happened in this country, too.

Italy stretches from northwest to southeast, but its climate does not depend entirely on latitude. Its weather is mod-ified by surrounding seas, mountain ranges, and prevailing winds. These agencies produce such widely different conditions that somewhere in Italy most grains and fruits of the temperate and subtropic zones find a favorable soil and climate.

AN IDEAL FARM

In discussing the purchase of an estate, Cato says that the ideal location was at the foot of a hill facing south. It was important to choose a healthful locality with a plentiful supply of water, and soil that was rich but not too heavy. The land should not be entirely level, for that made drainage difficult. The farm should be in a prosperous neighborhood near a market town, and on a good road if not near a river or the sea. A farm should have land and buildings in good condition. There should be a local supply of labor that could be hired for the harvest or other times of extra work. His choice was a farm of two hundred forty *jugera*,

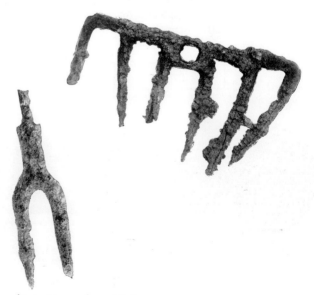

Ancient iron rake and fork

about one hundred fifty acres, suitable for diversified farming.

Pliny the Younger, discussing land that adjoined his, says, "The farms are productive, the soil rich, the water supply good; they include pastures, vineyards, and timberland that gives a small but regular return." He speaks of the saving in equipment, supervision, and skilled service gained by concentration of holdings—a good indication of the rise of great estates as small-scale farming became less profitable. On the other hand, Pliny said that to own much land in one neighborhood was to be greatly exposed to the same climatic risks.

SMALL FARMS

Evidence of farm life before 200 B.C. comes chiefly from tradition. Early farms were little—some only two jugera (about an acre and an eighth). Such a holding seems too small to support a family unless the farmer also had rights in community land. Holdings of seven jugera (a little less than five acres) are frequently mentioned. Farms of that size were assigned to individuals when allotments were made of public lands in 393 B.C. A farm of seven jugera could be worked by the owner with a paid laborer or one or two slaves. Farmhouses were grouped together in villages, from which the men went to the fields each day—as is still done in European countries. With hand labor and simple tools, Romans did intensive farming—rather like gardening.

FEWER SMALL FARMS

Various conditions led to a gradual decrease in the number of small farms and an increase of large estates. The devastation of southern Italy by Hannibal in the Second Punic War (218–202 B.C.) ruined many farms, so that much land had to be abandoned. Loss of life in that war and others brought a great decrease in free labor. Rich men bought or leased large tracts of public land, and worked them with slave labor. Since a small farmer without capital could not do this, he found competition with rich landowners increasingly difficult.

When the importation of grain made wheat-growing in Italy no longer profitable, or when the surface soil in Latium

Farm animals with cart, and plow made from the forked branch of a tree

was exhausted, a poor man had to give up the struggle. A wealthy landowner could afford to plant his acres with vines or olives or turn large tracts into pasture, and wait for his investment to become profitable. However, in remote or hilly sections, small farms were worked at all periods.

THE FARM MANAGER

Great estates were operated by slaves under a *vilicus*, a manager who was himself a slave. These slaves made up the *familia rustica* (country household—the term *rustica* implied that an estate was not the only home of its master). However, free labor on farms did not entirely disappear, for we read that extra hands were hired at times. Tenant farmers are rarely mentioned during the Republic, but increased in number later. Horace had five tenants on part of his Sabine farm; the remaining acres he worked himself through his vilicus.

All work on a farm was supervised by the vilicus. He was proverbially a hard taskmaster because his hope of freedom depended on the amount of profit that he could turn over to his owner. His job was not simple, for he had to plan all the work of the estate and supervise the slaves who did it. A good manager kept his men busy; slaves were in turn plowmen and reapers, vinedressers and treaders of the grapes, perhaps even quarrymen and lumbermen, according to season and locality. Farming on a large estate required not only strong men who could do different kinds of hard labor but also many skilled craftsmen. If necessary, a small farmer might hire craftsmen from a richer neighbor.

A vilicus also handled the group that took care of the other slaves. Practically everything needed for a large estate was produced or manufactured on the place unless conditions made only specialized farming profitable. Enough grain to feed family and slaves was raised, ground, and made into bread. Wool was sheared, cleaned, carded, spun, and woven into cloth, which was made into clothes by women slaves under the eye of the manager's wife (*vilica*).

Buildings were erected by slaves, and farm tools and implements were repaired or even made by them. Such labor required the work of carpenters, smiths, and

Tenants bringing produce to the owner of the farm

masons, though not necessarily highly skilled men. Among the implements were different kinds of hoes and rakes, spades and forks, mattocks, pruning knives, sickles, and scythes. There were carts and wagons and primitive harrows as well as plows. On farms where grapes and olives were grown, presses and storage jars were part of the permanent equipment.

DUTIES OF THE OWNER

Cato listed the duties of the owner of a large estate on his arrival there. After saluting his household gods, he was to go over the farm himself before calling in the manager to give his report. When he had discussed this and given further orders, he was to check the accounts and make plans for selling produce on hand and any superfluous stock. Pliny the Younger lamented the amount of time he had to give to accounts and the affairs of his tenants, to the hindrance of his literary work.

FARMER'S ALMANAC

An elementary knowledge of astronomy served farmers as a basis for their calendar. The beginning and ending of the seasons was fixed by the positions of stars or constellations and the rising and setting of certain stars indicated the seasons even to the day. This knowledge was especially important before 45 B.C., when Caesar reformed the calendar, which was eighty days ahead.

DRAINAGE AND FENCING

Farm land was carefully drained. In heavy soil open ditches were used; in light soil, covered drains. The latter were filled halfway with stones, gravel, or brush, and then with soil to the top. Open furrows were left across fields, so that water could run into the ditches. Careful drainage produced thriving farms in sections that later fell into neglect and be-

An owner inspecting work on his estate

MENSIS IANVAR DIES XXXI NON QVINT DIES HOR VIIIS NOX HOR XIIII SOL CAPRICORNO TVELA IVNONIS PALVS AQVITVR SALEX HARVNDO CAEDITVR SACRIFICAN DIS PENATIBVS

MENSIS FEBRAR DIES XXVIII NON QVINT DIES HOR XS NOX HOR XIIS SOL AQVARIO IVTELNEPTVNI SEGETIS SARIVNTVR VINEARVM SVPERFICCOLI HARVNDINES INCENDVNT PARENTALIA LVPERCALIA CARACOGNATIO TERMINALIA

MENSIS MARTIVS DIES XXXI NON SEPTIMA DIES HOR XII NOX HOR XII AEQVINOCTIV VIII KAL APR SOL PISCIBVS IVTELMINERVAE VINEAE PEDAM IN PASTIN VI PVTANTVR

One face of an altar on whose four sides an almanac was inscribed gives a list of farm duties and feasts for January, February, and March

came marshes, where for centuries people could not live or work because of malaria. Now this marshland has been drained again and is productive and habitable, as it was in Roman times.

In North Africa careful conservation of water and the use of aqueducts, dams, and cisterns made land productive where now only ruins of Roman cities lie in sandy wastes. In recent years plans have been proposed to reclaim some of this land by restoring Roman reservoirs and methods there.

Four kinds of fencing were used: hedges; fences of pickets interlaced with brush or of posts pierced with holes for connecting rails; military fences of ditch and bank; walls of stone, brick, or concrete. Trees were often planted along roads, property lines, and fences—sometimes serving as windbreaks.

PLOWING AND MANURING

Cato said that the first and second rules of good farming were to plow well, and that the third was to fertilize well. Plows were small and light, straight or curved, made of iron or wood. (In parts of Italy where the surface soil is light and the ground stony, wooden plows are still used.) Heavy tilling was done with a straight plow. A field was turned over twice; the first time the plow was held straight in the furrow, the second time, at an angle. A modern plow does the same work in one operation. Oxen were used for cultivation, and one hundred twenty Roman feet—the length that a team of oxen were supposed to plow without resting—was a traditional measure of land. (A Roman foot was equivalent to 11.64 inches in our measure.)

Plowing was done in close furrows, which were then plowed crosswise. The ground was thus worked over until the soil was almost as fine as dust. Harrowing to cover the seed was considered by the Romans evidence of poor plowing. Good plowing left no mark of the implement. Pliny the Younger gives an account of land that needed to be turned over nine times.

The Romans understood and practiced contour plowing, which is being slowly adopted in this country. In general, Roman farming methods were superior to those of our colonial ancestors and of even later farmers.

Farmyard manure was stored in piles, old and new separately. Ancient writers advised a farmer who did not keep stock to have a compost heap such as is now made for gardening, piling together leaves, weeds, straw, and the like, with ashes from the burning of hedge-clippings and other rubbish that does not decay readily. The Romans understood green manuring, and though without knowledge of nitrogen-fixing bacteria, they knew how to enrich the soil by planting legumes and plowing them under while still green. Though they did not have litmus paper, they were able to test soil for sourness.

Plowman with oxen

FARMERS AS HUSBANDMEN

Roman farmers understood something of seed selection, and practiced rotation of crops. They followed wheat with rye, barley, or oats. The second or fourth year, beans or peas might be planted, sometimes to be plowed under while green, or alfalfa might be sowed. Alfalfa was well established in Italy before the beginning of our era; according to Pliny the Elder, it was brought from Asia to Greece, and thence to Italy. Sometimes a field was left fallow the year before wheat was planted; then it was plowed in the spring and summer as well as in the fall. In other cases the land was left fallow every second or third year.

PARTS OF A FARM

Cato lists the different parts of a farm in order of their importance in his time. He puts vineyard first, then vegetable garden, willow copse, olive grove, meadow, grain fields, wood lot, orchard, and oak grove. That he lists grain fields sixth shows how much more important other crops had become. The transportation problem was a factor in decreasing the amount of grain raised. The difficulty and expense of moving grain overland by wagon made it cheaper to import food from the provinces by sea than to grow it at home.

RAISING WHEAT

Wheat sown in the fall matured in the spring or summer according to soil and rainfall. It was ordinarily harvested by hand. Sometimes reapers cut the stalks close to the ground, and after the sheaves were piled in shocks, cut off the heads for threshing. Sometimes the heads were cut first, and the standing straw later. There

The farm manager is at upper right; below, slaves drive horses and cattle to tread out grain on a threshing floor

was a simple form of header pushed by an ox, but it could be used only on level ground.

Threshing was done with a flail on the threshing floor—as for centuries afterwards—or the grain was trodden out by oxen, or beaten out by a simple machine. Grain was winnowed by being tossed in baskets or shovels, so that the breeze blew the chaff away. Such methods are still used in Italy on hilly land, where modern machinery is not practicable.

VINE-GROWING AND VINEYARDS

When grapes, which meant wine, and olives, which meant oil, became the most important products of the soil, vineyards and olive orchards were planted wherever conditions were suitable.

It is believed that grapevines were not native to Italy, but were introduced in very early times, probably from Greece. The first name for Italy known to the Greeks was *Oenotria*, which may mean Land of the Vine. Ancient legends ascribe to Numa, second of the kings, restrictions on the use of wine. Until the middle of the second century B.C., wine was probably rare and expensive. Although more and more wine was produced as the cultivation of cereals declined and that of grapes increased, the quality long remained inferior to the fine wines imported from Greece and the East. By Cicero's time scientific attention was being given to viticulture and wine-making, and by the time of Augustus, Italian vintages could compete with the best imported wines. Pliny the Elder says that of the eighty really choice wines known to the Romans in his time, two thirds were produced in Italy. Italian wines became famous as far away as India.

The sunny side of a hill was the best place for a vineyard. Vines were supported by trellises or poles, or planted at the foot of trees to which they were trained, as they often are still in Italy. The elm was preferred, because it flourished every-where, could be closely trimmed without endangering its life, and furnished good fodder when its leaves were picked off to admit sunshine to the vines. Vergil speaks of "marrying the vine to the elm," and Horace calls the plane tree a bachelor because its dense foliage made it unfit for the vineyard. The chief labor of the vineyard was keeping the ground well cultivated; it was spaded once a month and plowed in the spring. Then, too, vines had to be carefully pruned. One man could care properly for about four acres.

WINE GRAPES GREW EVERYWHERE

Grapes could be grown almost anywhere in Italy, but the best wines were made south of Rome in Latium and Campania. The towns of Praeneste, Velitrae, and Formiae were famous for wines from grapes grown on the sunny slopes of the Alban hills. A little farther south, near Terracina, the Caecuban wine was made, which Augustus declared the noblest of all wines. In Campania the Ager Falernus on the southern slope of Mount Massicus produced Falernian wine, even more fa-

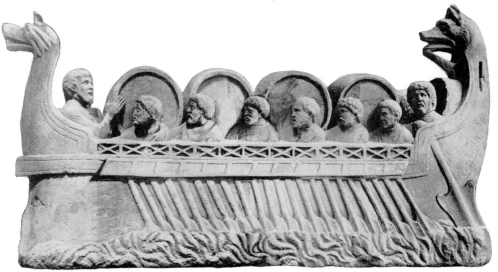

Boat loaded with casks of wine

Cupids picking grapes

mous than the Caecuban. On the lower slopes of Vesuvius and in the surrounding country, especially near Naples, Pompeii, Cumae, and Sorrento, excellent wine grapes grew. Less noted wines were made in the extreme south and to the east and north of Rome. The wines of Etruria and Gaul were not so good as others.

WINE-MAKING

Usually grapes were gathered and wine made in September, but the season of harvest varied with soil and climate. On the nineteenth of August the *vinalia rustica* was celebrated—a festival probably intended to ensure favorable weather for gathering grapes. After grapes were picked, they were carried to a vat, where they were trodden with men's bare feet and then crushed in a press. The fresh juice (*mustum*) that came from the press was often drunk. It could be kept sweet from vintage to vintage if sealed in jars smeared inside and out with pitch and then immersed for several weeks in cold water, or buried in moist sand. Mustum was also preserved by boiling; sometimes it was reduced to a jelly, which was used as a basis for various beverages.

A restored wine press in a villa outside Pompeii

Olive trees

Fermented wine (*vinum*) was made by storing the juice in huge jars (*amphorae*), each of which might hold a hundred gallons or more. These jars were lined with pitch. After being filled, they were left uncovered during the process of fermentation, which usually lasted about nine days. They were then tightly sealed, and partially buried in the ground in cellars or vaults. They were opened only when the wine required attention or was to be removed. Spoiled wine was used as vinegar (*acetum*) or rationed to slaves.

Cheaper wines were served directly from the amphorae, but the finer kinds were drawn off after a year into smaller jars, clarified, and even "doctored" in various ways, and then stored away again. A favorite place for storing wine in the house was a room in the upper story, where it was aged by warm air rising through the house or even by smoke from the hearth. Often jars were marked with the name of the wine they contained, and dated by the names of the consuls for the year when they were filled.

OLIVE GROVES

The olive tree was also brought to Italy from Greece, and as in other Mediterranean countries, its fruit became, next to wheat, the chief staff of life. Many different varieties of olives were grown, according to the type of soil and climatic conditions. Although olive trees come slowly into production, they are extremely long-lived, and provide an income for many years.

Olives required much less care than grapevines, but had to be pruned, manured, and cultivated. Budding, layering, and grafting were practiced to increase the number of trees. While the trees were growing, the ground between the rows could be used for other crops. (This is still done in Italy, as it sometimes is in young orchards in this country.) Cato advised planting olive trees in a sunny location facing southwest, and cultivating and manuring them in the fall. Trees were pruned low, so that the fruit could be easily picked.

OLIVE OIL

Although olives were much eaten as a fruit, they were most important for their oil. Olive oil not only was an indispensable article of food but also served as fuel in lamps. It was used to rub the body after bathing—especially by athletes; and it was a base for perfumes.

Olives yielded two fluids when pressed. The first to flow (*amurca*) was dark, bitter, and unsuitable for food. The second, which required greater pressure, was oil (*oleum olivum*). The best quality was made from olives not fully ripe, but the largest quantity came from ripe fruit.

Olives used for oil were picked from the trees, for fruit that fell was considered of lower grade. The olives were first spread on sloping platforms, so that part of the amurca might run out. Here the fruit remained until a slight fermentation took place. Then it was put into a machine that bruised and pressed it to separate the pulp from the stones. The pulp was then crushed in a press, and the oil that flowed out was put into earthenware containers, where amurca and other impurities sank to the bottom. The oil was then skimmed off into another container and again left to settle. This process was repeated (sometimes as many as thirty times), until all impurities were removed.

The best oil was made by first giving the fruit gentle pressure. Then the bruised olives were taken out and the pits removed from the pulp, which was pressed again a second or even a third time. The quality of oil became poorer with each pressing. Finally, the oil was placed in jars glazed on the inside with wax or gum to prevent absorption. After the covers were carefully fastened, the jars were stored in vaults.

A Roman merchant once stored oil in these jars

FRUIT ORCHARDS

From early times apples, pears, plums, and quinces were cultivated, and by Cicero's time orchards were numerous. Figs were raised in large quantities. Later on, peaches, apricots, cherries, and other fruits, as well as several varieties of nuts, were introduced from the provinces. Oranges were not grown at all by the Romans, and lemons not until the third century of our era.

FARM GARDENS

A farm garden contained vegetables for home use, herbs for seasoning and home remedies, bee plants, and flowers. Flowers were cultivated mainly for garlands to wear at banquets or to deck hearths on festival days when the household gods were honored. Near towns market gardening was profitable, and besides vegetables and fruits, flowers were raised for sale. In early days there was a garden behind each house, and excavations at Pompeii show occasional traces of small gardens even behind large town houses.

USEFUL TREES

Willows and reeds were planted in damp places. The slender shoots of willow trees were useful for making baskets, for tying vines, and other farm purposes; the wood made a quick, hot fire in the kitchen. Vergil knew the willow as a hedge plant, whose early blossoms were loved by the bees.

The word *arbustum*, usually translated "orchard" does not refer to what we call an orchard, but to regular rows of trees—elm, poplar, fig, or mulberry—for the training of vines, with grass, alfalfa, or vegetables between rows. They are still planted thus in Italy. Oak groves, as well as beech and chestnut trees, furnished mast to fatten pigs.

STOCK, POULTRY, AND GAME

Varro advised keeping stock and game on all farms. Cattle and hogs were raised in large numbers—cattle more for draft purposes and dairy products than for beef; hogs, because pork was the favorite meat of the Romans. Oxen were used for plowing. Goats were kept for their milk, although the meat was also eaten. Sheep were valued for their wool as well as for milk and meat. The milk of goats and sheep, like cow's milk, was made into cheese, which was produced in large quantities—all the larger because butter was not eaten. Sheep could be pastured in olive groves where grass grew between the rows of trees. In summer when lowland pastures dried up, flocks and herds were driven to the hills—as they still are in Italy and in some of our western states.

Every estate had a large poultry yard. Cato said that it was the business of the

Mosaic from a Pompeian dining room

vilica to see that there were plenty of eggs. Chickens, geese, ducks, and guinea fowl, pigeons, thrushes, peacocks, and other birds were raised for market. On most estates a great variety of game was bred. Bees were kept for honey, which was the Romans' only sweetening, and also for wax.

FARM BUILDINGS

The ordinary farmhouse (*villa rustica*) was part of a group of buildings around a court or courts and was somewhat regular in plan. Remains of villas have been discovered near Pompeii, and in other parts of the Roman world. They varied with the size and needs of the farm, its locality, and with the means and taste of the owner. If a working farmer tilled his own land, his farm buildings were small and simple. On large estates the villa naturally included comfortable and even luxurious quarters for the master's use. Sometimes these were in the second story. Cato recommended that the master's quarters be comfortable, so that he might spend more time on the farm, and Columella said that they should please the mistress, too.

The manager's room was near the gate, so that he could check on comings and goings. There were quarters for slaves, and barracks—partly underground and heavily barred—to house dangerous slaves, who worked in chains. In the large kitchen the slaves had their breakfast; they might also gather there in the evening if there were no servant's hall such as Varro advised. Vitruvius, writing on architecture in the time of Augustus, says that the bathroom should be near the kitchen, for convenience in heating bath water. Such an arrangement has been found in a number of villas near Pompeii.

Press and storage rooms for wine were supposed to face north; similar rooms for making olive oil faced south. There were stables and granaries, toolrooms and wagon sheds; Varro's comments show that even in Roman times some farmers had to be urged to keep their implements under cover. Water was provided by springs or wells, or rain water was stored in cisterns. In the court there was sometimes a pool. If a villa was located on a main-traveled road, its owner might use some of the rooms for a wineshop or tavern.

OTHER RURAL INDUSTRIES

Besides the raising of crops and other activities associated with farming, distinct and separate businesses were carried on in the country. Of these perhaps the most important was quarrying. Bricks and tiles were also manufactured, timber was cut and worked into rough lumber, and sand was prepared for builders. The last industry was especially necessary because of the extensive use of concrete in Rome.

For some of this work, intelligence and skill were required—as they are today—but in general, strength and endurance were the qualities most needed, because slaves were used to do rough, heavy work which is now done by machinery. The rude and ungovernable slaves employed in the quarries, who worked in chains by day and slept in dungeons by night, had to be unusually strong to survive at all.

LANDED PROPRIETORS AND THEIR ESTATES

Besides farms operated entirely or chiefly for profit, there were great estates kept up entirely for pleasure. Such a one was called *villa urbana* instead of *villa*

Houses with terraces and balconies, from a Pompeian fresco

were set in the hills and some near the water. They might even overhang the water, as at Baiae, a fashionable seaside resort, where houses were built on piles, extending from the shore out over the sea.

Cicero did not consider himself a rich man, but he had eight or more villas in different localities. This number is less surprising when one remembers that there were no seaside or mountain hotels, so that it was necessary to stay in a private house—one's own or another's—when leaving the city for change or rest. Cicero's wealthy friend Atticus had no seaside villa, and when his wife, Pilia, needed sea air, Cicero lent her his house near Pompeii, and went to his villa at Cumae.

Naturally an estate was provided with everything considered essential for open-air luxury; pleasure grounds, parks, and game preserves, fish ponds, and artificial lakes or canals. Great numbers of slaves were required to keep such places in order. Many of these were highly skilled, such as landscape gardeners and experts in the culture of fruit or flowers, while others were trained in breeding and keeping birds, game, and fish—a food which the Romans liked especially. These men had assistants of every sort, but all were under the supervision and authority of the vilicus.

The location of the house and the arrangement of rooms and courts varied, according to the owner's wishes. Remains of villas in different styles and plans have been found in many parts of the Roman world, and detailed accounts of some are given in Latin literature. Of special interest are the descriptions of two of his villas by Pliny the Younger. The location of the villa on the Sabine farm that Horace loved has been identified.

The architect Vitruvius says that in a country house the peristyle was usually

rustica. Owners of these estates lived in the city and visited their land only for pleasure. These villas were chosen with great care for their nearness to the city or to fashionable resorts, their healthful location, and the natural beauty of their surroundings. For coolness, some villas

next to the front door. Then came the atrium, surrounded by colonnades opening on the *palaestra*, a court for games and exercises, and walks. In such houses there were places for all occasions and seasons: baths, libraries, covered walks, gardens—everything was designed for convenience, ease, and comfort. Rooms and colonnades for hot weather faced north; those for winter use caught the sun. Views were considered in planning the arrangement of the rooms and their windows.

PLEASURE GARDENS

Gardens of large estates were carefully planned and tended. We may call them architectural in design, for they were laid out in straight lines and regular curves. The *xystus* was a parterre of trim flower-beds in geometrical shapes, edged with clipped box or rosemary. Such box-edged beds may be seen at Mount Vernon, in Williamsburg, and in old gardens in England. Favorite flowers of the Romans were roses—cabbage, damask, and a few other varieties—lilies, and violets. *Violae* seem to have included stocks, wallflowers, and perhaps sweet rocket as well.

Roadways for driving or riding led through the grounds, as did paths for walking or for an airing in a litter. Colonnades and clipped hedges provided shelter from the sun or wind, as did carefully planted shade trees, of which the plane was very popular. Garden houses commanded charming views and sometimes included dining rooms. If the water supply permitted, there were pools, fountains, and canals, while terraced hillside gardens gave opportunity for effective use of water as it fell from level to level. Grapevines were trained on trellises or arbors; ivy, on trellises, walls, and trees. This work was done by a *topiarius*, who was also an expert in clipping hedges of box, myrtle,

or cypress, and in trimming box into the symmetrical or fantastic shapes known as topiary work.

If these gardens afforded less color in summer, and less variety of flowers and shrubs in season than ours do, they were probably much more effective the year round with their careful design and use of evergreen foliage, water, and statuary. During the Renaissance, Roman gardens were revived and may be studied today in the grounds of famous old Italian villas.

DAILY LIFE IN THE COUNTRY

Though a busy city man fled to the country to escape the social duties of the city as well as for rest, there was no lack of social life among the villas, and interruptions from this source were sometimes as annoying as the responsibilities of the estate. As in town, exercise, bath, and dinner formed part of the day's routine. In addition to exercise in the palaestra, the owner might walk, ride, or drive over his property. There were hunting and fishing for the sporting landlord and his guests. Not only friends of the host, but sometimes other visitors were numerous, for the lack of good inns made hospitality a constant duty of the landowner.

Ancient as well as modern poets have sketched charmingly idyllic pictures of the small farm and life there when people still lived and worked as "in the brave days of old." The average farmer probably labored hard for seven days a week, going to town on market days to sell his produce, see his friends, and hear news and gossip. His wife looked after the house and family, supervising the slaves who did the actual work. Rural festivals added color and enjoyment to a farmer's life, and old religious customs were longest observed in country regions, where they had begun.

Garden with pool in the restored House of Castor and Pollux

ROMAN HOUSES

Peristyle and garden in the restored House of the Golden Cupids

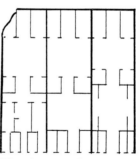

Three houses in Rome, from the Marble Plan

EARLY HOUSES

The earliest houses in Italy of which we know were small round huts with thatched roofs. These houses have vanished, but in prehistoric cemeteries ashes of the dead have been found in pottery urns shaped like the houses where the living dwelt. Such a house had one room, with a door, sometimes a window, and an opening in the roof from which smoke escaped.

Later there were oval huts, and still later, rectangular ones. The circular shape was always retained in the Temple of Vesta, goddess of the hearth, whose worship had begun at the hearth of the early round huts.

The single room of an early house was called the *atrium*. In it lived all members of the household—father, mother, children, and dependents. In this one room simple meals were cooked and eaten, indoor work done, and sacrifices offered to household gods. The space opposite the door seems to have been reserved for the father and mother. Here was the hearth where the mother cooked, and near it were her implements for spinning and weaving. Here also was the strongbox in which the father kept his valuables. At night the family spread their bedding on the dirt floor.

LARGER HOUSES

We cannot trace the various steps in the development of the early round hut into the enlarged house of historical times, but we can follow further changes in plans, construction, and decoration. There came to be town and city houses, apartment buildings, farmhouses, and country mansions. In Latin literature there are a few descriptions of houses or parts of them, and many casual allusions to rooms and their decorations and furnishings. In Vitruvius' book on architecture, he states his own principles of construction.

Archaeology has given us much more information. In many parts of the Roman world, scholars have found and studied remains of houses belonging to different periods. These are of many types, varying with region and climate, as well as with the finances and tastes of their owners.

Roman houses in Britain or in Africa were not like those in Italy. Since the eruption of Vesuvius buried—and thus preserved—Pompeii and Herculaneum, towns with paved streets, water systems and sewers, and solidly built public and private buildings, we can see and follow changes in the structure of Roman houses for nearly four hundred years.

LATER HOUSES

In larger and later houses the chief room was the atrium. The name originally denoted the whole house, but came to be applied to the characteristic room. It had no windows; light and air came through

Plan of a simple Roman house

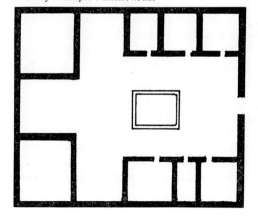

Life in the House of Cornelius Rufus, restored by a modern painter

the quadrilateral opening in the center of the roof—called *compluvium*—because rain entered there. The rain water fell into a space hollowed in the floor—*impluvium*—from which it ran into a cistern, and was used for household purposes.

The entrance of a Roman house opened directly on the street. Inside, on the right and left, were small rooms cut off from the atrium. At the end farthest from the entrance, the atrium kept its full width so that there was an open alcove at each side. These alcoves were called *alae* (wings). Opposite the outside door there was a wide recess—really an open room (*tablinum*)—which sometimes was fully

open at the rear, and at other times had a wide window in that wall. Behind this was a veranda, looking out on an enclosed garden.

Later houses retained the atrium with tablinum and alae, compluvium and impluvium. These are the characteristic features of a Roman dwelling.

DEVELOPMENT OF THE ATRIUM

The most conspicuous features of the atrium were the compluvium and impluvium. Vitruvius says that there were four styles of atrium, named from the kind of compluvium. In a Tuscan atrium the roof was supported by two pairs of beams that crossed each other at right angles. The square space enclosed formed the compluvium. This style could not be used for very large rooms. The *atrium tetrastylon* took its Greek name from the four pillars that supported the roof beams at the corners of the compluvium. The Corinthian room had more than four pillars. In the *atrium displuviatum* the roof sloped to the outer walls and the water was carried off by gutters on the outside, so that the impluvium collected only water that fell directly into it. We are told that there was also another type of atrium, the *testudinatum*. How this atrium was lighted we do not know, for it was roofed all over, and had no compluvium. It may have had clerestory windows.

CHANGE IN THE ATRIUM

By Cicero's time the atrium was no longer the center of family life, but had become a formal reception room used only for display. Perhaps the rooms at the sides were first used as bedrooms, for greater privacy. When the peristyle was adopted, kitchen and dining room were placed near it, with additional rooms, including bedrooms. Later, if these rooms were needed for other purposes, sleeping rooms were provided in an upper story. When second stories were first built we do not know, perhaps when city lots became small and expensive and when the use of concrete made walls strong enough to support an upper floor. Even little houses in Pompeii show remains of staircases.

As wealth and luxury and desire for beautiful surroundings increased, the atrium came to be decorated with all the splendor and magnificence that the owner could afford. The opening in the roof was enlarged to let in more light, and support-

ing pillars were made of marble or beautiful wood. Statues were placed between pillars and along the walls. The impluvium became a marble basin, often carved or decorated with figures in relief, and sometimes there was a fountain. Floors were of mosaic; ceilings were paneled, carved, and decorated with ivory and gold. Walls were brilliantly painted or paneled with colored marble. In such an atrium the master greeted guests, the patron received clients, and the husband welcomed his bride to her new home. And here his body lay in state after his death.

In spite of the changes, some traditions of earlier times were preserved even in the most elegant atria of Augustus' time. Though regular sacrifices were now made at a shrine in the peristyle, the altar to

Tetrastyle atrium in the House of the Silver Wedding

Modern curtains and sliding doors show how a portion of a house in Herculaneum could be shut off

Garden of the House of the Menander

the household gods—lares and penates—often remained near the place where the early hearth had been. Even in the finest houses, implements for spinning were kept where the matron in early times had sat working among her maids, as Livy (first century B.C.) described her in the story of Lucretia. The marriage couch still stood opposite the entrance, where in accordance with tradition, it had been placed on the wedding night. It had become a mere symbol, for no one slept in the atrium. In the country, however, the atrium continued to be used as in the old days, and poor people everywhere lived as poor men had always lived.

ALAE

The alae were rectangular recesses, or alcoves, on each side of the atrium. They opened on the atrium and formed a part of it. Within these alcoves, there were cabinets containing *imagines*—wax busts of ancestors who had held curule offices. Cords running from one bust to another and inscriptions under each one showed the relationship of these men. When Roman writers mention these busts as being in the atrium, they really mean in the alae, or wings. Stories of great deeds of their ancestors were proudly told to children, who learned Roman history from their own family.

TABLINUM

The tablinum was the master's office or study. It may have been so named because his account books (*tabulae*) and his business and private papers were kept in it. Here, too, was his *arca*—a heavy chest, sometimes chained to the floor, which served as a safe for money and valuables.

By its position, the tablinum commanded the whole house, for other rooms could be entered only from atrium or peristyle, and the tablinum lay between them. By closing folding doors or drawing curtains to shut off the peristyle, and using curtains to close the opening into the atrium, the master could secure privacy. But when the tablinum was left open, guests entering the house had a charming view of the entire house, including peristyle and garden. When the tablinum was closed, there was free passage through the house by a corridor at one side.

ROOMS USED FOR BUSINESS

As business spread from the center of a town to residence districts, owners of houses sometimes converted front rooms into shops. This was easily done, for the rooms of a Roman house opened on the interior. There were few windows in the outer walls, and frequently the only outside door was the one in front. So, if a house faced a business street, front or side rooms could be used for shops, without disturbing the family's privacy or cutting off light. A hallway between two outer rooms gave the family access to the front door. If the house stood on a corner, side rooms could also be used for shops or other business purposes. Sometimes there were small apartments or single rooms, as well as shops.

Perhaps such rooms were first planned by an owner for his own business, but even men of position and wealth supplemented their incomes by renting extra rooms. We know of one house, covering a whole block in Pompeii, which had rented rooms on three sides.

When a business required more space than these small shops, the owner of a private house converted it for the purpose, instead of putting up a building planned to meet the need.

VESTIBULUM

City houses were usually built on the street line. In a small dwelling the entrance door was in the front wall, separated from the street only by the threshold, and opening directly into the atrium. In larger houses, the separation of the atrium from the street by shops made the entrance more imposing. Sometimes there was an open court in front of the door, with an ornamental pavement extending from door to street. Such a court was called a *vestibulum*, but was quite different from the part of a house known today as a vestibule. It was planted with shrubs and flowers and adorned with statues, or even with trophies of war if the owner was a rich and successful general. In small houses the name *vestibulum* was given to the narrow space between the door and the inner edge of the sidewalk.

In the vestibulum wedding processions were assembled. From it a son was escorted to the Forum on the day he laid aside his purple-bordered boy's toga and put on the plain white toga of a Roman citizen. Here clients (free dependents)

A cutler's shop

Doorway

Cave canem

gathered for morning calls, sometimes arriving before daylight and waiting to be admitted, and here, later in the day, they received their dole of food or money.

DOORWAYS

The term *ostium* included both the doorway and the door. It also was applied to either, though *fores* and *janua* are more precise words for the door itself. Originally the ostium opened directly into the atrium, and in poorer houses, it was right on the street. Later, when a hallway separated the vestibulum from the atrium, the ostium opened into this hall, and eventually gave its name to it. The street door was set well back, leaving a broad threshold, which often bore in mosaic the greeting *Salve* (good health)! Sometimes words of good omen were placed over the door, such as *Nihil intret mali* (may no evil enter), or a charm against fire.

In some houses a doorman (*janitor*) was kept on duty. His place was behind the door, although sometimes he had a small room. Often a dog was chained inside the ostium. In some houses a picture of a dog was painted on the wall or worked in mosaic on the floor, with a warning: *Cave canem* (beware of the dog)! The ostium could be closed off from the atrium with curtains. Otherwise, when the outside door was open, traffic in the street was visible to anyone in the atrium.

PERISTYLE

The *peristylum*, an early addition to the Roman house, was apparently adopted from the Greeks. This was an open court at the rear of the tablinum, planted with flowers, trees, and shrubs. It was surrounded by rooms in front of which ran a paved corridor or veranda, with a roof

Colonnade and replanted garden in the House of the Vettii

supported by columns. Strictly speaking, these porches or colonnades were the peristyle, but the name came to be applied to this whole section of the house—court, colonnade, and surrounding rooms. Often there was a pool or fountain in the center of the garden. From the atrium the peristyle could be reached through the tablinum, or by a narrow hallway beside it. Often a passage led to a street, and sometimes there was a small garden behind the peristyle.

The court was usually open to the sun, and here, protected from the wind, many varieties of rare and beautiful plants and shrubs flourished. Often the space was laid out as a small formal garden, in neat geometrical beds edged with bricks. Care-ful excavation at Pompeii has given an idea of the planting, and in a number of gardens the original beds have been replanted, and water connections for fountains and pools restored. Statuary adorned these gardens, and the colonnades around them provided cool or sunny walks.

In homes of the upper class, the peristyle became the center of household life, while the atrium was reserved for formal functions. The peristyle then was the more important and often the larger of the two main sections of the house. All the rooms in this part of the dwelling received light and air through doors or latticed windows that opened on the columned and covered peristyle.

Cooking utensils and stove, underneath which fuel could be stored

The arrangement and uses of the rooms around the peristyle varied. The need of separate rooms for cooking and eating must have been felt as soon as the peristyle was adopted. Bedrooms were added later. According to the means and tastes of the owner, there were kitchen, dining rooms, bedrooms, library, drawing rooms, storerooms, baths, and toilet (*latrina*), simple quarters for the slaves, and sometimes even a stable.

KITCHENS

Of the rooms about the peristyle the kitchen (*culina*) was most important. An open fireplace, without a chimney, was used for roasting or boiling. There was also a charcoal stove of masonry, built against the wall, with a place for storing fuel beneath it. Sometimes a portable stove was used. Kitchen utensils, including spoons, strainers, pots and pans, kettles and pails, were graceful in form and often of beautiful workmanship. Interesting pastry molds have also been found. Trivets were used to hold pots and pans above the glowing charcoal on the stove, and some pots stood on legs.

Sometimes the shrine of the household gods was in the kitchen instead of in the atrium. Near the kitchen there might be a small bakery, with a built-in oven. Bathroom and toilet were also not far from the kitchen, so that the same water and sewer connections might be used. If there was a stable, it also was near the kitchen.

DINING ROOMS

A dining room (*triclinium*) was not always close to the kitchen. Large numbers of slaves made it possible to have it in almost any location, for food could be carried quickly, course by course. Sometimes there were separate dining rooms for different seasons. One room might be warmed by the sun in winter, and another shaded from the heat of summer. Since the Romans were fond of air and sky, the peristyle, or part of it, was frequently used for dining. There is an outdoor dining room in the House of Sallust at Pompeii.

In the House of the Silver Wedding, which is also at Pompeii, couches and a table for dining were built of masonry at one side of the peristyle. In the table a small fountain was set, which played when the table was not in use. Horace gives us a charming picture of a master, attended by a single slave, eating under an arbor, as the poet himself may have dined at his Sabine farm.

SLEEPING ROOMS

Cubicula were small and scantily furnished sleeping rooms; often there was an alcove for the bed. Some had anterooms where a slave might wait on call. Bedrooms used for rest in the daytime (*cubicula diurna*), were placed in the coolest part of the peristyle. Others, *cubicula nocturna* or *dormitoria*, were regular sleeping rooms located on the west side of the court to catch the morning sunshine. In large houses bedrooms were usually in the second story of the peristyle.

LIBRARIES

In the houses of many educated Romans there was a library (*bibliotheca*). Collections of books were made not only by booklovers but also by men who cared nothing for their contents but wished to be considered cultured. Books—which were papyrus rolls—were usually kept in cases or cabinets around the walls. In a library at Herculaneum a rectangular case was found in the middle of a room. Libraries were decorated with statues of Minerva and the Muses, and with busts and portraits of men of letters. Vitruvius recommends that a library face east, perhaps as a safeguard against dampness.

OTHER ROOMS

There were other rooms besides the ones mentioned, some so rare that we scarcely know their uses. A room with a shrine where images of the gods stood was called a *sacrarium*. *Oeci* were rooms for the entertainment of large groups, perhaps banquet halls. Rooms furnished with permanent seats, apparently for lectures, readings, or other entertainments, were known as *exedrae*. A *solarium* was a sun deck, laid out as a garden with flowers and shrubs, sometimes on a terrace, often on a flat roof. There were also pantries and storerooms. A few houses even had cellars.

Dining room with built-in couches

House of Pansa—model

Interior plan

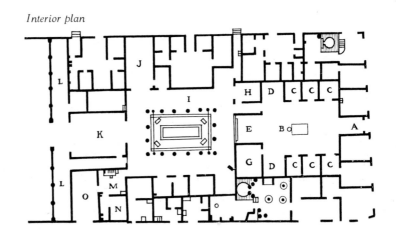

HOUSE OF PANSA

One house at Pompeii is called Pansa's because that name occurs in an election notice painted on an outer wall. It occupied an entire block, facing a little south of east, and most of the rooms on the front and sides had no connection with the rest of the house, but were rented as shops or apartments. In the rear was a garden.

In the plan, the vestibulum is the open space between two shops in front. Behind it, opening into the atrium, is the ostium (A) with a mosaic dog in the floor. The atrium (B) has three rooms (C) on each side, the alae (D) in the usual location, the impluvium in the middle, and the tablinum (E) opposite the street entrance, with the passage beside it. The atrium is of the Tuscan type and is paved with concrete, while the tablinum and the passageway have mosaic floors.

Steps lead down into the peristyle (I), which is lower than the atrium. It measures sixty-five by sixty feet, and had a colonnade of sixteen pillars surrounding the basin in the center. This was about two feet deep; its rim was decorated with figures of plants and fish. Next to the atrium are two rooms, one on each side of the tablinum. One (G) has been called the library, because a manuscript was found in it, but its purpose is not certain. The other (H) may have been a dining room. In the peristyle on the side toward the front of the house, there are two exedrae, each seven feet square, much like the alae. From one a passage runs to the street.

The uses of the rooms on the west and of the small room on the east have not been definitely determined. The large room (J) on the east was the main dining room; the remains of dining couches can be seen. The kitchen (M) is at the north-west corner, with the stable (N) next to it. Off the kitchen is a paved yard (O) with a gateway from the street by which a cart could enter. East of the kitchen and the yard is a narrow passage connecting the peristyle with the garden. East of this are two rooms, the larger of which (K) is one of the most imposing rooms in the house. It is thirty-three by twenty-four feet, with a large window guarded by a low balustrade, and opens into the garden. This was probably an oecus, used for entertaining.

At the back of the house is a long veranda (L), overlooking the garden, in which vegetables were grown. There are stairs in the rented rooms, but not in the residence itself, suggesting that the upper rooms were not occupied by the family of the owner.

Of the rooms facing the street, the one connected with the atrium was probably used for some business enterprise of the

Entrance to House of Pansa

owner. The suites on the east side seem to have been apartments used as dwellings. The others were shops. The four connected rooms on the west, near the front, were used as a bakery. First was the salesroom, and in the large room opening off it were troughs for kneading dough, a sink with a faucet, a built-in oven, and three stone mills—since bakers ground their own flour.

The middle picture shows the probable appearance of the house if it were cut in half through the middle from front to rear, and shows how the partitions and roof may have been arranged.

HOUSE OF THE SURGEON

One of the oldest dwellings in Pompeii is known as House of the Surgeon. It received this name because some surgical instruments were found in one of the rooms. It is a typical Roman house with a Tuscan atrium and surrounding rooms, without the peristyle which came to be an important part of later houses. The original building, shown in the plan by heavy lines, was later enlarged to fill the entire lot on which it stood, except for a tiny garden (K) in one corner. The added parts are shown by double lines.

The ancient house was probably built before 200 B.C. The walls of the atrium are made of large cut blocks of limestone. The inner walls are not so solidly constructed.

The first house had entrance hall (A), atrium (B), with sleeping rooms (C) and alae (D) adjoining. On each side of the tablinum (E) there was a square room (F). Both these may have been dining rooms. The two rooms (G), one opening on the street, may have been used as shops, perhaps by the owner, since both have doors opening into the atrium. The corner shop (I) is part of the later addition, as are the veranda at the rear (H), the kitchen (J), and adjoining rooms, which were slave quarters and storerooms.

The ceiling of the atrium was about twenty feet high, with no upper floor. Over the back part of the house was a second story reached by stairs leading from the veranda.

Plan of House of the Surgeon

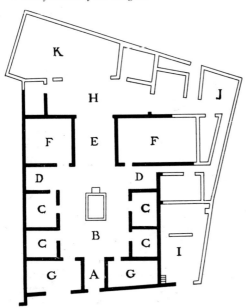

Façade of House of the Surgeon today

NEWPORT VILLA

In outlying provinces of the Empire, especially in Britain, there were houses of very different design. One such that has been excavated and studied is Newport Villa, on the Isle of Wight. Here, instead of an atrium with rooms around it, the central feature is a corridor (A) over fifty feet long. From it opens the main room of the house (B); other living rooms (E, M) are near. The bath occupied four rooms (F, G, H, I). Under one of these (F) there was a furnace, and two of the large rooms (E, N) were also heated by separate furnaces. Room E had also a fireplace—an unusual feature. Rooms C, K, and J were passages; nothing remains to show the exact use of rooms C and L. Sleeping rooms were probably on the second floor.

HEATING

Even in the mild climate of Italy, houses must often have been too cold for comfort. On chilly days people probably moved into rooms warmed by the sun, or wore wraps or heavier clothing. In severe winter weather, portable stoves were used. These were braziers made of metal for holding hot coals.

Wealthy people sometimes had furnaces with chimneys. The fire was under the house, and warm air circulated in tile pipes or in hollow walls and floors without coming directly into the rooms. Such a heating arrangement was called a *hypocaust*. Most baths in Italy had hypocausts, as did some of the great houses. Because of the mild climate in Italy, furnaces were not used so often in private houses as in northern provinces, particularly in Britain, where furnace-heated houses were apparently common in the Roman period.

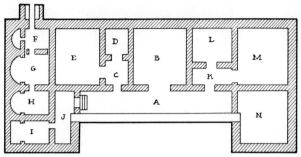

Plan of Newport Villa

Excavating Newport Villa—hypocaust at lower right

Hypocaust, underneath the mosaic floor

Pipes and joints

WATER SUPPLY

Every important town in Italy and many cities throughout the Roman world had abundant supplies of water brought by aqueducts from the mountains, sometimes for a long distance. Mains were laid down the middle of the street, and from them water was piped into houses. Often there was a tank in the upper story from which water was distributed. Not many rooms had plumbing, for slaves carried water as needed. There was often a fountain in the peristyle and in the garden, and water was piped into the bathroom and the toilet. People who could not afford to have water supplied to their homes carried it from public fountains in the streets, as is still done in Italian towns. From early times there were drains and sewers to carry off rain water and sewage. The *Cloaca Maxima* (main sewer), said to have been built in the time of the kings, continued to serve Rome until early in the present century.

BUILDING MATERIALS

Building materials used in houses varied with the period, place, and cost of transportation. For temporary structures wood was commonly used. From early times, permanent buildings were made of stone and unburned brick. Walls of dressed stone were laid in regular courses as they are today. Tufa, the soft volcanic stone easily available in Latium, was dull and unattractive in color, but could be covered with fine white marble stucco, which gave it a brilliant finish. For ordinary houses, sun-dried bricks—like the adobe of our southwestern states—were largely used until the beginning of the first century B.C. For protection against the weather, as well as for decoration, these also were covered with stucco.

An unusually large brazier

In classical times a new material was developed, better than brick or stone, cheaper and more durable, more easily worked and transported. This came to be used almost exclusively for private homes, and generally for public buildings. Walls built of this material were called *opus caementicium* (cement work).

The materials of the cement wall varied with the place. At Rome lime and volcanic ash were used, reënforced with pieces of stone the size of a fist. Brickbats were sometimes used instead of stone, and sand for volcanic ash. Broken pottery, crushed fine, was sharper and better than sand. The best concrete was made with pieces of lava, the material of which roads were generally built, for the harder the stones, the better the concrete. The Romans made a concrete that would harden under water.

Cement was also combined with crushed terra cotta to make a waterproof lining (*opus Signinum*) for cisterns.

CONCRETE WALLS

Concrete walls were built as they are now. Along the line planned for the wall, upright posts were set about three feet apart. To them were nailed, horizontally, boards ten or twelve inches wide. Cement, with stones, was poured into the space between the boards. After this had hardened, the framework was removed and raised, until the wall was built to the desired height. Such walls varied in thickness from a seven-inch partition wall in a dwelling house to the eighteen-foot walls of the Pantheon of Agrippa. They were far more durable than stone walls, for the concrete wall was like a single slab of stone throughout its whole extent, and large parts of it might be cut away without diminishing the strength of the part remaining.

Examples of opus incertum, opus reticulatum, and brick facing

WALL FACINGS

Although concrete walls were weatherproof, they were usually faced with stone or burned bricks. The stone was commonly soft tufa, though it would not stand weather as well as the concrete it covered. The earliest method was to place bits of stone having one smooth face, but no regular size or shape, with their smooth sides against the framework as fast as the concrete was poured. Such a wall was called *opus incertum* (irregular work). Later tufa was used in small blocks of uniform size with a square outer face. Such a wall gave the appearance of being covered with a net, and so was called *opus reticulatum* (network). Bricks used for facing were triangular in shape, set horizontally, with the point in the concrete. No walls were built of brick alone.

Even thin partition walls had a core of concrete. In any case, the outer face of the wall was usually covered with a fine limestone or marble stucco, which gave a smooth, white, hard finish.

FLOORS AND CEILINGS

In small houses the floor of the first story was made by smoothing the ground in each room, covering it thickly with small pieces of stone, brick, tile, or pottery, and pounding all down solidly and smoothly with a heavy rammer. Such a floor was called *pavimentum*—a name which came to be used for all kinds of floors. In better houses the floor was made of stone slabs fitted smoothly together. More elaborate houses had concrete floors, often with a mosaic surface. In the upper stories, floors were made of wood, or of concrete poured over a temporary flooring of wood, but such a floor was very heavy and required strong walls for support. It made a perfect ceiling for the room below, needing only a finish of stucco. Other ceilings were made much as they are now—of laths nailed on rafters and covered with mortar and stucco.

ROOFS OF HOUSES

Roman roofs were much like ours; some were flat, some sloped in two directions, others in four. The earliest roof was a thatch of straw. Shingles replaced straw, and these gave way to tiles. At first, roof tiles were flat, like our shingles, but later were made with a flange on each side so that the lower part of a tile would slip into the upper part of the one below it on the roof. Tiles were laid side by side, and flanges were covered by semicircular tiles inverted over them. Gutters of tile ran along the eaves to carry rainwater into cisterns.

HOUSE DOORS

A Roman doorway, like our own, had four parts—lintel, two jambs or doorposts, and threshold. The lintel was a single massive piece of stone, to carry the weight of the wall above. The doors were like ours, but lacked hinges. A door was mortised to and supported by a cylinder of hard wood, a little longer and thicker than the door, with a pivot at each end, which turned in sockets in threshold and lintel. (See ill., p. 78.) The weight of both cylinder and door was on the lower pivot. Roman comedies are full of references to the creaking of street doors.

The outer door of a house was properly called *janua*, an inner door *ostium*, but the words were often confused. Double doors were called *fores;* a back door, *posticum*. Doors opened inward; outer doors were provided with bolts and bars. Locks and keys were heavy and clumsy, but with a doorkeeper constantly on duty, locks on outer doors were not often needed. Inside private houses, curtains were preferred to doors.

WINDOWS

The principal windows of a city house opened on the peristyle. First-floor rooms used for household purposes rarely had windows on the street. Country houses sometimes had windows in the first story. In the upper floors of both private houses and apartment buildings there were outside windows in rooms that did not look out on the peristyle.

Some windows were provided with shutters, which slid in a framework on the outer wall. If these were in two parts, so that they moved in opposite directions, they were said to be *junctae* (joined) when closed. Some windows were latticed, others covered with a fine network

Street in Herculaneum, showing house with balcony and, on the right wall, an example of opus incertum

to keep out mice and other animals. Though glass was made during the Empire, it was too expensive to use commonly in windows. Occasionally talc or other translucent material was used to keep out cold.

APARTMENTS

Before the end of the Republic, in Rome and other cities, only wealthy people could afford to live in private homes. The greater part of the population lived in apartments and tenements. These were called *insulae* (islands), a name originally applied to city blocks. Apartment buildings were usually built around a court, and were sometimes six or seven stories high. Augustus limited their height to seventy feet; Nero (A.D. 54–68), after the great fire in his reign, set a limit of sixty feet. Often apartment buildings were built poorly and cheaply for speculative purposes. The satirist Juvenal (A.D. 60?–130?) told of the great danger of fire and collapse.

Except for the lack of glass in the windows, these buildings must have looked much like modern ones. Outside rooms were lighted by windows, and balconies sometimes overhung the street. These, like windows, could be closed by wooden

Large insula at Ostia—model

shutters. Inside rooms were lighted from the courts, if at all.

Insulae were sometimes divided into apartments of several rooms, but frequently single rooms were rented. Remains of insulae have been found at Ostia in which each of the upper apartments had its own stairway. The ground floor was regularly occupied by shops. The *insularius*, a slave of the owner, looked after the building and collected the rents.

CITY STREETS

In downtown city streets, galleries and balconies of apartment buildings were full of life in warm weather, while flower pots or window boxes gave color to upper windows. But in the residence quarter of an ordinary Roman city or town, streets were plain and monotonous in appearance. No lawns or gardens faced the street. The houses were all of one style, finished in stucco with few windows, mainly in the upper stories. To lend variety or please the eye, there was little except a decorated vestibulum, an occasional balcony, or a public fountain.

During the day, the open fronts of small shops in business streets, as well as balconies and windows above, gave color and variety. At night, shops were shuttered and blank. Along the fronts of buildings in Pompeii there were occasionally colonnades, which gave shade and shelter to shoppers and passers-by. The protected walls were sometimes decorated with paintings. Advertisements and notices of elections were painted on walls.

Streets were paved, with sidewalks twelve to eighteen inches higher than the roadway. At Pompeii stepping stones can still be seen. They extend from one walk to the other, and are fixed in the pavement at convenient intervals for crossing. They are usually oval with flat tops, about three feet long and eighteen inches across. Wagons often wore the paving into deep ruts between the stones, and the ruts show that the wheels were set about three feet apart.

In Rome most of the streets were narrow and crooked. Private carriages were not used in the city; people went on foot or were carried in litters. Juvenal gives a vivid description of the discomfort, even danger, in working one's way through a crowd. At night, conditions were worse because of the lack of street lighting. A rich man in his scarlet cloak with attendants carrying torches passed safely, while a poor man hurrying home alone was in danger from robbers and drunken brawlers.

Street in Pompeii with stepping stones

INTERIOR DECORATION

Frescoes from the House of the Vettii, showing cupids acting as fullers, goldsmiths, and perfumers

WALL DECORATION

Until the last century of the Republic, houses were small and simple with little decoration. Although outer walls were usually plain, interiors, even in small houses, were often charming because of the simple use of bright colors. At first stuccoed walls were merely marked off into rectangular panels, colored in deep, rich shades, especially reds and yellows. Later, in the center panel of each wall, a picture with a frame was painted. Still later, large pictures—figures, interiors, or landscapes—were frescoed all over the walls.

After this, walls were decorated with panels of thin marble slabs and had baseboards and cornices. Pieces of marble with different tints were combined—the Romans ransacked the world for strikingly colored marble. Finally, raised figures were used, modeled in stucco, bright with gold leaf, colors, and mosaic work, in which minute pieces of colored glass were set to give a jeweled effect.

DECORATED CEILINGS

Ceilings were vaulted and painted in brilliant colors; or they were divided into deeply sunk panels by heavy wood or marble beams—often carved and gilded. The panels were decorated with raised stucco work, with gold or ivory, or with gilded bronze plates. Such ceilings are sometimes imitated by modern architects.

CARVED DOORS AND MOSAIC FLOORS

Doors were richly paneled and carved, or plated with bronze, or made of solid bronze. Many thresholds were of mosaic. Doorposts were sheathed with marble, beautifully carved. Floors were covered with marble tiles of contrasting colors arranged in geometrical figures, or with mosaic pictures only slightly less beautiful than those on the walls. The most famous of these mosaic pictures, "Darius at the Battle of Issus," measured sixteen feet by eight with about a hundred fifty separate pieces in each square inch.

Battle of Issus—a mosaic, made of pieces so tiny that it resembles a painting

Mosaic floor in which pygmies hunt hippopotami and crocodiles on the Nile

ROMAN FURNITURE

Some articles of furniture made of stone or metal have come down to us; others have been restored from casts made in Pompeii and Herculaneum by pouring plaster into shells of hardened ashes or volcanic mud that were left when their wooden contents decayed. Many articles of furniture are described in Latin literature or shown in wall paintings.

The Romans cared little for luxurious comfort and had few pieces of furniture in their houses, but those were usually of rare and expensive materials, fine workmanship, and graceful form. A few articles of artistic elegance were far more in keeping with the richly colored background than our thickly upholstered furniture would have been. Although the great mansions on the Palatine had been enriched with spoils from Greece and Asia, there probably was not a really comfortable bed in any of them.

Wealthy men often collected bronze or marble statues to decorate atrium, peristyle, or garden. Some who could not afford originals had reproductions—shown by the numerous pieces of sculpture found in excavating ancient cities.

Many of our common and useful articles of furniture were entirely unknown to the Romans. No mirrors hung on their walls. There were no desks or writing tables, no chests of drawers, no cabinets with glass doors to display objects of art or other treasures. Even the houses of the rich were furnished chiefly with essential articles: couches, chairs, tables, and lamps. If we add chests, wooden cabinets with doors, an occasional brazier for hot coals, and more rarely a water clock, the list of household furnishings is complete except for tableware and kitchen utensils.

COUCH—BOTH BED AND SOFA

Couches were found everywhere in Roman houses. A couch (*lectus*) was often a sofa by day, a bed at night. In its simplest form a lectus was a wooden frame with straps interwoven across the top, on

The metal parts of this couch are ancient; all wooden parts, restored

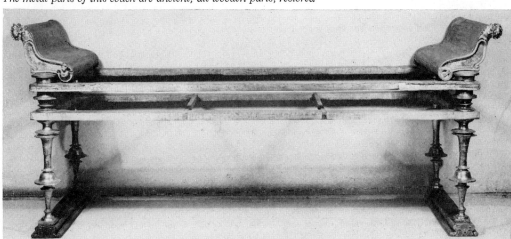

which a mattress was laid. There was an arm at one end—sometimes one at each end—and a back. The latter seems to have been a Roman addition to an earlier form of lectus. A couch was always provided with mattress, pillows, and coverlets. Early mattresses were stuffed with straw; later they were made of wool, and even of feathers. In some bedrooms in Pompeii no remains of a couch were found; perhaps the mattress was laid on a built-in support. Some bed-couches seem to have been larger than those used for sofas; these were so high that stools or small stepladders were needed to climb into them, as with some old-fashioned beds in this country.

In the absence of easy chairs a lectus was used in the library as a sofa for reading or writing. In the dining room it had a permanent place and in the atrium the wedding couch kept its honorary position.

Empress Agrippina seated on a cathedra

Roman bedroom in a museum

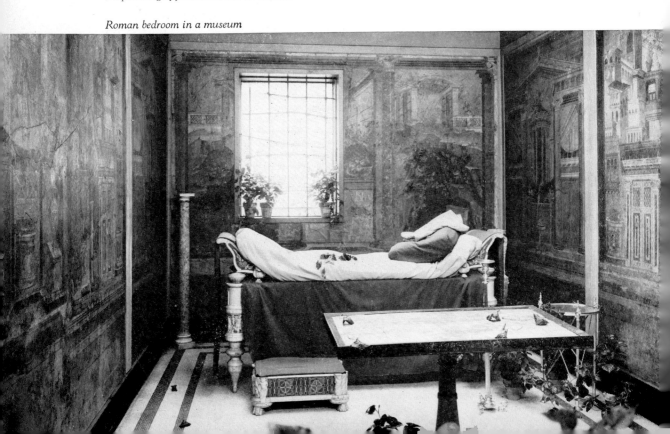

A lectus was often an extremely ornamental piece of furniture. Beautifully grained woods were used for legs and arms, which were carved and sometimes inlaid or plated with tortoise shell, ivory, or precious metals. Even frames of solid silver are mentioned in literature. Couch coverings were of fine fabrics, dyed in brilliant colors and embroidered in gold.

STOOLS, BENCHES, AND CHAIRS

The primitive form of seat among the Romans was a stool or bench with four legs and no back. Some stools, like our campstools, could be folded. A stool was the ordinary seat for one person, used by men and women resting or working, and by children and servants at meals. The famous curule chair, to which only high magistrates were entitled, was a folding stool with curved legs of ivory and a purple cushion. Benches were used in private houses, by jurors in court, by boys in school, and by senators in the curia. There were also footstools to keep the feet from the cold floor.

The first improvement on the stool was the *solium*, a stiff, straight, high-backed chair with solid arms, so high that a footstool was necessary. The solium looked as if it had been cut from a single block of wood. This was the chair in which a patron sat when he received clients in the atrium. In fact, it was a chair of such dignity that poets represented it as a seat for gods and kings.

After the solium came the *cathedra*, an armless chair with a curved back, sometimes fixed at an easy angle (*cathedra supina*), the most nearly comfortable chair the Romans knew. At first it was used only by women, for it was regarded as too undignified for men; finally it came into general use. Because teachers in schools of rhetoric sat in cathedrae, *ex*

Philosopher seated on a stool

cathedra came to mean an authoritative utterance of any kind. The use of this expression by bishops explains the derivation of the word *cathedral*.

Chairs were not upholstered, but cushions were used. Like couches, chairs provided opportunity for skillful workmanship and elaborate decoration.

A VARIETY OF TABLES

Tables were not only useful but often very beautiful, and high prices were paid for some kinds. They differed as much in shape and style as our own, many of which are copied from Roman ones. Their

Monopodium

Mensa delphica

Carved base of a table from Pompeii

Chest of wood, covered with iron plates

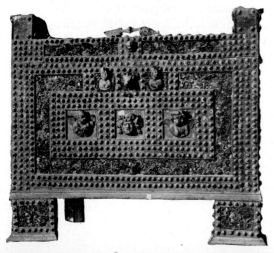

supports and tops were made of fine materials—stone or wood, solid or veneered, or even covered with thin sheets of precious metal. The most expensive were round tables made from cross sections of citrus wood, the African cedar. This wood was beautifully marked, and single pieces three or four feet in diameter could be sawed out. Cicero paid $40,000 for such a table, and prices ran up to $120,000.

In atria at Pompeii we sometimes find carved marble table supports still standing, though the top, probably originally a marble slab, was crushed by the weight of ashes and stones. These tables were between the tablinum and impluvium, just as a dining table had stood in the atrium in earlier days.

Special names were given to tables of certain styles. The *monopodium* was a table or stand with one support, used to hold a lamp or toilet articles. The *abacus* was a rectangular table with a raised rim; it was used as a sideboard to hold dishes. A *mensa delphica*—of marble or bronze— had three legs. Tables were frequently made with adjustable legs, so that they could be raised or lowered. A table of solid masonry or concrete, with a top of polished stone or mosaic, was often built into the dining room or peristyle. Tables gave an even better opportunity than couches or chairs to display elaborate workmanship, especially in the carving or inlaying of legs and tops.

CHESTS AND CABINETS

Every house was supplied with chests of various sizes for storing clothes and other articles, and for the safekeeping of papers, money, and jewelry. Usually made of wood, chests were often bound with iron and had ornamental hinges and locks of bronze. Small chests, used as jewel cases, were sometimes made of silver or gold. The head of the family had a strongbox in the tablinum in which he kept his ready money. Made of metal or of wood reënforced with metal, so that it could not easily be opened by force, it was too heavy to move, and sometimes it was chained to the floor. Such chests were often richly ornamented.

Cabinets were made of the same materials as chests and were often beautifully decorated. They were frequently divided into compartments, but they had no sliding drawers, and their wooden doors were without hinges or locks. The cabinets kept in the library held books, while those in the alae held wax masks of ancestors.

Mosaic showing sea creatures—so realistic that species can be identified

A realistic mosaic, delicately made

STOVES AND TIMEPIECES

The Romans' charcoal stoves, or braziers, were metal boxes which held hot coals. They were raised on legs, so that they would not damage the floors, and provided with handles so that they could be carried from room to room. Frequently design and decoration made such a stove a handsome piece of furniture.

Shakespeare's famous reference to the striking of the clock in *Julius Caesar* is an anachronism. In the peristyle or garden there was sometimes a sundial, such as we occasionally see now in a park or garden, which measured the hours of the day by the shadow of a stick or pin. The sundial was introduced into Rome from Greece about 268 B.C.

A sundial gives the correct time twice a year if it is calculated for the spot where it stands. As the first ones at Rome were brought from Greek cities, they did not give the exact time. The largest at Rome was set up by Augustus, who used an Egyptian obelisk for the pointer, and had the lines of the dial laid out on a marble pavement.

The water clock (*clepsydra*) was also borrowed from the Greeks. It was more useful than the sundial, because it marked the hours of night as well as day and could be used indoors. This was a container filled with water, which escaped from it at a fixed rate, the changing level marking the hours on a scale. It could not be accurate because Roman hours varied in length with the season of the year.

Above are the pictures in the side panels which show the seaside villas painted on the wall of this Pompeian house

Legs of this stand have the form of satyrs; handles make it easily movable

Pottery lamp

Elaborate bronze lamp

Bronze lamp

Bronze candelabrum

Monopodium

Lamp stand with four hanging lamps, each with two spouts

ILLUMINATION

A Roman lamp was merely a container for olive oil or melted fat, with loosely twisted threads for a wick, or wicks, drawn out through one or more holes in the cover or the top. Usually there was also a hole through which the lamp was filled. Its light must have been uncertain and dim, for it had no chimney to keep the flame steady. As works of art, however, lamps were often very beautiful. Many made of cheap material were graceful in form and proportion, while the skill of craftsmen gave additional value to those made of precious metals and rare stones.

Some lamps had handles so that they might be carried from room to room; some were suspended from the ceiling by chains. Others were kept on stands— monopodia used in bedrooms, or tripods. Some stands were adjustable in height. For lighting public rooms there were also tall stands like those of our floor lamps, from which several lamps could be hung. Such a stand, called *candelabrum*, must originally have been intended for candles, but they were rarely used; the Romans seem not to have been skillful in candlemaking.

A supply of torches (*faces*) of dry, inflammable wood, often soaked in pitch or smeared with it, was kept near the outer door for use on the unlighted streets at night.

In a Roman house, light was reflected from polished floors and from water in the impluvium. Brilliant color shone on the walls, and shrubs and flowers decorated the peristyle. Furnishings might be scanty, but they were never clumsy or ugly; so that even without the art collections of the wealthy, a house was beautiful.

Members of the family of Augustus

ROMAN FAMILIES

THE HOUSEHOLD

In the sense nearest that of the English word "family," a Roman *familia* (house) was made up of all persons under the authority of the head of a house (*pater familias*). In addition to the head of the house, a familia consisted of his wife, his unmarried daughters, and his sons (by birth or adoption), whether married or not. Wives, sons, and unmarried daughters of his married sons were also included, as were even more remote descendants through the male line. No matter how many of these persons there were, they were considered one familia. The head of such a house was always *sui juris* (of his own right), that is, independent, while the members of the familia were *alieno juri subjecti* (subject to another's authority), or dependent.

Our word "family" does not correspond exactly with any of the meanings of the Latin familia. "Household" or "house" is the nearest English word. Among the Romans, husband, wife, and children did not necessarily constitute an independent family. Individuals whom we think of as members of a family group did not always belong to the same familia, as for example, married daughters and their children.

OTHER MEANINGS OF FAMILIA

The word *familia* was sometimes used in a wider sense to include clients, slaves, and all real estate and personal property belonging to the pater familias himself or

Augustus as imperator

acquired and used by persons under his authority. *Familia* was also used of slaves alone, and occasionally of property alone. In the widest sense the word was applied to the *gens* (clan), which included all those households whose heads were descended through males from a common ancestor.

Finally, *familia* was often applied to a branch of a gens whose members had the same cognomen, the last of a Roman citizen's three names. For this sense of familia a more accurate word is *stirps*. A branch, or stirps, might include few or many households, and great clans sometimes had both patrician and plebeian branches.

PATRIA POTESTAS

The authority of the pater familias over his descendants was called *patria potestas*. In theory, the head of the family had absolute power over his children and all other descendants in the male line. He decided whether a newborn child should be reared. If his right to a child was disputed, or one of his children was stolen, he used the same legal processes as in recovering a piece of property. If for any reason he wished to transfer one of his children to another person, the transaction was effected by the same legal form used in transferring inanimate property. He could punish what he regarded as misconduct with penalties as severe as banishment, slavery, or death.

He alone of the household could own or exchange property. In strict legality, those subject to him were his personal property and everything that they earned or acquired was his. This complete authority came down from early days, when for safety it was necessary that a family act as a unit, and it was carried to greater length by Romans than by any other

Roman children

people we know. Jurists boasted that this power was enjoyed by Roman citizens alone.

The Latin language itself testifies to the headship of the father. We speak of our "mother tongue," but a Roman expressed this idea by the words *sermo patrius*. As *pater* was to *filius* (son), so *patronus* (patron) was to *cliens* (client), *patricii* (patricians) to *plebeii* (plebeians), *patres* (senators) to other citizens, and *Juppiter* (Jove the Father) to other gods.

LIMITATIONS OF PATRIA POTESTAS

However stern the authority of patria potestas was in theory, it was greatly modified in practice—under the Republic by custom, under the Empire by law. According to legend, Romulus, founder and first king of Rome, ordered that no child should be put to death until its third year, unless it was seriously deformed, and that all sons and first-born daughters should be reared. This at least secured life for young children, though a father still could decide whether a baby should be admitted to his household with all social and religious privileges, or be disowned and become an outcast. Married sons were protected against being sold into slavery by a decree of Numa, second of the kings, who was said to have forbidden the sale of a son who had married with the consent of his father.

Of much greater importance than the law was the check established by custom and public opinion on arbitrary and cruel punishments. Custom compelled the head of the house to call a council of relatives and friends when he was considering severe punishment for a child, and public opinion forced him to abide by their verdict. In a few cases where the death

Pater and mater familias

penalty was inflicted, a father, who happened to be in office at the time, either acted as a magistrate, or he anticipated the penalties of the ordinary law, perhaps to avoid the disgrace of a son's public trial and execution.

The marriage of a son did not make him a pater familias or release him from the authority of his father or the head of his house. His wife and their children also became subject to that head. The pater familias might free (*emancipare*) his sons—a formal proceeding by which each son became the head of a new house, even if he was unmarried, had no children, or was himself still a mere child. An unmarried daughter might also be emancipated, and thus become in her own right an independent familia, or she might be given in marriage to another Roman citizen. In the latter case, she passed into her husband's family, and her father could not count her children in his own familia. Children, if legitimate, were under the same authority as their father, in case he was not independent. An illegitimate child was from birth an independent familia.

Roman husband and wife

TERMINATION OF POTESTAS

Patria potestas could be terminated in various ways: first, by death of the pater familias; second, by emancipation of a son or daughter; third, by loss of citizenship of either father or son; fourth, by a son's becoming a priest of Jupiter (*Flamen Dialis*), or a daughter a vestal virgin (*Virgo Vestalis*); fifth, by the adoption of either father or child by a third party; sixth, by the marriage of a daughter, through which she passed into the power of her husband or the head of her husband's house; seventh, by a son's becoming a public magistrate. In the last case, potestas was suspended during his period of office, but after it expired, the father might hold his son accountable for his acts, public and private, during his term of office.

All but the first and third of these conditions required the consent of the head of the house, so that with these exceptions, the father's authority was regularly terminated by his own decision.

THE MASTER'S AUTHORITY

The authority of a Roman citizen over his property was called *dominica potestas* (master's power). While the master lived and retained his Roman citizenship, he alone could end these powers. He owned his property completely and absolutely, and could dispose of it by gift or sale as freely as one can now. His ownership included slaves as well as inanimate things, for slaves were mere property in the eyes of the law. Until imperial times there was no court to which a slave could appeal; the judgment of his master was final.

Restrictions on ownership of property were not so hard as the letter of the law makes them appear. It was customary for a father to assign to his children property (*peculium*, originally, "cattle of their own"), which they could manage for their own benefit. In theory he held legal title to all their acquisitions, but in practice all property was acquired for and belonged to the family as a whole.

The head of the house was, in effect, little more than a trustee to hold and manage property for the benefit of his family. This is shown by the fact that it was a grave offense against public morals and a blot on his private character for a father to prove untrue to his trust and squander family property. The long continuance of patria potestas is in itself proof that its severity was more apparent than real.

A HUSBAND'S AUTHORITY

A husband's authority over his wife was called *manus*. By the oldest and most solemn form of marriage a wife passed entirely from her father's family into her husband's power or hand (manus). If he was not independent, they were both subject to the head of his house. If she had been independent before her marriage, her property passed to her husband's father. Otherwise, the head of her house gave a dowry which met the same fate. In case of divorce, the dowry had to be returned. If a woman acquired any property while the marriage lasted, it became her husband's, subject to the authority under which he lived. So where property rights were concerned, manus put the wife in the position of a daughter, and on her husband's death she took a daughter's share in his estate.

In matters other than property, the authority of manus was more limited. A husband could get a divorce only for serious offenses. Both by law and custom he was required to refer misconduct of his wife to a family council, which was composed partly of her blood relations. Romulus is said to have ordained that a man should lose all his property if he divorced his wife without good cause. Under no circumstances did manus give a husband the right to sell his wife. In short, public opinion and custom protected wives more strongly than they did children. The chief distinction between manus and patria potestas lay in the fact that manus was a legal relationship based on the consent of the weaker party, while the other was a natural relationship independent of law and choice.

FORMATION OF NEW HOUSEHOLDS

A household usually was dissolved only by the death of its head. When he died, as many new households were formed as there were persons directly subject to his authority at the moment of his death: wife, sons, unmarried daughters, widowed daughters-in-law, and children of deceased sons. The children of a surviving son merely passed from the authority of their grandfather to that of their father. A son under age or an unmarried daughter was put under the guardianship of someone in the same gens, very often an older brother.

Emancipation of a child by his father was not common, but when it occurred, the son or daughter became independent and constituted a new familia.

The table on this page shows how individual members were affected by the splitting up of a household. The sign = means married; the sign † means deceased.

According to the diagram, Gaius, a widower, had three sons and two daughters. Aulus and Appius had married, and each had two children; Appius was dead. Publius and Terentia were unmarried when their father died. Terentia Minor

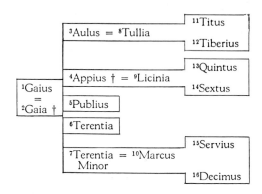

had married Marcus, and they had two children. Gaius had not emancipated any of his children.

Gaius had ten living descendants (3, 5, 6, 7, 11, 12, 13, 14, 15, 16); his son Appius was dead.

Nine persons (3, 5, 6, 8, 9, 11, 12, 13, 14) were subject to the potestas of Gaius at the time of his death.

Terentia Minor had passed out of her father's potestas by her marriage to Marcus. Therefore, the only descendants of Gaius not subject to him were his daughter's children (15, 16).

At Gaius' death six independent familiae were formed, one consisting of four persons (3, 8, 11, 12), the others of one person each (5, 6, 9, 13, 14).

Titus and Tiberius merely passed out of the potestas of their grandfather, Gaius, to that of their father, Aulus.

Since Quintus and Sextus were minors, guardians were appointed for them.

AGNATES

All persons related to each other by descent from a common male ancestor through the male line were called *agnati* (agnates). *Agnatio* was the closest tie of relationship known to the Romans. Included among agnati were two persons whom the definition would seem to ex-

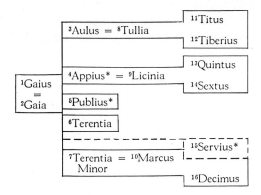

clude: a wife, who passed by manus into her husband's family, and an adopted son. On the other hand, a son who had been emancipated (indicated in the table by the sign*) was excluded from agnatio with his father and his father's agnates. He had no agnates of his own until he married or was adopted into another familia.

Gaius and Gaia had five children (Aulus, Appius, Publius, Terentia, Terentia Minor) and six grandsons (Aulus' sons, Titus and Tiberius; Appius' sons, Quintus and Sextus; and Terentia Minor's sons, Servius and Decimus). Gaius emancipated two of his sons, Appius and Publius, and adopted his grandson Servius, who had previously been emancipated by his father, Marcus. There are, then, four sets of agnati.

Gaius, his wife, and those whose pater familias he is: Aulus and his wife Tullia, Terentia (unmarried), Titus, Tiberius, and Servius, a son by adoption (1, 2, 3, 6, 8, 11, 12, 15).

Appius, his wife Licinia, and their two sons (4, 9, 13, 14).

Publius, who is himself a pater familias, but has no agnati at all.

Terentia Minor, her husband Marcus, and their son Decimus (7, 10, 16).

Notice that their other child, Servius (15), who was emancipated by Marcus,

is no longer agnate to his father, mother, or brother, but has become one of the group of agnati mentioned first.

COGNATES

Cognati were related by blood, regardless of whether they traced their relationship through males or females, and no matter what authority had been over them. Loss of citizenship was the only legal barrier to *cognatio* and even this was not always regarded. Thus in the table there are five sets of cognates, all related to one another by blood.

Gaius, Aulus, Appius, Publius, Terentia, Terentia Minor, Titus, Tiberius, Quintus, Sextus, Servius, and Decimus.

Gaia and all her descendants—the same as those of her husband, Gaius.

Tullia, Titus, and Tiberius.

Licinia, Quintus, and Sextus.

Marcus, Servius, and Decimus.

Husbands and wives (Gaius and Gaia, Aulus and Tullia, Appius and Licinia, Marcus and Terentia Minor) are not cognates of each other, although marriage made them agnates.

The twenty-second of February was set aside to commemorate the tie of blood (*cara cognatio*). On this day presents were exchanged and family reunions were probably held. Cognates, however, did not form an organic body in the state as agnates formed the gens, and blood relationship alone gave no legal rights or claims under the Republic.

Public opinion strongly discouraged the marriage of cognates within the sixth degree—later, the fourth degree—of relationship. Persons within this degree were said to have *jus osculi* (right to kiss). The degree was calculated by counting from one of the interested parties through the common kinsman to the other.

This table shows the male relatives of Marcus on his father's side. Terms for corresponding female relatives are these.

Column one, *tritavia, atavia, abavia, proavia, avia, mater—filia, neptis, proneptis, abneptis, atneptis, trineptis.*

Column two, *abamita, proamita, amita magna, amita, soror.*

Column three, *filia propatrui (proamitae), propior sobrinā, patruelis, filia fratris (sororis), neptis fratris (sororis), proneptis fratris (sororis), abneptis fratris (sororis).*

For corresponding relatives on the mother's side the same Latin words as those on the father's side are used, with these exceptions.

(1) *avunculus* (uncle), *matertera* (aunt)

(2) *avunculus magnus* (great-uncle), *matertera magna* (great-aunt)

(3) *proavunculus* (gt.-granduncle), *promatertera* (gt.-grandaunt)

(4) *abavunculus* (gt.-gt.-granduncle), *abmatertera* (gt.-gt.-grandaunt)

(5) *consobrinus* (male first cousin), *consobrina* (female first cousin)

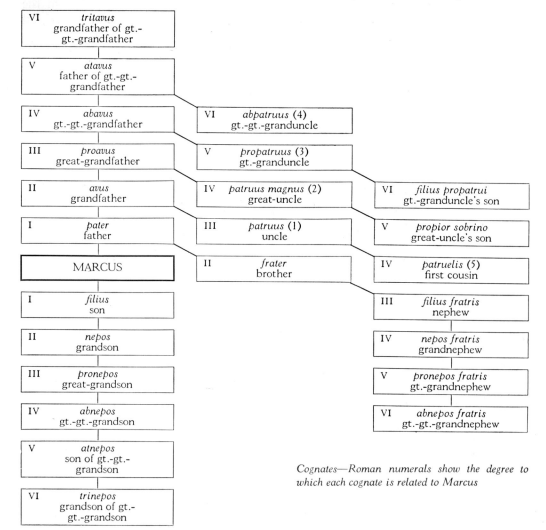

Cognates—Roman numerals show the degree to which each cognate is related to Marcus

Family being carried in a litter

RELATIVES-IN-LAW

Persons connected by marriage only, as a wife with her husband's cognates and he with hers, were called *adfines* (in-laws). There were no formal degrees of *adfinitas*, as there were of cognatio. The kinds of adfines for whom distinctive names were in common use were *gener*, son-in-law; *nurus*, daughter-in-law; *socer*, father-in-law; *socrus*, mother-in-law; *privignus*, *privigna*, stepson, stepdaughter; *vitricus*, stepfather; *noverca*, stepmother. Comparison of these names with the awkward compounds used in English as their equivalents gives additional proof of the importance attached by the Romans to family ties. Two women who married brothers were called *janitrices*, a relationship for which we do not have even a compound.

The terms used for blood relations tell the same story. A glance at the table of cognates shows how strong the Latin is here, how weak the English. We have "uncle," "aunt," and "cousin," but to distinguish between some relationships we use descriptive phrases as "uncle on my father's side." The Romans had two words for "uncle"—*avunculus* was a mother's brother, *patruus*, a father's; two words for "aunt"—*matertera*, a mother's sister, and *amita*, a father's; two words for "cousin"—*consobrinus* and *patruelis*, meaning first cousin on the mother's side and first cousin on the father's. For *atavus* (father of a great-great-grandparent) and *tritavus* (father of *atavus*) we use the indefinite "forefathers."

THE FAMILY CULT

The closest tie known to the Romans was agnatio. The importance attached to the agnatic group is largely explained by the Romans' conception of life after death. They believed that men's souls continued to exist, though separate from the body, but they did not originally think of the soul as being removed from the earth. They thought that it hovered near the burial place, and for its peace and happiness required regular offerings of food and drink. If the offerings were discontinued, they believed that a soul would be unhappy, and might even become a spirit of evil, bringing harm to those who had neglected the proper rites. The maintenance of these rites and ceremonies fell naturally to the descendants from generation to generation. In return the spirits would guide and guard their descendants. Later, contact with Etruscan and Greek art and mythology developed ideas of a place of torment or of possible happiness such as Vergil describes in the *Aeneid*.

The head of the house was priest of the household, and those under his authority assisted in prayers and offerings. As long as he lived, a Roman was obligated to perform these acts of affection and piety. He likewise had to provide for their performance after his death by perpetuating his line and the family cult. Since a curse was believed to rest on a childless man, marriage was a solemn religious duty. It was entered into only with the approval of the gods as shown by the auspices, taken by the proper rites before a marriage ceremony. When he married, a Roman brought his bride home to share his family rites, and thus separated her entirely from her family worship. In the same way, he later surrendered his daughter, on her marriage, and she no longer worshiped at her father's altar, but at the altar of her husband's family.

If a marriage was childless, or if the head of a family survived his sons, he had to face the prospect of the extinction of his family, with no one to carry on proper rites for his ancestors and himself after his death. Two alternatives were open to him. He might give himself in adoption and pass into another family, or he might adopt a son to perpetuate his own family. He usually preferred the latter course, in order to secure peace for the souls of his ancestors as well as for his own.

ADOPTION

The person adopted was chosen from a family of the same rank as that into which he would pass. Sometimes the adopted son was a pater familias himself. More often he was a *filius familias*. In the latter case, the Romans used a complicated procedure called *adoptio*, by which a father conveyed his son to the adopter, transferring him from one family to the other.

The adoption of a pater familias (*adrogatio*) was a much more serious matter, for it involved the extinction of one family in order to prevent the end of another. This was an affair of state. It had to be sanctioned by the *pontifices* (high priests), who probably made sure that the *adrogatus* (man being adopted) had brothers to attend to the proper rites for the ancestors he was abandoning. If the pontifices gave their consent, the adrogatio still had to be sanctioned by the old patrician assembly (*comitia curiata*), since the act might deprive the gens of its succession to the property of a man without children.

If consent was given, the adrogatus sank from the position of head of a house to that of a filius familias in the household of his adoptive father. If he had a wife and children, they passed with him into the new family, as did all his property. His adoptive father had the same authority over him as over a son of his own, and looked on him as his son. We can have only a feeble and inadequate idea of what adoption meant to Romans.

THE CLAN

In the widest sense the term *familia* was applied to a larger group of related persons, the gens, which consisted of all households whose heads could trace their descent from a common ancestor through the male line. These were, of course,

Husband and wife

agnates, and this remote ancestor, if he could have lived for centuries, would have been the pater familias of all the members of the gens, and they all would have been subject to his authority. Membership in the gens was proved by the possession of the *nomen*, the name of the gens, the second of a Roman's three names.

Theoretically a clan originated as one of the familiae whose union in prehistoric times for political purposes had formed the State. The pater familias of such a clan was supposed to have been one of the heads of houses from whom, in the days of the kings, the patres (Senate) had been chosen. The splitting up of this prehistoric household into separate families, generation after generation, was believed to account for the large number of familiae that in later times bore the names of the great old gentes, claimed connection with them, and through their gentile affiliations, wielded great political power in the Republic. There were also clans of later origin that imitated the organization of the older ones.

Little is known of the organization of the gens. It passed resolutions binding on its members. It furnished guardians for minor children, insane persons, and spendthrifts. When a member died without heirs, his gens succeeded to any property not disposed of by his will, and administered it for the common good of all. The *gentiles* (clansmen) were obliged to take part in the religious rites of their clan and had a claim to the common property. Those who chose might be buried in the common burial ground if the clan had one.

Gessia Fausta, P. Gessius Romanus, P. Gessius Primus

ROMAN NAMES

Part of a roster of soldiers' names

THE TRIPLE NAME

Most of the Romans whom we know from history or literature had three names, such as *Gaius Julius Caesar, Marcus Tullius Cicero, Publius Vergilius Maro*. Three names—each of which had its own significance—were customary in the great years of the Republic. In earlier times names were simpler, while under the Empire the system ended in utter confusion.

The earliest legends of Rome show single names: *Romulus, Remus, Faustulus;* but there were also double names: *Numa Pompilius, Ancus Marcius, Tullus Hostilius*. Possibly single names were the original usage, although in some early inscriptions two names are found, with the second in the genitive case, representing the father, or head of the house, as *Marcus Marci, Curtia Rosci*. A little later such a genitive was followed by *uxor* (wife), or by the letter *f* for *filius* or *filia*, to show the relationship. Later, but still in very early times, a freeborn man had three names—*nomen* to indicate his clan, *cognomen* to designate his family, and *praenomen* to mark him as an individual. The regular order of the three names is praenomen, nomen, cognomen, although exceptions are found.

Great formality required the use of even more than three names. In official documents and in state records it was usual to insert between a man's nomen and cognomen the *praenomina* of his father, grandfather, and great-grandfather, and sometimes the name of the tribe in which he was registered as a citizen. Cicero might have written his name *M. Tullius M.f. M.n. M.pr. Cor. Cicero*, that is, Marcus Tullius Cicero, son (*filius*) of Marcus, grandson (*nepos*) of Marcus, great-grandson (*pronepos*) of Marcus, of the tribe *Cornelia*.

Tomb of Caecilia Metella

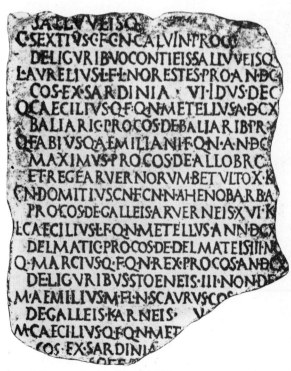

Inscription mentioning three Metelli

Inscription in honor of the distinguished general Lucullus—a name now associated with love of good food

ORDER OF NAMES

Since formal inscriptions give names in full, they are the best sources of information. In Latin literature shorter forms of names are commonly used.

A man's full name was too long for everyday use. Children, other relatives, intimate friends, and even his slaves addressed him by his praenomen only. Mere acquaintances used the cognomen, with the praenomen prefixed for emphasis. In earnest appeals the nomen also was used, with the possessive *mi* or the praenomen sometimes prefixed. When only two of the three names were used in conversation,

the order varied. If the praenomen was one of the two, it usually came first. Sometimes the order was reversed by poets for metrical reasons, and a different order is found in prose in a few places where the text is uncertain. The order also varied when the praenomen was omitted. Earlier writers put the cognomen first, as Cicero usually did; as, *Ahala Servilius*—but contrast *Gaius Servilius Ahala*. Caesar put the nomen first, as did Pliny the Younger. Horace, Livy, and Tacitus used both arrangements.

PRAENOMEN

The number of praenomina in general use seems small compared with that of our Christian names, to which they most nearly correspond. There were never many more than thirty, and by Sulla's time the number had dwindled to eighteen. The following are the ones found frequently in authors read in school and college: *Appius (APP)*, *Aulus (A)*, *Decimus (D)*, *Gaius (C)*, *Gnaeus (CN)*, *Lucius (L)*, *Manius (M')*, *Marcus (M)*, *Publius (P)*, *Quintus (Q)*, *Servius (SER)*, *Sextus (SEX)*, *Spurius (S)*, *Tiberius (TI)*, and *Titus (T)*. Abbreviations vary: for Aulus we regularly find *A*, but also *AV* and *AVL;* for Sextus, *SEXT* and *S* as well as *SEX*. Similar variations are found in abbreviated forms of other praenomina. *C* originally had the value of *G* and retains it in the abbreviations *C* and *CN* for Gaius and Gnaeus. *M'* is a modern form. The Romans' abbreviation for Manius was a five-stroke *M* that we do not have.

Conservative Roman families found in this short list more than enough names. Great families repeated the same praenomina from generation to generation, so that identification of individuals is often very difficult for us. The *Aemilii* used seven of these praenomina: Gaius, Gnaeus,

Lucius, Manius, Marcus, Quintus, and Tiberius—but added one not found in any other gens—*Mamercus* (*Mam*). The *Claudii* had six: Decimus, Gaius, Lucius, Publius, Quintus, and Tiberius—with the additional name *Appius* (*App*), which is of Sabine origin. The *Cornelii* used seven: Aulus, Gnaeus, Lucius, Marcus, Publius, Servius, and Tiberius. A still smaller number served the Julian gens: Gaius, Lucius, and Sextus—with the praenomen *Vopiscus*, which was dropped in early times. The use of even these names was limited. The praenomina *Decimus* and *Tiberius* were taken by only one branch of the gens *Claudia*—the *Claudii Nerones*. Of the seven praenomina used in the gens *Cornelia*, the branch of the Scipios (*Cornelii Scipiones*) had only three—Gnaeus, Lucius, and Publius. A gens might discard a praenomen as the gens *Antonia* dropped the praenomen Marcus after the downfall of the famous triumvir *Marcus Antonius*.

From the praenomina used in his family, a father chose one to give his son on

Inscription in honor of Appius Claudius, builder of the Appian Way and Aqueduct

Woman and man of the Furii family

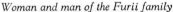

Tombstone of a lady of Britain

indicated succession in the family. Perhaps *Servius* was connected with *servire* (serve), and *Gaius* with *gaudere* (rejoice). Others are associated with the name of a divinity—*Marcus* and *Mamercus* with *Mars; Tiberius* with the river god *Tiberis*. In time the original meanings of names, even when numerals, were forgotten, just as the significance of many of our given names has been lost. Cicero's only brother was called *Quintus*.

Abbreviation of the praenomen was not a matter of caprice, as is the writing of initials with us, but a fixed custom, perhaps indicating Roman citizenship. The praenomen was written out in full when used alone or when it belonged to a person in one of the lower classes of society; when abbreviated it was pronounced in full (as it should be when carried over into English in reading or translating).

NOMEN

The most important name, the nomen, is called more precisely *nomen gentile* or *nomen gentilicium* (name of the gens). It was inherited as a surname is now, with no choice in its use. Originally it ended in -*ius*, -*eius*, -*aius*, -*aeus*, or -*eus*, and patrician families sacredly preserved this ending. Other endings point to a non-Latin origin of the gens. Names ending in -*acus* (*Avidiacus*) are Gallic; in -*na* (*Caecina*), Etruscan; -*enus* or -*ienus* (*Salvidienus*) shows that the clan originated in Umbria or Picenum.

By custom the nomen belonged to plebeian branches of the gens as well as to patrician—to men, women, clients, freedmen, without distinction. Perhaps patrician families used a limited number of praenomina to avoid those used by clansmen of lower social standing. Plebeian families who had gained political nobility, and could display in their alae busts of

the ninth day after his birth—*dies lustricus* (day of purification). As often now, a father usually gave his own praenomen to his first-born son. Cicero's full name shows the praenomen *Marcus* repeated for four generations.

When a praenomen was first given, it must have been chosen for its original meaning. *Lucius* (*lux*) meant "born by day," *Manius* (*mane*), "born in the morning." *Quintus, Sextus, Decimus, Postumus*

ancestors holding curule office, showed a similar exclusiveness in choosing praenomina for their children.

COGNOMEN

To his individual name and the name of his gens the Roman often added a third name—cognomen—to indicate the branch of the gens to which he belonged. Almost all great gentes were divided in this way—some into numerous branches. The gens Cornelia included the plebeian *Dolabellae, Cethegi, Cinnae,* and *Lentuli,* and others, as well as the patrician *Scipiones, Maluginenses, Rufini,* and other branches. In the full official name the cognomen followed the name of the tribe. Because of this, it is believed that even the oldest *cognomina* came into use after the people were divided into tribes.

Cognomina seem to have been originally nicknames from some personal peculiarity or characteristic, sometimes as a compliment, sometimes in derision. Many cognomina were adjectives pointing to physical traits—*Albus, Barbatus, Cincinnatus, Claudius, Longus* (White, Bearded, Curly, Lame, Tall). Nouns were also used, as *Naso,* man with a nose; *Capito,* man with a head. Some cognomina refer to temperament, as *Benignus, Blandus, Cato, Serenus, Severus* (Kind, Pleasant, Smart, Serene, Severe). Such names as *Gallus, Ligus, Sabinus, Siculus, Tuscus* show the place of the owner's origin.

Since these names descended from father to son, they gradually lost their appropriateness, until their meanings, like those of the praenomina, were forgotten. This is true of our own surnames, many of which suggest place of origin, occupation, or personal appearance.

During the Republic most patricians had the third or family name, but there was at least one, Gaius Marcius, who did not. With plebeians the cognomen was not so common. In the Cornelian, Tullian, and other gentes, the plebeian branches had cognomina, but the great plebeian families of the *Marii, Mummii,* and *Sertorii* had none.

The cognomen came to be prized as an indication of ancient lineage, and individuals whose nobility was new were anxious to acquire cognomina to pass on to their children. Such men often chose their own. Some names were given in mockery; others were conceded by public opinion, as in the case of *Gnaeus Pompeius,* who took *Magnus* as his cognomen. Under the Empire a cognomen was hardly more than an indication of freedom.

Inscription mentioning Pompey

L. Caecilius Jucundus, a Pompeian banker

ADDITIONAL NAMES

Often we find a fourth or fifth name. These additional names were called *cognomina* by a loose extension of the word until in the fourth century of our era grammarians began to call them *agnomina*. There were four types. In the first, the division of a clan into branches might be continued, that is, a stirps was often divided. Such a subdivision had no better name than the vague term *familia*. The gens Cornelia included among others a stirps of *Scipiones*, and this, in turn, threw off a family, or house, of *Nasicae*. Thus we find the fourfold name *Publius Cornelius Scipio Nasica*, in which the last name was probably given in much the same way that the third had been bestowed earlier.

Second, when a man passed from one family to another by adoption, he regularly took the three names of his adoptive father and added his own gentile name with the suffix *-anus. Lucius Aemilius Paulus*, son of *Lucius Aemilius Paulus Macedonicus*, after his adoption by Publius Cornelius Scipio, was called *Publius Cornelius Scipio Aemilianus*. When *Gaius Octavius Caepias* was adopted by *Gaius Julius Caesar*, he became *Gaius Julius Caesar Octavianus;* hence, he is called *Octavius* or *Octavianus* in our histories.

Third, an additional name, sometimes called *cognomen ex virtute* (surname of merit, title of honor) was often given by acclamation to a great statesman or victorious general. It was written after his cognomen. To *Publius Cornelius Scipio*, the title of *Africanus* was given after his defeat of Hannibal; his grandson by adoption won an honorary title after he had destroyed Carthage, so that he was called by the full name *Publius Cornelius Scipio Aemilianus Africanus*. Other examples are *Macedonicus*, the title given to Lucius Aemilius Paulus (mentioned above) for his defeat of Perseus, the last king of Macedonia, and the title *Augustus*, given by the senate to Octavianus in 27 B.C.

Fourth, a man who had inherited a nickname from his ancestors as a cognomen sometimes received another because of some characteristic of his own. To an early Publius Cornelius the nickname *Scipio* (staff) was given, because, as the story goes, he served as a staff to his blind father. This title was taken by all his descendants, and so became a cognomen, although the original significance had been lost. Then, for personal reasons, to one descendant another name, *Nasica* (*nasus*, nose), was given, which later became the name of a whole family. Another member of the family was called *Corculum*, so that his full name was *Publius Cornelius Scipio Nasica Corculum*. This expansion might continue indefinitely. Hence it is not always possible to distinguish between a nickname that applied merely to an individual and an additional cognomen that marked one family.

CONFUSION OF NAMES

Such an elaborate system of nomenclature was almost sure to be misunderstood or misapplied. In the late Republic and under the Empire, the established order in names was disregarded, and confusion was caused by misuse of praenomina. Sometimes two are found in one name: *Publius Aelius Alienus Archelaus Marcus*. In very early times, the familiar praenomen *Gaius* must have been a nomen.

Similar irregularities occur in the use of *nomina*. Two in a name were not uncommon, one of which was sometimes derived from the mother's family. Occasionally three or four nomina were used;

a consul in the year A.D. 169 had fourteen. As a nomen might later become a praenomen, so a praenomen might become a nomen. Cicero's enemy, *Lucius Sergius Catilina*, had the nomen *Sergius*, which once had been a praenomen.

The cognomen was similarly abused. It ceased to denote a whole family, and was used to distinguish members of the same family, as the praenomina had originally been. The three sons of *Marcus Annaeus Seneca* were called *Marcus Annaeus Novatus, Lucius Annaeus Seneca,* and *Lucius Annaeus Mela*. The arrangement of the parts of a name might vary from time to time. In the consular lists we find the same man called *Lucius Lucretius Tricipitinus Flavus* in one place and *Lucius Lucretius Flavus Tricipitinus* in another.

There is even greater variation in the names of persons who passed from one family to another by adoption. Some formed their additional name from the cognomen, instead of from the nomen. Others used more than one nomen. The Elder Pliny adopted his sister's son, who then was called not *C. Plinius Secundus Caecilius,* but as we find in inscriptions, *C. Plinius Caecilius Secundus*.

The confusion increased during the Empire. The Younger Pliny had a friend *Pompeius Falco,* who in one inscription has thirteen names, while in a later one, his son has thirty-eight.

NAMES OF WOMEN

No definite system was followed in the choice and arrangement of women's names. Praenomina for women were few, and when used were apparently not abbreviated. More common were the adjectives *Maxima* and *Minor,* and the numerals *Secunda* and *Tertia*. Unlike the numerals sometimes used as praenomina for men, these seem to have designated accurately

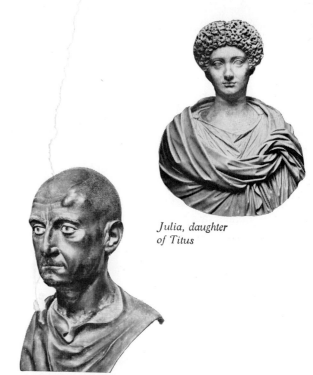

Julia, daughter of Titus

P. Cornelius Scipio Africanus Major

Probably Octavia, sister of Augustus

the individual's position among a group of sisters. Usually an unmarried woman was called by her father's nomen in its feminine form. To this was added her father's cognomen in the genitive case—later followed by the letter *f* (*filia*) to mark the relationship—as *Caecilia Metelli*. Julius Caesar's daughter was called *Julia;* Marcus Tullius Cicero's, *Tullia.*

Sometimes a woman used her mother's nomen after her father's. Originally when a married woman came under her husband's authority by the old patrician ceremony, she took his nomen, just as an adopted son took the name of the family into which he passed. It cannot be proved, however, that this custom was generally observed. In later forms of marriage a wife retained her maiden name. Under the Empire the threefold name for women was in general use, with the same confusion in selection and arrangement as that which appeared in names of men.

NAMES OF SLAVES

Slaves had no more right to names of their own than they had to any property. They took such names as their masters gave them, and these did not descend to their children. In the simple life of early times a slave was called *puer* (boy). Until late in the Republic a slave was known only by this name, corrupted to *por* and affixed to the genitive of his master's praenomen—*Marcipor* (*Marci puer,* Marcus' slave); *Olipor* (*Auli puer,* Aulus' slave). When slaves became numerous, they were given individual names, which were usually foreign and indicated the slave's nationality. Sometimes, perhaps in mockery, slaves were given high-sounding names of Eastern potentates—such as *Afer, Eleutheros, Pharnaces.* By this time a slave had come to be called *servus* instead of *puer.*

Marciana, sister of Trajan

Toward the end of the Republic a slave's name consisted of his own name followed by the nomen and praenomen (the order is important) of his master. The last two names were in the genitive case, followed by the word *servus: Pharnaces Egnatii Publii servus.* When a slave passed from one master to another, he took the nomen of his new master, and added to the cognomen of his old master the suffix *-anus.* When Anna, the slave of *Maecenas,* became the property of Livia, she was called *Anna Liviae serva Maecenatiana.*

NAMES OF FREEDMEN

A freedman received the nomen of his master with any praenomen assigned, using his own name as a sort of cognomen. A master's praenomen was frequently given, especially to a favorite slave. The freedman of a woman took the name of her father, as, *Marcus Livius Augustae l*

Ismarus. The letter *l* (*libertus*, freedman), was inserted in all formal documents.

A master might give a freedman any name he pleased. When Cicero freed Tiro and Dionysius, he called Tiro, according to custom, *Marcus Tullius Tiro*, but to Dionysius he gave his own praenomen with the nomen of his friend *Titus Pomponius Atticus*, so that the new name was *Marcus Pomponius Dionysius*. Descendants of freedmen, eager to hide traces of servile descent, dropped their individual names.

NATURALIZED CITIZENS

When a foreigner became a Roman citizen, he took a new name, formed on much the same principles as that of a freedman. He chose his own praenomen, and received the nomen of the person— always a Roman citizen—to whom he owed his citizenship. His original name was kept as a sort of cognomen. The most familiar example of a naturalized name is that of the Greek poet *Archias*, whom Cicero defended. When Archias was naturalized, his name became *Aulus Licinius Archias*. Because he had been attached to the family of the *Luculli*, he took as nomen that of his distinguished patron, *Lucius Licinius Lucullus*. His reason for selecting the praenomen *Aulus* is unknown. *Gaius Valerius Caburus*, a Gaul mentioned by Caesar in the *Gallic War*, took his name from *Gaius Valerius Flaccus*, the governor of Gaul when Caburus became a Roman citizen. This custom of taking names of governors and generals is the reason for the frequent occurrence of the name *Julius* in Gaul, *Pompeius* in Spain, and *Cornelius* in Sicily.

The name on the sarcophagus is Cornelius Lucius Scipio Barbatus

MARRIAGE CUSTOMS AND ROMAN WOMEN

Portrait of a Roman matron, dressed as Juno

EARLY MARRIAGE CUSTOMS

Throughout the early centuries of their history Roman citizens held marriage sacred, and were married in a solemn religious ceremony. For five hundred years after the founding of the city, divorce was unknown. So long as patricians were the only citizens, they intermarried only with patricians or members of surrounding communities who had the same social and religious rank.

They used the stately form of marriage called *confarreatio*. With the direct consent of the gods, as shown by the auspices, while the high priest celebrated the solemn rites, in the presence of representatives of his gens, a patrician took his bride from her father's family into his own. She was to be mater familias, to rear children who would preserve family traditions, carry on the ancient race, and help maintain and extend the power of Rome. By this—the one legal form of marriage at the time—a wife passed *in manum viri* (under her husband's authority), and her husband acquired over her almost the same rights that he would have over his children and other dependent members of his family.

USUS

During this time free noncitizens—plebeians—were joined by their own form of marriage—*usus*. It consisted essentially of the living together of a man and woman as husband and wife. Common-law marriages, legal in some of our states, correspond to usus. There were probably other forms and ceremonies of which we know nothing. Since plebeians were not citizens, patricians held that such unions were not hallowed by the gods and could not be recognized by civil law. But to plebeians themselves, their unions were

Possibly Berenice, a favorite of Emperor Titus

undoubtedly as sacred, their family ties as strict and pure, as those of patricians.

A plebeian husband might have the same rights over the person and property of his wife as those of a patrician over his, but usus in itself did not involve manus. A wife might remain a member of her father's family and hold whatever property her father allowed her by staying away from her husband for three nights in succession each year. If she did this, her husband could not control her property.

COEMPTIO

Another Roman form of marriage—ancient, but not so old as usus—was called *coemptio*. This was a fictitious sale by which the pater familias of the woman, or her guardian if she had one, transferred her to the man in marriage. This form may have been a survival of the ancient custom of purchase of wives. It carried manus with it as a matter of course, since in form it was a transfer of property, and it seems to have been considered socially a better form than usus. The two forms continued in use for centuries, but coemptio survived usus as a form of marriage with manus.

JUS CONUBII

When plebeians became citizens, their forms of marriage were legalized, but they still did not have the right of intermarriage (*jus conubii*) with patricians. Although many plebeian families were almost as ancient as patricians and many were rich and powerful, it was not until 445 B.C. that marriage between the two classes was formally sanctioned by law.

The objections of patricians to intermarriage were based largely on religious grounds. Since the gods of the State were their gods, auspices could be taken only by patricians, and therefore only marriages of patricians were sanctioned by the gods. Patrician orators protested that unions of plebeians were not *justae nuptiae* (legal marriages).

Much of this was class feeling, but when intermarriage between patricians and plebeians was legalized, new conditions were fixed for justae nuptiae.

By a sort of compromise, coemptio became the usual form of marriage when one party was plebeian. Marriage with manus became less common as patrician women realized the advantages of marriage without it. Taking the auspices before the ceremony became a mere form, and marriage gradually lost its sacramental character. Later, these changes resulted in a laxness in marriage and a freedom of divorce that seemed in the time of Augustus to threaten the life of the Roman commonwealth.

By Cicero's time marriage with manus was probably uncommon, and consequently confarreatio and coemptio were not generally used. However, confarreatio was retained to a limited extent down to Christian times because certain Roman priesthoods could be held only by men who had been married by the old patrician sacramental form, and whose parents also had been married by that form. To induce women to be married by the confarreate ceremony, Augustus offered exemption from manus to a wife after she had three children. This was not enough; and under Tiberius, in order to fill even the few priestly offices, manus was eliminated from the confarreate ceremony.

Portraits of husband and wife from their tomb

A nuptial sacrifice in the center; bride and groom with hands joined, at right

LEGAL MARRIAGES

Certain conditions had to be met before a legal marriage could be contracted even by citizens.

The consent of both bride and groom had to be given, or that of the pater familias if both were in patria potestate. Under Augustus it was provided that the pater familias could not refuse his consent without showing valid reason.

Both parties had to be adult; there could be no marriage between children. Probably fourteen and twelve were the minimum ages for groom and bride.

Both man and woman had to be unmarried; polygamy was never sanctioned at Rome.

The contracting parties could not be closely related. In general, marriage was absolutely forbidden between ascendants and descendants, between other cognates within the sixth (later the fourth) degree, and between the nearer connections by marriage.

If bride and groom met these conditions, they might be legally married, but other distinctions might affect the civil status of their children, without casting doubt on their legitimacy or on the moral character of their parents.

If all requirements were fulfilled and both parties were Roman citizens, the marriage was legal; the children were legitimate and by birth possessed of all civil rights.

If one of the parties to a marriage was a Roman citizen and the other a member of a community having jus conubii but not full Roman citizenship, the marriage

Wedding ceremony with gods and goddesses in attendance

was still legal; the children, however, took the civil standing of their father. If the father was a citizen and the mother a foreigner, the children were citizens, but if the father was a foreigner and the mother a citizen, the children were foreigners, like their father. If either party was without jus conubii, the union, although legal, was an irregular marriage; the children were legitimate, but took the civil position of the parent of lower degree.

BETROTHAL

A formal betrothal before marriage was considered good form but not legally necessary; it carried with it no obligations that could be enforced by law. In betrothal the girl was promised in solemn form by her pater familias or guardian. If the man was independent, the promise was given to him directly. Otherwise it was made to the head of his house, who had asked for the girl in marriage for him. The form of betrothal was probably something like this.

Spondesne Gaiam, tuam filiam (or if the girl was a ward, *Gaiam Luci filiam*), *mihi* (or *filio meo*) *uxorem dari?* Do you promise to give me (or my son) Gaia, your daughter (or Gaia, Lucius' daughter) as wife?

Di bene vortant! Spondeo, May the gods grant their blessing. I promise.

Di bene vortant! May the gods grant their blessing.

The word *spondeo* was used for this promise, and the maiden was henceforth *sponsa* (promised, engaged). The person making the promise had the right to cancel it at any time. This was usually done through a third person, a *nuntius* (messenger); the formal expression for breaking an engagement was *repudium renun-*

tiare (to send a rejection), or simply *re-nuntiare*. While the contract was entirely one-sided, a man's reputation was likely to suffer if he formed two engagements at the same time, and he could not recover presents made with marriage in mind if he himself broke the engagement.

A man almost always presented gifts to his betrothed. Articles for personal use were common, but a ring was usual. This ring was worn on the third finger of the left hand because there was a belief in Roman times and for centuries later that a nerve or sinew ran directly from this finger to the heart. Engagement and wedding rings are still worn on this finger. Also the girl usually made a gift to her betrothed.

DOWRIES

It was a point of honor with the Romans, as it still is with many European peoples, for the bride to bring her husband a dowry (*dos*). In case of a girl in patria potestate this was furnished by the head of her house. If she was independent, she supplied her own dowry, or if she had no property, a dowry might be contributed by relatives. If they were unwilling to provide it, she might, by process of law, compel her parents or grandparents to furnish it. In early times when marriage with manus prevailed, all property brought by the bride went to her husband or his pater familias. Later, when manus was less common, part of the bride's property was set aside for her own use and part was made over to the groom as her dowry, the size of the shares varying with circumstances. The bride's family gave her slaves, clothing, and jewels according to their means.

THE ESSENTIAL CONSENT

There were really no legal forms necessary for the solemnization of a Roman marriage; there was no license to be obtained from the civil authorities; it was

A Roman wedding

A Roman lady, sometimes called Livia, wife of Augustus

not necessary that ceremonies be performed by state officials. The one essential thing was the consent of both parties if they were independent, or of their patres familiae if they were dependent. A father could refuse consent for valid reasons only; he could command the consent of persons under his authority. Usually family affection made this parental authority much less severe than it now seems to us.

This consent had to be shown by some act of personal union between the parties; that is, marriage could not be entered into by letter, messenger, or proxy. Such a public act was the joining of hands in the presence of witnesses, the bride's letting herself be escorted to her husband's house, or in later times, the signing of the marriage contract. Escorting a bride to her new home was a custom never omitted when those concerned had any social standing. It was not necessary for a valid marriage that the parties should live together as man and wife, though in usus living together in itself constituted a legal marriage.

CHOOSING THE WEDDING DAY

Superstition influenced arrangements for a wedding of two thousand years ago, just as it sometimes does now. Special pains were taken to name a lucky day. The Kalends, Nones, and Ides of each month, and the day following each one, were unlucky. So was all of May and the first half of June, because of certain religious ceremonies observed in these months: in May the Argean offerings and the Lemuria, both associated with death; in June the holy days connected with Vesta.

The memorial days, February 13–21, and the days when the entrance to the lower world was supposed to be open,

August 24, October 5, and November 8, were also carefully avoided. Nearly one third of the year, therefore, was absolutely barred. The great holidays, too—and these were legion—were avoided, not because they were unlucky, but because friends and relatives were sure to have many engagements then. A woman marrying for the second time chose one of these holidays, so that her wedding would not be conspicuous.

PREPARATIONS FOR A WEDDING

On the evening before her wedding day a bride dedicated to the lares of her father's house her *bulla* (locket), and if she was not much over twelve years of age, her childish toys. For the sake of a favorable omen she tried on her wedding dress, the *tunica recta* (straight tunic), woven in one piece and falling to the feet. It was said to derive its name *recta* from being woven in the old-fashioned way at an upright loom.

On the morning of her wedding day a bride was dressed for the ceremony by her mother. Roman poets show unusual tenderness as they describe a mother's solicitude for her daughter. A bride's most important garment was the tunica recta, which was fastened around the waist with a band of wool tied in the knot of Hercules, probably because Hercules was the guardian of wedded life. This knot only the husband was privileged to untie. Over the tunic the bride wore a flame-colored veil. So significant was the veil that *nubere* (to veil oneself) is the word regularly used for the marriage of a woman.

Special attention was given to the arrangement of a bride's hair. It was divided into six locks by the point of a spear, or comb of that shape—a practice surviving perhaps from the ancient cus-

tom of marriage by capture. These locks were coiled and held in position by ribbons. Since the Vestal Virgins wore their hair this way, the style must have been an extremely early one. In addition, the bride wore a wreath made of flowers and sacred plants which she had gathered herself.

The groom, wearing a toga, had a similar wreath of flowers on his head. He was accompanied to the home of the bride at the proper time by relatives, friends, and clients, who were bound to show him every honor on his wedding day.

Dressing the bride—a fresco from Herculaneum

FORMS OF WEDDING CEREMONIES

In connection with wedding ceremonies it must be remembered that only the consent and the act expressing it were necessary, and that all other rites were nonessential and variable. The ceremonies depended on the particular form used, but even more on the wealth and social position of the families concerned. Probably most weddings were much simpler than those described by our chief authorities.

The house of the bride's father, where the ceremony was performed, was decked with flowers, boughs of trees, bands of wool, and tapestries. When the guests arrived, before sunrise, the omens had already been taken. In the ancient confarreate ceremony these were taken by the public *augur* (soothsayer), but in later times, no matter what the ceremony, the unofficial interpreters of omens merely consulted the entrails of a sheep which had been sacrificed.

If the omens were pronounced favorable, bride and groom appeared in the atrium, and the wedding began. It consisted of two parts: the ceremony proper, varying according to the form used (confarreatio, coemptio, or usus), and the festivities, including the feast at the bride's home, the taking of the bride from her mother's arms, the escorting of the bride to her new home (the essential part), and her reception there.

CONFARREATE CEREMONY

The confarreate ceremony began with the joining of hands. Bride and groom were brought together by the *pronuba*, a matron who had been married only once and was still living with her husband. They joined hands before ten witnesses, representing the ten clans of the curia, an old patrician division of the people.

Then followed the words of consent spoken by the bride: *Quando tu Gaius, ego Gaia* (When—and where—you are Gaius, I then—and there—am Gaia). The formula, which goes back to a time when Gaius was a nomen, not a praenomen, was the same no matter what the names of bride and groom were. Its use implied that the bride was entering the gens of the groom, and it was probably chosen for the lucky meaning of the names. Even in marriages without manus the old formula was used, although its meaning was lost with the lapse of time.

After the words of consent, bride and groom took their places side by side at the left of the altar and facing it. They sat on stools covered with the skin of the sheep which had been killed for the sacrifice.

Dextrarum junctio

A bloodless offering was made to Jupiter by the high priest and the priest of Jupiter. This offering consisted of a cake made of *far* (spelt, an old variety of wheat), from which the ceremony got the name *confarreatio*. The cake was then eaten by the bride and groom. While the offering to Jupiter was being made, the priest recited prayers to Juno, goddess of marriage, and to gods of the countryside and its fruits. Utensils necessary for the offering were carried in a covered basket by a boy called a *camillus*, whose parents were both living. Then followed congratulations, the guests using the word *feliciter* (good luck, happiness).

Bronze statue of a camillus

should become more alike as time went on. But even so the rite involving the cake of spelt remained exclusively part of the confarreate ceremony, as did the use of the scales and scale-holder in coemptio.

CEREMONY OF COEMPTIO

The ceremony of coemptio began with the fictitious sale of the bride in the presence of at least five witnesses. The purchase money was represented by a single coin laid in scales held by a scale-holder. The scales, scale-holder, coin, and witnesses were all essential in the ceremony. Then followed the words of consent by the bride and the joining of hands, borrowed from the confarreate ceremony. Originally the groom had asked the bride whether she wished to be mater familias for him. After she assented, she asked the groom the corresponding question. He assented, a prayer was recited, and perhaps a sacrifice offered, after which came congratulations, as in the other ceremony.

USUS AND CEREMONIES

The third form, the ceremony preliminary to usus, has not come down to us. Probably hands were clasped, words of consent spoken, and congratulations offered, but we know nothing of special customs or usages. It was almost inevitable that the three forms of marriage

WEDDING DINNER

After the marriage ceremony, there was a wedding dinner, which in early times lasted until evening. It was usually given at the house of the bride's father. We know of a few cases when it was given at the groom's house, but there must have been exceptional circumstances. Dinner seems to have ended with the distribution among the guests of pieces of wedding cake, as is often done now. In time these feasts became so extravagant that under Augustus it was proposed to limit the cost by law to the equivalent of fifty dollars.

BRIDAL PROCESSION

After the wedding dinner the bride was formally escorted to her husband's house. Since this ceremony was essential to the validity of a marriage, it was never omitted. It was not a private function, for anyone might join the procession and take part in the merriment that distinguished it; we are told that even persons of rank waited in the street to see a bride. As evening approached, a procession formed before the bride's house with torchbearers and flute-players at its head.

When all was ready, the marriage hymn was sung and the groom took the bride with a show of force from her mother's arms. The Romans saw in this custom a reference to the seizing of the Sabines, but it probably goes back far beyond the founding of Rome to the custom of marriage by capture which prevailed among many primitive peoples.

The bride then took her place in the procession. She was attended by three boys whose parents were both living; two walked beside her, holding hands with her, while the other carried before her the wedding torch of hawthorn. Behind the bride were carried a distaff and spindle, emblems of domestic life. The camillus with his basket also walked in the procession.

During the march were sung the *versus Fescennini*, songs full of coarse jests and personal remarks. The crowd also shouted the ancient marriage cry, the significance of which the Romans themselves did not understand. We find it in at least five forms, all variations of *Talassius* or *Talassio*, the name probably, of a Sabine divinity, whose functions are unknown. Livy derives the term from the supposed name of a senator in the time of Romulus.

On the way the bride, who was carrying three coins, dropped one as an offering to the gods of crossroads; another she later gave to the groom as an emblem of the dowry she brought him; and the third she offered to the lares of his house.

The groom meanwhile scattered nuts, sweetmeats, and sesame cakes through the crowd. Catullus suggests that this act of the groom symbolized putting away childish things, for nuts were used in a number of children's games. However, nuts were also a symbol of fruitfulness. We have a similar custom—that of throwing rice after the bride and groom.

Roman musicians with a lyre

ARRIVAL AT THE NEW HOME

When the procession reached the groom's house, the bride wound the doorposts with bands of wool, probably a symbol of her future work as mistress of the household, and anointed the door with oil and fat, emblems of plenty. She was then lifted carefully over the threshold, in order, some say, to avoid such a bad omen as a slip of the foot on entering her new home for the first time. Others, however, see in the custom another reminder of marriage by capture. The bride spoke again the words of consent: *Ubi tu Gaius, ego Gaia*. Then the doors were closed against the general crowd; only invited guests entered with the newly married pair.

In the atrium the husband offered his wife fire and water in token of the life they were to live together and of her part in the home. On the hearth, wood was ready for a fire; this the bride kindled with the marriage torch, which had been carried before her. The torch was afterwards tossed among the guests to be scrambled for as a lucky possession—as the bride's bouquet now is.

A prayer then was recited by the bride, after which the pronuba led her to the wedding couch, which was always placed in the atrium on the night of the marriage. There it remained afterwards, but only as a piece of ornamental furniture.

On the next night the newly married pair were hosts at a second wedding dinner for friends and relatives. At this meal the bride made her first offering to the gods as a Roman matron. A series of dinner parties followed, given in honor of the bride and groom by friends of their families.

A ROMAN MATRON

With her marriage to a citizen of Rome a Roman woman reached a position never attained by the women of any other nation in the ancient world. Nowhere else were women held in such high respect; nowhere else did they exert so strong and beneficent an influence. A Roman matron was not kept at home in special women's

Cupids stage a Roman wedding, with a bride wearing a veil

A Roman matron—perhaps the wife of Balbus

apartments as were her sisters in Greece; the whole house was open to her—she was its absolute mistress. She directed its management and supervised the tasks of the household slaves, but did no menial work herself. She was her children's nurse and conducted their early training and education. Under her eyes her daughters were trained to be mistresses of their own homes. They remained her closest companions until she herself had dressed them for their weddings and their bridegrooms had torn them from her arms.

A Roman matron was her husband's helpmeet in business as well as in household matters, and he often consulted her on affairs of state. She received her husband's guests and sat at table with them. Even when she was subject to the manus of her husband, any restraint was tempered by law and custom.

When she went abroad, her matron's costume (*stola matronalis*) secured for its wearer profound respect. Men made way for her in the street; she had a place at public games, at theaters, and at great religious ceremonies of state. She could testify in court and until late in the Republic, might even defend a case. Often she managed her own property. The first book of Varro's work on farming—dedicated to his wife—was intended to guide her in managing her own land.

A matron's birthday was sacredly observed and made a joyous occasion by the members of her household. The Roman *Matronalia* was very much like our own Mother's Day. It was universally celebrated on the kalends (first day) of March; presents were given to wives and mothers.

Finally, when a woman of a noble family died, she might be honored with a public eulogy, delivered from the *rostra* in the Forum.

While the education of women was not

carried far at Rome, and their accomplishments were useful rather than elegant, their husbands were probably no more accomplished. In the early days of our country, girls had little education; in 1684, girls of New Haven, Connecticut, were not allowed to attend grammar school.

CHANGES IN CUSTOMS

In the last years of the Republic, the inflow of wealth from conquests brought about a gradual decay in the moral fiber of the Romans. Family ties were relaxed, divorce was frequent, and the way of life no longer simple and austere, but frivolous and extravagant. Under such influences the character of the Roman matron tended to deteriorate, as did that of her father and her husband.

Ancient writers do not say much about the domestic subjects that are popular with us. Poets and essayists of Rome took for granted the simple joys of childhood, home life, and family relationships and felt no need to dwell on them. The mother of the poet Horace may have been a gifted woman, but she is never mentioned by her son.

The descriptions of domestic life that have come down to us are either from Greek sources such as the comedies, or else deal only with social circles where fashion, profligacy, and impurity made easy the work of the Roman satirist. It is safe to say that the characterizations in the verses of Catullus and Juvenal were not true of all Roman women in the times of which they wrote. The strong, pure woman of early days must have had many to imitate her virtues even in the darkest times of the Empire. There must have been noble mothers then, as well as in the time of the famous mother of the Gracchi, and wives as noble as the wife of Marcus Brutus.

Antonia, wife of Drusus

ROMAN CHILDREN

Roman children with pets—a lamb, two doves, and a snake

LEGAL STATUS OF CHILDREN

The fact that Roman children were by law little better than the property of the head of the house makes their position seem unduly hard to us. It is true that the head granted them the right to live, that whatever they earned was his, and that they married under his direction. But custom, *pietas* (sense of duty), and family affection made their condition easier than we are apt to think it.

ACKNOWLEDGING A CHILD

As soon as a child was born, it was laid at its father's feet. If he raised the child in his arms, by that act he acknowledged it as his own and admitted it to all rights and privileges of membership in a Roman family. If he did not take it up, the child became an outcast, without a family, without the protection of the spirits of dead ancestors—friendless and forsaken.

Disposal of the child did not call for murder, as was intended in the case of Romulus and Remus and was afterwards forbidden by Romulus when king. The child was exposed; that is, taken from the house by a slave and left by the roadside. It is improbable, however, that a Roman father often made use of his theoretical right. Although exposure and recognition appear frequently in Roman comedies, they are probably convenient dramatic devices taken over from Greek originals, rather than a portrayal of actual cases in everyday life. No actual instances of exposure are known during the Republic.

BIRTHDAYS

The Romans believed that a *genius* (guardian spirit) came into the world with a child at birth. The guardian spirit of a girl was called her *Juno*. Birthdays were celebrated as festivals of the genius with offerings of wine, flowers, incense, and

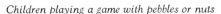

Children playing a game with pebbles or nuts

142

Wax tablet—birth certificate of a girl of Roman Egypt

Crepundia

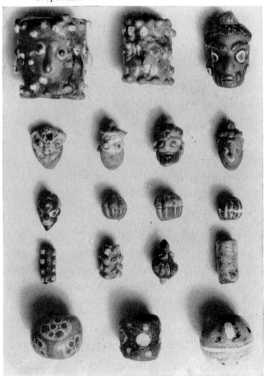

cakes. The family wore fresh white clothes, friends called or sent letters of congratulation, and the member having the birthday received presents both from friends and family. Horace wrote a graceful ode for a birthday of his friend and patron Maecenas. The festival usually ended with a dinner party.

EARLY DAYS

During the first eight days of a baby's life there were various religious ceremonies. The child was called *pupus* (baby) until a praenomen was given it. Delicate children were often named soon after birth. Usually on the ninth day in the case of a boy, and the eighth in that of a girl, the praenomen was bestowed with due solemnity. A sacrifice was offered and the ceremony of purification performed, from which the day was called *dies lustricus* (day of purification), although it was also called name day. This seems to have been a family ceremony in the home.

Marcus Aurelius was the first emperor to require birth registration. He ordered a father to register the name of his child and the date of its birth within thirty days—at Rome, before the secretary of the treasury; in the provinces, before the registrars. A boy was enrolled as a citizen when he put on a man's toga.

The day of purification was one of rejoicing and congratulation among relatives and friends, and even household slaves. They presented the baby with tiny metal toys or ornaments in the form of flowers, swords, axes and other tools, and especially, lucky charms shaped like a half moon. These, strung together and hung around the baby's neck to amuse him with their jingling or rattling, were called *crepundia* (rattles). They were often made of valuable material. If a child was lost or stolen, the rattles served as identification.

Two sides of a golden bulla

BULLAE

More important than the crepundia was the bulla, which a father hung around his child's neck on the day of purification, if he had not put it on when first he took the baby in his arms. Often it was made of two concave gold pieces, like a locket, fastened together by a wide spring. It contained an amulet as a protection against evil, and was worn on a chain, cord, or strap.

For a long time only children of patricians were allowed to wear golden bullae. A plebeian had to be contented with leather imitations on a narrow strap. By Cicero's time a gold bulla might be worn by a child of any freeborn citizen. A girl wore her bulla until the eve of her wedding day, when she laid it aside with other childish belongings. A boy wore his until the day he became a citizen, when it was dedicated to the lares. His bulla was carefully preserved, for if the owner became a general and so successful that he won the honor of a triumph, he wore his bulla in the triumphal procession as a protection against envy.

CHILDREN'S NURSES

A Roman woman nursed her baby if possible; if not, her place was taken by a slave nurse (*nutrix*), whom later the child affectionately called *mater*. A mother supervised the slaves who helped care for her children. A slave washed and dressed

Nurse with baby in her lap

Baby in a cradle

Glass nursing bottle

the baby, told it stories, sang it lullabies, and rocked it to sleep in her arms or in a cradle. Outdoors a child was carried in a litter by slaves.

After wars of conquest brought Rome into contact with Greek ways of life, a Roman often selected a Greek nurse for his child, so that he might learn Greek as naturally as Latin. Many passages in Latin literature show affection between nurse and child that lasted even after the child was grown. Frequently a young wife took her old nurse with her to her new home. The faithfulness of such slaves was often repaid by the gift of freedom. The Younger Pliny gave his old nurse a farm.

Roman toys

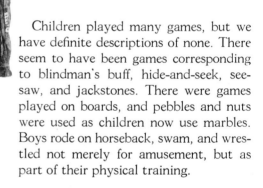

TOYS, PETS, AND GAMES

There are occasional references to toys, pets, and games of Roman children in literature; something has been learned from objects found, and in art there are representations of children playing. A child's first toys were the tiny ones of the crepundia. Then there were rag dolls and dolls of clay or wax, some with jointed arms and legs.

The famous teacher Quintilian (first century of our era) speaks of ivory letters, used by children as letter blocks are now; little wagons and carts were common; and Horace tells of hitching mice to carts, of building houses, and of riding on hobbyhorses. Children spun tops with a whiplash, as they still do in Europe. Hoops were driven with sticks, and had bits of metal attached, to jingle and warn people in their way. Boys walked on stilts and played games with balls.

Dogs were common and favorite pets; cats began to be known at Rome in the first century of our era. Many kinds of birds were pets: doves, pigeons, ducks, crows, quail, and geese. Monkeys were known but were not common.

Children played many games, but we have definite descriptions of none. There seem to have been games corresponding to blindman's buff, hide-and-seek, see-saw, and jackstones. There were games played on boards, and pebbles and nuts were used as children now use marbles. Boys rode on horseback, swam, and wrestled not merely for amusement, but as part of their physical training.

HOME TRAINING

The training of children was conducted by their parents, with emphasis on moral rather than intellectual development. Reverence for the gods, respect for law, unquestioning and instant obedience to authority, truthfulness, and self-reliance were the most important virtues for a child to acquire. Much was learned from constant association with parents, which was the characteristic feature of the home training of the Romans. Children sat at table with their elders; in early times they helped serve the meals.

Until the age of seven, boys and girls had lessons from their mothers, who taught them to speak Latin correctly, and do elementary reading, writing, and arithmetic. At seven a boy went on to a regular teacher, while a girl remained her mother's constant companion. Her formal education was cut short because a girl married early, and there was much to learn of home management. From her mother a girl learned to spin, weave, and sew; even Emperor Augustus wore garments woven by his wife.

After this training a girl was able to take her place as mistress of her own household—to become a Roman matron, the most dignified position to which a woman could aspire in the ancient world.

FATHER AND SON

Except during school hours a boy was usually his father's companion. If his father was a farmer, as all Romans were in early times, the son helped in the fields; he learned to plow, plant, and reap. If the father was a man of high position in Rome, his son stood beside him in the atrium, correctly dressed in toga and high shoes, when callers were received. In this way a boy came to know faces, names, and rank of callers, and began

Roman mother and son, called Agrippina and Nero

Scenes from the life of a child

M·CORNELIO·M·F·PAL·STATIO·P   FECER

Girl with shawl and street shoes

exercises, as well as in riding, swimming, wrestling, and boxing. The object of this training was strength and agility, rather than the grace of movement and symmetrical development which the Greeks stressed. On great occasions, when the cabinets in the alae were opened and wax busts of great ancestors displayed, boys and girls of noble family were always present to learn the history of their own forefathers, and with it the history of Rome.

END OF CHILDHOOD

No special ceremony marked a girl's passing into womanhood, but when a boy reached his majority, he discarded the crimson-bordered toga (*toga praetexta*) that boys wore and donned the pure white toga of a man. There was no fixed year, corresponding to the twenty-first with us, in which the boy became a man; it depended somewhat on his physical and intellectual development, somewhat on his father's decision, more perhaps on the time in which he lived. In general, a man's toga was assumed between the fourteenth and seventeenth years—the later age being customary in earlier times when citizenship carried with it more responsibility than under the Empire, and consequently demanded greater maturity.

In the classical period the boy's age was usually about sixteen. After that, a man placed his son in the care of some man who was prominent in the army or in civil life; with this man, the youth spent a year in training for his career. He would then be seventeen years old, the age at which a young Roman could be called for military duty.

We should expect the day when a boy came of age to be the birthday at the beginning of his seventeenth year, but it seems to have been usual to select the birthday that came nearest to March

early to gain some practical knowledge of politics and affairs of state. He could also observe and practice the dignified and pleasant courtesy that marked a Roman gentleman.

If his father took him to make calls, a boy answered politely any questions asked about his school and his studies. In early times, a senator took his son to the senate-house to hear debates and listen to great orators. It is said that this custom was given up because his mother asked too many questions when a boy came home.

Since every Roman boy was expected to become a soldier, fathers trained their sons in the use of weapons in military

17. This was *Liberalia* (the festival of *Liber*), which appropriately suggested the wider freedom of manhood.

COMING-OF-AGE CEREMONIES

Festivities began in the early morning, when the boy laid before the lares of the house his bulla and bordered toga. A sacrifice was then offered, and the bulla was hung up, only to be worn again if a time came when its owner was in danger of the envy of men and gods. The boy then dressed himself in a white tunic, which his father adjusted. If he was the son of a senator, this had two wide crimson stripes; if his father was a knight the tunic had two narrow ones. Over this the *toga virilis* (toga of the grown man) was carefully draped. This was called also *toga libera*, contrasting the restrictions of boyhood with the freedom of a man.

The toga was not necessarily bestowed at Rome, even if the family usually lived there. When Cicero was governor of Cilicia in A.D. 50, he gave his nephew Quintus the white toga at Laodicea, on the Liberalia. Later in March of the following year when he gave the toga to his son, young Marcus, in his home town of Arpinum, the townspeople considered this a compliment.

When the boy was ready, the procession to the Forum began. The father had gathered his slaves, freedmen, clients, relatives, and friends, using all his influence to make his son's escort numerous and imposing. If the day of the Liberalia had been chosen, the Forum was crowded with similar gay processions. Here the boy's name was added to the list of citizens, and formal congratulations were extended. Then the family climbed up to the temple of Liber on the Capitoline Hill, where an offering was made to the god. Finally they all returned to the house, where the day ended with a dinner party given by the father in honor of the new Roman citizen.

A Roman boy

EDUCATION

Boy reading

THE FIRST SCHOOLS

In early days a Roman father was both companion and teacher of his sons, but the actual instruction he gave them depended on his own education. Moreover, his teaching must often have been interrupted by private business affairs or public duties. Because of these difficulties, if one of his slaves was competent to give instruction, a father would turn over to him the regular teaching of the children. Slaves taken in war were often much better educated than their Roman masters.

Since many households did not include a competent teacher, the fortunate owner of such a slave frequently permitted the children of friends and neighbors to come to his house at fixed hours and be taught elementary subjects with his own children. For this privilege he either charged the parents a fee which he kept—as Cato did—or instead of direct payment, he allowed the slave to take as his *peculium* (personal property) little presents brought him by his pupils.

SCHOOLROOMS

The next step, taken in very early times, was to establish a school in a central and easily reached location and to accept all children whose parents could pay a small fee. There were no special buildings, but frequently a school was set up in an open room like a shop, or in a gallery attached to a public building, roofed against sun and rain, but open toward the street. The only furnishings were rough benches without backs. Pupils were exposed to the distractions of busy town life about them, and neighbors were annoyed by noisy recitations and even noisier punishments.

SCHOOLS AND DEMOCRACY

A knowledge of the elements of education was more generally diffused among the Romans than among any other people of the ancient world. Their elementary and grammar schools were open to all, and fees were low.

These schools were not "public" in our sense of the word—they were not supported or supervised by the government, and attendance was not compulsory. They were democratic—in discipline and treatment of pupils no class distinction was made between children of humble parents and those of noble families. The pupils who attended these schools were mostly boys, because girls were married so young that most of them had no more teaching than their mothers could give. If a girl carried her studies further, she usually belonged to a family that could afford to educate its daughters at home and preferred to do so.

Children with attendant

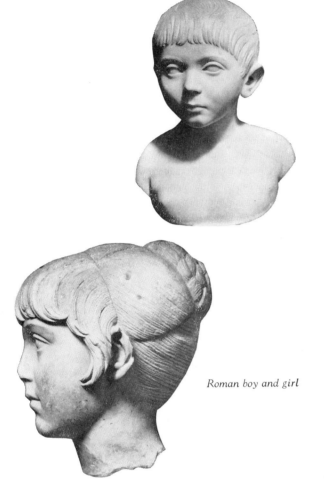

Roman boy and girl

TEACHERS

Since a teacher was usually a slave or a freedman, his position was not considered honorable, although his character sometimes made it so. His pupils feared him, but seem to have had little respect for him. Fees varied from three dollars a year for an elementary pupil to five or six times as much for a grammar-school student. In addition to fees, pupils brought the master little presents from time to time as in early days when there was no charge. Fees also differed with the qualifications of the master. Some masters with established reputations and fashionable schools charged no set fees, but left the amount to the generosity of their patrons.

There were no teachers' licenses, and no requirements in education to be met. Anyone might set up a schoolroom and wait for pupils, just as, in 1833, Stephen A. Douglas walked into Winchester, Illinois, and opened a school for three months at three dollars a pupil.

A Roman school—one boy is tardy

PAEDAGOGI

A boy of good family was attended by a *paedagogus* (Greek for child leader), a trustworthy slave who escorted him to school, stayed during the session, and saw him safely home again. A boy from a wealthy family might have also one or more slaves to carry his satchel and tablets.

A paedagogus, usually elderly and always of good character, was expected to keep his charge from all moral or physical harm. A paedagogus was not a teacher, but Latin names given him indicate his role of companion, guardian, adviser, and director. After a knowledge of Greek became common, the paedagogus was usually a Greek slave, who could help the boy remember the Greek he had learned. The boy called him master, and the slave seems to have had the right to punish mildly. His duties ended when the boy put on a man's toga, but often the same affection continued between the young man and his paedagogus as between a woman and her old nurse. An epigram of Martial describes a paedagogus who still lectured and scolded his former charge after he was a grown man.

SCHOOL DAYS AND HOLIDAYS

The school day began before sunrise, as did all work at Rome. Pupils brought candles to study by until daybreak, and the ceiling of a schoolroom was black from smoke. The session lasted until lunch time and was resumed in the afternoon after the siesta.

We do not know whether there was a fixed length for the school year, but it began regularly on the twenty-fourth of March. There were many holidays, among them the *Saturnalia*, beginning the seventeenth of December and lasting several days, and the *Quinquatria*, March nineteenth to twenty-third.

The great religious festivals, especially those celebrated with games, were naturally observed by the schools, and apparently market days, like our Saturdays, were also holidays. Since the children of wealthy parents were usually away from Rome during hot weather, some schools were closed while the pupils were out of the city.

DISCIPLINE

Judging from grim references in the poems of Juvenal and Martial to the use of rod and ferule, discipline in schools was thoroughly Roman in its severity. Horace has given deathless fame to his teacher Orbilius by the adjective *plagosus* (thrasher). The biographer Nepos says that teachers appealed at times to the natural rivalry between well-bred boys, and we know that prizes were sometimes offered. Punishment may well seem deserved when we read of the schoolboy's trick immortalized by the satirist Persius.

Paedagogi with their charges

Wax tablet with cursive writing

"Often, I remember, as a small boy I used to give my eyes a touch with oil, if I did not want to learn Cato's grand dying speech, sure to be vehemently applauded by my wrong-headed master."

ELEMENTARY SCHOOLS

The famous teacher of oratory in the first century of our era, Quintilian, gives a clear and interesting account of preschool and elementary education, which enables us to compare Roman methods with modern ones.

In elementary schools only reading, writing, and arithmetic were taught. In reading, great stress was laid on pronunciation. The teacher pronounced the words —first, syllable by syllable, then as separate words, and finally read a whole sentence. The pupils imitated him at the top of their voices. The sounds of the letters were easy, but the quantity of vowels was hard to master. Since Latin is written phonetically, it was not necessary to teach spelling as a separate subject.

In learning to write, pupils used wax tablets, much as American children once used slates. A boy wrote with a *stilus*, a pointed piece of wood, bone, or metal

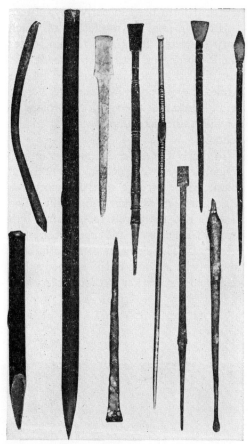

Pens and stili—the flattened end of a stilus served as eraser by smoothing the wax

shaped like a pencil. The teacher traced letters to be copied, and then guided each pupil's hand until he learned to form them. (There were only capital letters to learn, for the small letters we use were not developed until centuries later.) Next, the pupil learned to use a reed pen and to write with ink on papyrus, the ancient paper. Blank sides of used sheets of papyrus served for practice work. If any books were used in these schools, they must have been written by the pupils from the teacher's dictation.

A less formal style of writing, a sort of script, which we call "cursive," is found in scribblings on walls, scratches on tiles before they were baked, and on tablets of memoranda or accounts.

The use of Roman numerals, as we still call them, made arithmetic more difficult than it is with Arabic numerals. Mental arithmetic was emphasized, but pupils were also taught to use their fingers in an elaborate method that we do not understand. Hard problems were worked out with an *abacus* (a counting-board).

Memory training was thought so important that every pupil had to memorize many wise sayings, and above all, the Twelve Tables of the Law. These were the first written codes of Roman law, and were so reverenced that they became a fetish to the Romans. Even after the language in which they were written was obsolete, pupils still learned and recited them. Not until the time of Cicero were the tables dropped from the course, and even so, he had learned them at school.

GRAMMAR SCHOOLS

One result of the contact with other peoples that followed the Punic Wars was the extension of education at Rome beyond elementary and strictly utilitarian subjects. The Greek language came to be generally known, and Greek ideas of education were gradually adopted. Schools were established in which the curriculum was based on study of the Greek poets. These schools we may call grammar schools because the chief subject studied in them was *grammatica*, which included not only grammar but also literature and simple literary criticism. The teacher of such a school was called *grammaticus*.

The epics of Homer were long the standard textbook; along with the Greek language, students were naturally taught such topics of geography, mythology, antiquities, history, and ethics as were suggested by the *Iliad* and *Odyssey*. The range and value of this instruction depended largely on the ability and resourcefulness of a teacher, and was at best fragmentary and disconnected. There was no systematic study of these subjects, not even of history, despite its interest and practical value to a world-ranging people like the Romans.

Soon the Latin language was studied in the same way as the Greek, though at first in separate schools. The dearth of Latin poetry to study (prose writings were not yet used as textbooks) led a Greek slave, Livius Andronicus, who was teaching at Rome in the third century B.C., to translate Homer's *Odyssey* into Latin. He wrote in Saturnian verse, a

metrical form used in early days. From this rough, jingling translation, of which only scattered fragments remain, dates the beginning of Latin literature. It was not until this verse was replaced by the works of great poets like Terence, Vergil, and Horace that the rough Saturnians of Livius Andronicus disappeared from the schools.

In both Greek and Latin grammar schools, boys were drilled especially in enunciation, because of the importance of oratory in Roman public life. The teacher had his pupils repeat after him words, then clauses, and finally, complete sentences. The elements of rhetoric were also taught in some of these schools, but technical instruction in that subject was

Pupil's exercise on a wax tablet

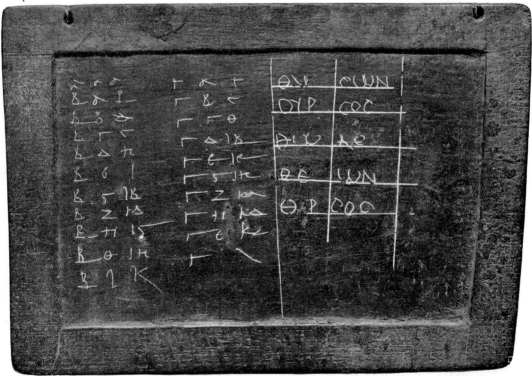

not given until early in the first century B.C., when special schools of rhetoric were established. Music and geometry completed the ordinary course of study in grammar schools.

SCHOOLS OF RHETORIC

Schools of rhetoric were formed on Greek lines and conducted by Greek teachers. They corresponded somewhat to our colleges, for those who attended them were young men—not mere boys. Usually they came from wealthy families. Here the study of prose authors and sometimes of philosophy was begun, but the main work was the practice of composition. This began with the simplest form—narrative—and continued to the practice of public speaking. There was an intermediate form in which the student took the part of a noted person who had to make a critical decision, and discussed possible courses of action. A favorite exercise was writing a speech to put into the mouth of some person famous in legend or history. How effective such speeches could be is shown by those inserted in their histories by Sallust, Livy, and Tacitus.

FOREIGN STUDY

For young men of noble and wealthy families, or for those whose talents promised a brilliant future, training in the schools of rhetoric was followed by travel and residence abroad. Greece, Rhodes, and Asia Minor were the places most frequently visited, for there a young man might observe scenes of historical significance and enjoy rich collections of books and works of art, or merely live a gay and luxurious life.

Athens offered the greatest attractions for serious study, and so many young

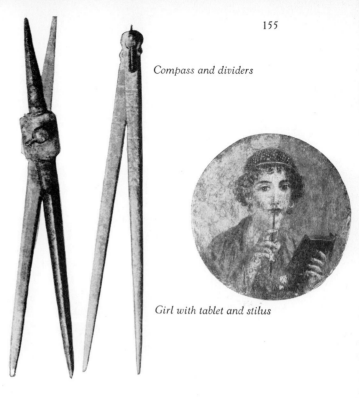

Compass and dividers

Girl with tablet and stilus

Archytas, a mathematician of Tarentum

Model of the Parthenon at Athens

Romans flocked there that it might almost have been called the university for Romans. In a letter to his father's secretary Tiro, young Marcus Cicero discusses his studies and his teachers in Athens. It must be remembered that a Roman who studied in Athens was already familiar with Greek, and so was better prepared to profit by the lectures he heard than are many Americans now studying in Europe, who have to cope with an unfamiliar language.

PROFESSIONAL TRAINING

No provision was made for formal training in certain subjects essential to successful public life—jurisprudence, administration, diplomacy, military tactics.

For observation and practical experience in duties that he would later undertake, a young man attached himself for a time as an apprentice to an older man distinguished in one of these lines. Thus Cicero studied Roman law under Quintus Mucius Scaevola, the most eminent jurist of the time; in later years young Marcus Caelius Rufus served the same voluntary apprenticeship under Cicero. Such an arrangement was considered highly honorable for both student and instructor and was certainly advantageous for the young man. In the same way, before law schools were common in this country, many youths studied in the offices of practicing lawyers.

Governors of provinces and generals in the field were attended by a voluntary staff of young men whom they took with them, at state expense, for personal or political reasons. These youths became familiar with the practical side of administration or war, while relieved of many hardships and dangers suffered by less fortunate soldiers who had to rise from the ranks. It was the inexperienced young men on Caesar's staff who hid in their tents or asked for leave of absence when he decided to meet Ariovistus in battle, although in later life some of them may have made gallant soldiers and wise commanders.

Few besides the sons of wealthy parents had the complete course of education, travel, and further training. An exception is the poet Horace, whose father, though himself only a freedman and by no means wealthy, was ambitious for his clever son, and proudly sent him to study in Athens. Horace probably knew Cicero's son and the young Messalla, for they were there at the same time. His father's confidence was justified by Horace's literary success.

Cursive scribbling on a tile, including the words "Conticuere omnes" (Aeneid, II, 1)

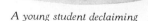

A young student declaiming

SLAVERY

Slave sharpening a knife

GROWTH OF SLAVERY

In very early times Romans were farmers and shepherds; the few slaves were used only for farm work. Because the Romans, their sons, and their free farm hands were often called from the fields to fight for their country, the use of slaves gradually increased, until they were more numerous than free men who worked for pay. In time, the use of slaves for personal service and in industry became general—one of the worst evils resulting from Rome's foreign conquests.

In the last century of the Republic most manual labor, many trades, and some professions were in the hands of slaves and freedmen. Occupations in which slaves were used were so despised by free men that manual labor was considered dishonorable. Competition with slave labor determined wages and living conditions of free workmen.

Gradually the number of sturdy Roman farmers grew smaller because many were killed in the constant wars, and competition with large slave-worked properties made old-style small farming unprofitable. Little farms were swallowed up in great estates, while slavery and manumission increased. By the time of Augustus most freeborn citizens were soldiers or slave owners unless they belonged to the idle poor class in the cities. Plebeians were largely of foreign, not Italian, descent.

Morally slavery was destructive. It was the chief cause of the changes in character even before the first century of the Em-

In a smithy the dog sleeps while slaves work

Blacksmiths' work was done by slaves

pire. Since slaves swarmed in the houses of the Romans, ministering to their love of luxury, directing their amusements, and educating their children, it is no wonder the masters lost their old virtues of simplicity, frugality, and temperance. And as they lost their strength of character in a life of ease and luxury, their sway over the civilized world decreased.

NUMBERS OF SLAVES

There is no direct evidence for the number of slaves in Italy at any given time or for the ratio of slaves to free men. (We do not even know the population of Rome at any date.) But there is some indirect evidence for statistics. That slaves were few in early times is shown by their names, for *Marcipor* and *Olipor* could not have distinguished one slave among many. The rapid increase in the number of slaves is shown by the number of captives sold into slavery by victorious Roman generals. Scipio Aemilianus is said to have disposed of 60,000 Carthaginians, Marius of 140,000 Cimbri, Aemilius Paulus of 150,000 Greeks, and Pompey and Caesar together of more than a million Asiatics and Gauls.

Even their insurrections, though unsuccessful, show the overwhelming numbers of slaves. Cicero's orations against Catiline in 63 B.C. show how much the conspirators' plan to call out the slaves was dreaded by the citizens.

For the number of slaves under the Empire there is more direct testimony. Horace implies that even a gentleman in moderate circumstances had to have at least ten slaves. He himself had two in town and eight on his little Sabine farm, though he was a poor man whose father had been a slave. Tacitus tells of a city prefect who had four hundred slaves in his mansion. Pliny the Elder mentions a man who left at his death over four thousand slaves. Athenaeus (A.D. 170-230), a Greek grammarian, tells us that some individuals owned as many as ten or even twenty thousand. The fact that house slaves were sometimes divided into "groups of ten" shows how many there were in some households.

SOURCES OF SUPPLY

During the Republic most slaves sold in Rome were prisoners of war. To avoid the trouble of feeding and guarding them in a hostile country, captives were sold soon after they were taken. The sale was conducted by a quaestor, the general's paymaster and financial officer. Buyers were wholesale slave dealers, who followed an army. A spear, the sign of a sale under public authority, was set up in the ground to mark the place. Captives, like victims offered in sacrifice, had wreaths on their heads, so *sub hasta venire* or *sub corona venire* (to be sold under the spear or under the crown) came to mean "to be sold into slavery."

Wholesale dealers assembled their purchases in convenient places and marched them to Rome in chains and under guard, to be sold there to dealers or private owners. These slaves, usually men, were likely to be physically sound and strong because they had been soldiers. For this reason they were hard to manage—many preferred suicide to slavery. Sometimes, of course, the inhabitants of towns and entire districts were sold into slavery without distinction of age or sex.

In imperial times Rome became one of the great slave markets of the world. From all the provinces slaves were brought: swift runners from Numidia; grammarians from Alexandria; able house servants from Cyrene; handsome boys and girls, and well-trained scribes, accountants, secretaries, and teachers from Greece; experienced shepherds from Epirus and Illyria; patient and tireless laborers from Cappadocia. Some of these were captives taken in boundary warfare; many had always been slaves. Some were victims of slave hunters, whose man hunts were not prevented by Roman governors.

A less important source of supply was the natural increase in slave population as men and women formed permanent connections with each other, called *contubernia*. Such connections were permitted by owners, but slaves could not be legally married. This source of supply became of general importance only late in the Empire, for in earlier times, especially during the period of conquest, it was cheaper to buy than to breed slaves.

To the individual owner, however, such an increase was a matter of as much interest as the increase in his flocks and herds. These slaves were more valuable at maturity than others, for they were acclimated and less liable to disease, and had been trained from childhood in the performance of special tasks. Also they might well feel a natural affection for their home and their master's family, especially since his children had often been their playmates. Therefore, slaves born in a household had a claim on their master's confidence and consideration that others lacked, and it is not surprising that they were proverbially impertinent and forward. As long as they remained the property of their first master, they were called *vernae*.

Barbarian trousers show that these slaves were captured in war

Orestes and Electra, the work of a freedman

SALES OF SLAVES

Slave dealers usually sold their wares at public auctions. These were supervised by aediles, who appointed the place and made the rules and regulations. A tax was imposed on imported slaves, who were offered for sale with their feet whitened with chalk; those from the East had their ears pierced, a common sign of slavery among oriental peoples.

When bids were to be asked for a slave, he mounted a stone or platform. From his neck hung a scroll describing his character, as a guarantee for the purchaser. If he had defects not shown in his guarantee, the dealer had to take him back in six months or make good the buyer's loss.

The chief items in the guarantee were the slave's name and nationality and a statement to the effect that he was free from disease—especially epilepsy—and from a tendency to steal, run away, or commit suicide. Slaves, usually stripped and made to move about, were closely examined by a buyer, and even looked over by a physician. If the dealer gave no guarantee, a cap was put on the slave's head at the sale, and the buyer took all risks.

A dealer might also offer his slaves at private sale. This was the rule for slaves of unusual value, especially for those of remarkable beauty. They were not shown to the crowd, but only to probable buyers. Private sales and exchanges of slaves between citizens were as common as sales

While waiting, the little slave has fallen asleep

Negro slave cleaning a boot

164

of other property, and carried no stigma. Although the dealer's trade was considered disreputable, great fortunes were often made in it. The vilest dealers sold female slaves for immoral purposes.

PRICE OF SLAVES

The price of slaves varied with the times and the supply and demand, as well as with their characteristics and accomplishments, and the requirements of a purchaser. Captives sold on a battlefield brought only nominal prices, because generals were eager for quick sales, and on the long trip to Rome, dealers

were sure of heavy losses from disease, fatigue, and especially suicide. The tragic piece of statuary showing a hopeless Gaul killing himself after slaying his wife indicates the despair that many captives felt at the loss of freedom.

Slaves were once sold in Lucullus' camp for less than a dollar each. In Rome male slaves varied in value from one hundred dollars paid for a common laborer in the time of Horace to $28,000 paid by Marcus Scaurus for a highly educated grammarian. Handsome boys, trained and educated, brought as much as four thousand dollars, and high prices were also paid for beautiful and accomplished

Slaves loading a boat

Slaves sifting grain

Grain measure and scoop

girls. Often slaves were matched in size and coloring, and a well-matched pair of boys brought a larger price than if sold separately.

PUBLIC SLAVES

Public slaves were owned by the State; private slaves, by individuals. Public slaves were thought better off than those privately owned; they were not so likely to be sold, were not worked so hard, and were not subject to the whims of an individual master. Their duties were to care for public buildings and serve magistrates and priests. Great numbers were used by quaestors (financial officials) and aediles. Some public slaves were drilled as night firemen. Others were *lictors* (attendants on an official), jailers, and executioners. Although the number of public slaves was large, it was inconsiderable compared with the number privately owned.

PRIVATE SLAVES

Private slaves were either employed in the personal service of their masters or kept for profit. The former were called *familia urbana*, the city household. The latter were kept for hire or were employed in their master's business affairs. Of these

Trajan and two companions, with lictors

Slaves making bread

the oldest and most important class was that of the farm hands (*familia rustica*).

Other slaves were used in all sorts of industries, but it was considered more honorable for a master to employ his slaves in enterprises of his own than to hire them out. However, slaves were always available for any purpose in any city.

INDUSTRIAL EMPLOYMENT

In ancient times most work now done by machinery was done by hand. Armies of slaves were employed as unskilled laborers: porters to transport materials and other merchandise, stevedores to load and discharge vessels, men to handle spade, pickax, and crowbar—men whose great physical strength alone made them worth their keep. Above these laborers came artisans, mechanics, and other skilled workmen: smiths, carpenters, bricklayers, masons, seamen. Merchants and shopkeepers required assistants, and so did millers and bakers, dealers in wool and leather, keepers of lodging houses and restaurants—all who helped to supply the countless wants of a great city. Such assistants were mostly slaves.

Even the professions were largely in the hands of slaves. Books were reproduced by slaves, who laboriously copied manuscripts. Artists who carved wood and stone, designed furniture, laid mosaics, painted pictures, and decorated the walls and ceilings of buildings were slaves. So were entertainers—musicians, acrobats, actors, gladiators—who amused the crowds at public games. So, too, were many teachers and most physicians.

If a slave showed executive ability as well as technical knowledge, his master often provided capital to carry on a business. A slave might manage an estate, a bank, or a commercial enterprise, even though such an occupation took him far beyond his master's observation, even into a foreign country. Sometimes such a slave was expected to pay his master a fixed annual sum from the profits of the business; at other times he was allowed to keep a share of the profits; occasionally he was merely required to repay the sum advanced, with interest. In any case, a slave's industry and intelligence were stimulated by the hope of acquiring money enough to buy his freedom and eventually make the business his own.

CITY SLAVES

The number of slaves kept by a Roman in his city household depended on the demands of fashion and the amount of his wealth. In early days a sort of butler had relieved a master of such household cares as buying, keeping accounts, seeing that house and furniture were in order, and looking after the slaves who did the actual work. Under the late Republic all this was changed. Other slaves relieved the butler of purchasing supplies and keeping accounts, and left to him merely the supervision of house and furniture. The duties of the slaves under him were, in the same way, distributed among many.

Each part of the house had its special staff of slaves, often divided into groups of ten, with a separate superintendent for each group—one for kitchen, another for dining rooms, another for bedrooms. The entrance door was guarded by its special slave; sometimes he was chained to the door like a watchdog, so that he was kept literally at his post. The duties of all the groups were again divided and subdivided—each slave had one task to perform, and only one. City slaves with their light tasks were the envy of farm slaves.

The names of the various functionaries of kitchen, dining rooms, and bedrooms are too numerous to mention, but an idea of the complexity of the service may be gained from the number of attendants that helped the master and mistress dress. The master had a slave to shave him, another to care for his feet, and a third to look after his clothes; the mistress, her hairdresser and personal maid. Besides these, each had no fewer than three or four attendants to assist with his bath. Every child had its own nutrix, while a boy had also his paedagogus and slaves who accompanied him.

PERSONAL SLAVES

When master or mistress left the house, a retinue was necessary. If either walked, slaves went ahead to clear the way, while other servants followed, carrying wraps, or for the mistress, a sunshade and fan. Such slaves were ready to perform any

Baking bread

Slave dressing her mistress' hair

service. Often a master was accompanied by his nomenclator, who prompted him with the names of those greeting him. Sometimes instead of walking, a Roman rode in a litter. This was a canopied and curtained couch set on poles, which the bearers carried on their shoulders. The bearers were strong men, by preference Syrians or Cappadocians. They were carefully matched in size and dressed in gorgeous liveries. Each member of the family had a litter and bearers. Attendants accompanied the litter just as they went with one of the family when he walked. At night, since there were no street lights, slaves carried torches. Probably even a poor man, like the poet Horace, was attended by at least one slave whenever he left the house.

When a Roman dined at the home of a friend, slaves attended him to the door. Some stayed to take care of his sandals, which were removed at the table, and others returned at a set time to see him home.

A journey out of the city called for pomp and display. The family rode in carriages drawn by horses or mules, while pack animals or wagons were loaded with baggage and supplies. There were mounted outriders, slaves that followed on foot, and occasionally a bodyguard of gladiators. Besides all these attendants, personal servants were taken along.

Slave tying his mistress' sandal

Roman tunic found in Egypt

Reconstructed litter

Iron collar identifying a runaway slave

SLAVES OF THE HIGHEST CLASS

Among the familia urbana were slaves who amused and entertained the master and his guests, especially during and after meals—musicians, actors, and readers—and for persons of less refined tastes, dancers, jesters, dwarfs, misshapen freaks, and under the Empire, even children.

Slaves of the highest class were the confidential assistants of their master—secretaries, accountants, and agents through whom he collected his income, audited the reports of his managers, made investments, and transacted all sorts of business. The greater the luxury and extravagance of the house, the more a master needed these trained and experienced men to relieve him of cares and make possible the gratification of his tastes.

Such a staff was found only in the home of a wealthy and ostentatiously fashionable man. Persons with good taste had only slaves who could be profitably employed. Cicero's friend Atticus—a man of sufficient wealth and social position to defy the demands of fashion—kept in his service only slaves born in the house. These he had so carefully trained that any one of them could read to him and write for him. But Cicero himself, who was not rich, thought it was not good form to have a slave do more than one kind of work.

LEGAL STATUS OF SLAVES

The master's power over the slave (*dominica potestas*) was absolute. He could assign laborious and degrading tasks to a slave, punish him until he died under the torture, sell him, and even kill him (or turn him out in the street to die) when age or illness made him useless. In the eyes of the law, slaves were mere chattels, like oxen or horses. They could not legally hold property, make contracts, or marry, and could testify in court only under torture. A free person under his father's authority was little better off legally, but there were two great differences between the circumstances of son and slave. A son became independent on his father's death, but the death of his master did not free a slave. Again, the condition of a son was improved by pietas and public opinion, but there was no pietas for the slave, and public opinion did little for him, except enabling him to own his savings, and sanctioning the permanent unions of male and female slaves.

Under the Empire various laws were passed that seemed to recognize a slave as a person; he could not be sold to fight wild beasts in the amphitheater; he could not be put to death by his master simply because he was old or ill; if he were "exposed," that is, turned out to die, he was freed by the act; and he could not be killed without due process of law. But these laws were generally disregarded, and only the influence of Christianity changed the condition of slaves for the better.

TREATMENT OF SLAVES

Nothing in the stern, selfish character of the Romans would lead us to expect from them gentleness or mercy in the treatment of slaves. At the same time, they were too shrewd in all matters of business to forget that a slave was valuable property, or to risk the loss or injury of that property by wanton cruelty. Much depended, of course, on the character and temper of an individual owner. Vedius Pollio, notorious for cruelty, once ordered a slave to be thrown alive into a pond as food for the fish because he had

Musicians, probably slaves, playing for a circus

broken a goblet, while Cicero's letters to his slave Tiro disclose real affection and tenderness of feeling. If we consider the age in which the Romans lived, and disregard for a moment the matter of their punishments, we may say that they were exacting taskmasters rather than habitually cruel masters to their slaves.

Of the treatment of farm slaves we get some information from the writings of the Elder Cato—a rugged farmer of his time. Cato held that slaves should always be at work except for the hours—few enough at best—allowed them for sleep, and he took pains to find plenty for his slaves to do even on public holidays. He advised farmers to sell immediately worn-out draft cattle, diseased sheep, broken implements, aged and feeble slaves, "and other useless things."

FOOD AND CLOTHING

Slaves were, of course, fed on coarse food, but when Cato tells us that besides the monthly allowance of grain (about a bushel), they were to have merely fallen olives, or else a little salt fish and sour wine, we must remember that this diet corresponded closely to that of the poor Romans. Grain was the only ration of the sturdy soldiers who won Caesar's battles for him.

A slave received a tunic every year and a cloak and pair of wooden shoes every two years. Worn-out clothing was returned to the slave manager to be made into patchwork quilts. We are told that a manager often cheated slaves by stinting their allowance for his own benefit, and it is probable that, even though a slave himself, he was more brutal and cruel than his master.

DIFFICULTIES OF ESCAPE

No matter how lenient a master might be, lack of freedom was torture enough in itself for a slave, since there was little chance for him to escape. In Greece, a country of small states, a slave was sometimes able to slip across a boundary and find refuge. But when Italy was no longer divided into independent communities, even if, by a miracle, a slave did reach the northern boundary or find passage over the sea, he was still in the Roman world, where there was no refuge for a fugitive.

If a slave escaped, he had to live the life of an outlaw, with organized bands of slave hunters on his track—knowing that there was a reward for his capture and that torture awaited him if he was taken back. He was a criminal, for he had stolen himself; he had set a bad example to other slaves, and if not caught he might become a bandit. He was branded on the forehead with the letter *F*, for *fugitivus*, and sometimes a slave had a metal collar riveted about his neck. One such collar, still preserved at Rome, has this inscription: *Fugi. Tene me. Cum revocaveris me d.m. Zonino, accipis solidum.* "I have run away. Catch me. If you take me back to my master Zoninus, you'll be rewarded."

No wonder that despairing slaves sometimes sought rest from their labors in death. It must be remembered, too, that many a slave was a man of good birth and high position in his own country—perhaps a soldier taken on the field of battle—to whom degradation as a slave was well-nigh intolerable.

SLAVES' PROPERTY

Although a freeman in patria potestate could not legally own property, his pater familias might allow him to hold, manage, and use property assigned to him as his own. In the same way a slave could hold property—called by the same name, *peculium*, as the property of a son. While a slave had no legal claim to property, his right to it was confirmed by public opinion and custom. Often an industrious, thrifty slave could scrape together a little fund of his own, if this was permitted by his master and by his own position in the familia.

A slave on a farm had few opportunities for building up such a fund, but by stinting himself he might save a little from his monthly allowance of food or he might work in the hours allowed for sleep and rest, perhaps cultivating a few square yards of garden for his own benefit. A city slave was often tipped by his master's friends and guests, and sometimes bribed to perform a bit of knavery or rewarded for succeeding in a trick. A slave who was a teacher received presents from his pupils.

A shrewd master sometimes taught a slave a trade and allowed him a share of the earnings which his deftness and skill brought. Frequently, too, a master would furnish capital and allow a slave to start in business, retaining a share of the profits. For a master such action was undoubtedly profitable in the long run. It stimulated the slave's energy and made him more contented and cheerful. It also furnished a means of control more effective than the severest corporal punishment, and that without physical injury to the chattel.

The peculium gave an ambitious slave a hope of freedom, for he might in time save enough to buy himself from his master. But many preferred to use their earnings for small luxuries rather than distant liberty. Some slaves who were held at a high price by their owners used their peculium to buy slaves for themselves, at a low price, whom they hired out, to increase their savings. The slave of a slave was called *vicarius*, and legally belonged to the owner of his master, but public opinion regarded him as part of the slave-master's peculium.

A private slave had only a life interest in his savings, could have no heirs, and could not dispose of his savings by will. If he died in slavery, his property went to his master. Public slaves were allowed, as a great privilege, to dispose of one-half their property by will.

At best the accumulation of a sum large enough to buy his freedom was pitifully slow and painful for a slave, especially since the more energetic and industrious he became, the higher his price would be. We must feel sincere respect for the man who obtained his freedom at so great an effort. We can sympathize, too, with the poor fellow who had to draw on his little hoard to make presents to members of his master's family on such occasions as a marriage, the naming of a child, or the birthday of the mistress.

PUNISHMENTS

Although terrible tortures were in some instances inflicted on slaves as punishment, such practices were not characteristic of ordinary correction. Certain punishments are mentioned in Latin literature. The most common one for neglect of duty or petty misconduct was a beating or a flogging with a lash.

The lash or rawhide was often a sort of cat-o'-nine-tails, made of cords or thongs of leather. When an offense was more serious, bits of bone, and even

Pepperbox in the shape of a slave

EX DONO DVCIS FLORTIAE SFORTIAE

A flagellum like that at the priest's left was used to flog slaves

metal buttons were attached to the lash, to tear the flesh. This instrument was called a *flagrum* or *flagellum*, and it is easy to believe that slaves died beneath its blows. To make the victim incapable of resistance, his arms were sometimes drawn up to a beam, and weights attached to his feet, so that he could not even writhe under the torture.

In Latin comedies there are references to such punishments, in which actors taking the part of slaves make grim jests on the rods and scourge, taunting each other with beatings they have had or deserve to have. But such jests are much commoner in comedies than was the actual portrayal of any sort of punishment.

Another punishment for trivial offenses

involved the use of something like the stocks of colonial days. The offender was exposed to the derision of his fellows with his arms and legs so fastened that he could make no motion at all—not even brush a fly from his face. In one variation of this, a heavy forked log was placed on the culprit's shoulders with his neck in the fork, and his arms fastened to the ends projecting in front. He had to carry the log around where other members of the familia might see him and take warning. This punishment was so common that *furcifer* became a mere term of abuse. Sometimes to this punishment was added a lashing as the culprit moved painfully along.

Minor punishments were inflicted at the order of the master or his manager by a fellow slave, called for the time *carnifex* (executioner).

Less painful and degrading for the moment, but even more dreaded by a slave, was a sentence to harder labor than he was accustomed to. The ultimate penalty for misconduct on the part of a city slave was banishment to the farm, where he might be given the hateful task of grinding at the mill or still worse, the backbreaking labor of the quarries. The last two were punishments for the better class of farm slaves, while the desperate and dangerous slaves who worked regularly in the quarries paid for their misdeeds by forced labor under the scourge, by wearing heavier shackles during the day, and by having fewer hours of rest at night. The lot of these unfortunate men may be compared with that of galley slaves. Utterly incorrigible slaves were sold to be trained as gladiators.

For actual crimes, not mere faults or offenses, punishments were severe. Slaves were so numerous and had such free access to their master that his life—and property, too—were always at their mercy.

It was a just and gentle master that did not sometimes dream of a slave holding a dagger at his throat. Nothing was so much dreaded throughout all Italy as an uprising of slaves. It was this haunting fear that led to the tortures inflicted on a slave guilty of an attempt to murder his master or destroy his property.

For an attempt on a master's life the penalty was death in a most agonizing form—crucifixion. This was also the penalty for taking part in an insurrection; Pompey erected six thousand crosses along the road to Rome, each bearing a survivor of the final battle in which their leader, Spartacus, fell.

This terrible punishment was inflicted not only on a guilty slave but also on his wife and children. If the crime could not be traced to any one slave, the guilty man still did not escape punishment, for then all the slaves of the murdered man were crucified. Tacitus says that in the reign of Nero four hundred slaves were executed because their master had been murdered by one of their number who had not been detected. The cross stood to slaves as the horror of horrors. The very word *crux* (cross) was used among them as a curse, especially in the expression [*I*] *ad* [*malam*] *crucem* ([Go] to the [bad] cross). The actual carrying out of a death sentence was performed by a public slave at a fixed place of execution outside the city wall.

MANUMISSION

A slave might buy his freedom, or he might be freed as a reward for faithful service or some special act of devotion. It was only necessary for his master to declare him free, before witnesses, although a formal act of manumission often took place before a praetor. A new-made freedman set on his head the cap of liberty

seen on some Roman coins. (This is the origin of the "liberty cap" of the French Revolution, and of that worn by the Goddess of Liberty on our coins.) A freedman was called *libertus* as an individual or in reference to his master, *libertinus* as one of a class. His former master was no longer his lord, but his patron.

The relation between patron and freedman was one of mutual helpfulness. Often a patron helped his freedman with funds to make a start in his new life. If a freedman died first, his patron paid for a decent funeral and had the body or ashes buried near the place where his own ashes would rest. He was the guardian of his freedman's children, but if there were no heirs, he inherited the property. In return a freedman was bound to show deference and respect to his patron at all times, attend him on public occasions, assist him in misfortune, and in short, stand to him as client stood to patron in the early days of Rome.

(Left) Such mosaics were frequently made by slaves

Manumission—one slave in a liberty cap shakes hands with his former owner, the other kneels in thanks

Jupiter, patron of hospitality

CLIENTES
AND
HOSPITES

CLIENTS—OLD AND NEW

In Roman history the word *cliens* (client) is used for two very different classes of dependents, who may be roughly distinguished as old clients and new clients. Old clients played an important part under the kings and were even more influential in the struggle between patricians and plebeians during the early years of the Republic, but by the time of Cicero they had nearly disappeared as a class. New clients, who are first heard of under the Empire, never had any political significance. There was no connection between the two classes except in name, and the later one was not a development of the earlier.

OLD CLIENTS

Clientage was one of the most ancient social institutions of the Italian tribes. The gentes who settled on the hills along the Tiber had, as part of their familiae, numerous free retainers, who helped farm their lands and tend their flocks. These retainers also performed personal services for the clans to which they were attached, in return for protection against cattle thieves, raiders, and open enemies. Although they had a share in the increase of flocks and herds, and bore the nomen of the gens, they were regarded as inferior members of the clan; they had no right of marriage with patrician members of the clan and no voice in its government.

The Mulvian Bridge over the Tiber

They were the original plebs, as the patrician members of the clan were the populus—the citizens, the governing body of Rome.

Rome's policy of expansion brought into the city a third element, distinct from both patricians and clients. Conquered communities, especially if they were dangerously near, were forced to destroy their own strongholds and move to Rome. Members of communities that were organized in gentes brought their clients with them and became citizens.

Those not organized in gentes attached themselves to clans as clients or else settled in and about the city to make an independent living as best they could. Some of these men may have been as wealthy as patricians, others were skilled artisans, and some were unskilled laborers; none of them had any political rights. They occupied the lowest position in the new state.

As Roman territory expanded, these people increased until they outnumbered the patricians and their retainers—with whom these conquered men could have had neither sympathies nor social ties. To them also the name *plebs* was given, and the original plebs—the clients—began to occupy an intermediate position in the State, though politically included with the plebeians. Many Roman clients, perhaps because of the dying out of ancient patrician families, gradually lost their old dependent relation, and became identified in interests with this newer element.

MUTUAL OBLIGATIONS

The relation between patrician patrons and plebeian clients is not thoroughly understood. We know that it was hereditary; great houses boasted of the number of their clients and were eager to increase them from generation to generation. The relationship was regarded as sacred, and a client stood to a patron almost as a son. Vergil tells us that a special punishment in the underworld awaited a patron who defrauded a client. There are instances of splendid loyalty of clients to their patrons —such loyalty as Highlanders displayed to the chief of the clan. There is very little definite information about the duties and obligations of clients and patrons to each other. A patron furnished means of support to a client and his family, helped him with advice and counsel, assisted him in transactions with third parties, and if necessary, represented him in court. A client was bound to advance the interests of his patron in every way possible. He cultivated his fields, herded his flocks, attended him in war, and in an emergency, even assisted him with money.

Scene on the Palatine

Atrium of a fine house where clients were received (reconstruction)

The value of this relation for both patron and client depended on the predominant position of the patron in the State. So long as patricians were the only citizens and plebeians had no civil rights, a client could afford to sacrifice his personal independence in return for protection. In a dispute over property, for example, the support of his patron assured a client of justice even against a patrician, and might secure him more than justice if the opponent were an independent plebeian.

This relationship could not long endure after patricians and plebeians became politically equal. For a generation or two patron and client might stand together against their adversaries, but sooner or later a client would see that he was getting no equivalent for services rendered, and he or his children or grandchildren would throw off the yoke. Although it is hard to tell whether the rapid growth of slavery was the cause or the result of the decline of clientage, the introduction of slaves helped make a patron independent of his clients. It is significant that the new relation of patron and freedman marked the disappearance of patron and client in the old and better sense of the words.

Roman coins

NEW CLIENTS

New clients came in with the upstart rich, who considered a long train of dependents as necessary to their position as a string of high-sounding names, or a mansion crowded with slaves. These dependents were merely needy men or women, usually obscure, who toadied to the rich and great for the crumbs that fell from their tables. There were among them occasionally men of talent—philosophers, or poets like Martial or Statius —but for the most part they were a swarm of cringing, fawning, timeserving flatterers and parasites. There was neither a hereditary nor a personal tie between a new client and his patron. A new client did not, as an old client had done, attach himself for life to one patron for better or for worse; frequently he paid court to several patrons at a time, changing often in the hope of better things. A patron might casually dismiss a client when tired of him.

DUTIES AND REWARDS

In his *Epigrams* Martial gives us many details of the life of a client. The service was easy, though humiliating. The chief duty of a client was the salutatio, or early morning call at his patron's house. Correctly arrayed in togas, his clients assembled in the great man's atrium to greet him as soon as he appeared. If this was the only duty required for the day, a client might have time to hurry through the streets to call on another patron— perhaps on several. On the other hand, a patron might command the attendance of his clients at home or on the street and keep them beside him the whole day long. Then there was no chance to call on the second patron, but every chance to be forgotten by him.

A client's rewards were no greater than his services: a few coins for a clever witticism or fulsome compliment, a cast-off toga or cloak occasionally—since a shabby appearance disgraced the salutatio—or an invitation to dinner if the patron was in a gracious mood. One meal a day was considered a client's due, but sometimes a patron did not receive his clients, and they were sent away hungry. After a day's attendance, tired and hungry clients were occasionally dismissed with only a little basket of cold food for each one—a poor substitute for the good cheer they had hoped for. From this basket the "dole"—as we should call it now—came to be named *sportula*, even when later a gift of money (about twenty-five cents a day) took the place of food.

But it was something to be admitted to the presence of the rich and fashionable, and there was always hope of a small legacy if one's flattery was adroit. Even the dole enabled a man to live more easily than by work, especially if he could keep on good terms with several patrons and draw the dole from each.

HOSPITES AND HOSPITIUM

Hospites, strictly speaking, should not be reckoned as dependents. The word *hospes* is used to mean both host and guest, and *hospitium* means their relation to each other. True, they were often dependent on others for protection and help, but they were equally ready and able to give help and protection to those

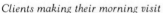

Clients making their morning visit

A Roman visiting Athens saw the Acropolis

who had the right to claim their assistance. Hospitium differed from clientage in that the parties to it were on a footing of absolute equality. Although at some time one might be dependent on the other for food, shelter, or aid, in another instance relations of protector and protected might be reversed.

Hospitium, in this sense, goes back to a time when there were no international relations—when the one word *hostis* was used for both "stranger" and "enemy." In early days when there were numerous independent communities, a stranger was regarded with suspicion and found it difficult to get his wants attended to even if his life was not in danger. Hence it became the custom that a man engaged in an occupation compelling him to visit a foreign land formed in advance a connection with a citizen of that country who would receive him as a friend, supply his needs, vouch for his good intentions, and act as his protector, if necessary. This relationship of hospitium was always strictly reciprocal. If a Roman agreed to entertain and protect an Athenian when he visited Rome, then the Athenian was bound in turn to entertain and protect the Roman when he came to Athens. Thus the word *hospes* has a double meaning, and we have no one word which translates it. It is sometimes translated "guest-friend."

OBLIGATIONS OF HOSPITIUM

The obligations imposed by the covenant of hospitium were most sacred, and failure to regard its provisions was sacrilege, bringing on the offender the anger of Jupiter, god of hospitality. Either party to the agreement might cancel the bond after formal and public notice of his intention. The obligations of the covenant descended from father to son, so that persons might be hospites who had never seen each other, or whose immediate ancestors had perhaps never even met.

The original parties exchanged tokens by which they might identify one another. These tokens were carefully kept and handed down to descendants. A stranger who claimed hospitium had to produce his token for examination. If it proved genuine, he was entitled to all the privileges of a hospes: hospitality so long as he remained in his host's city, protection —including legal assistance if needed— means for continuing his journey, nursing and medical attention if he fell ill, and honorable burial if he died.

Such arrangements are very similar to the duties of members of some of our great fraternal organizations when one of their brothers who is in distress appeals to them for help.

It was a point of honor to keep up the relationship of hospitium and to fulfill its obligations from generation to generation.

A token of hospitality (two sides)

The Erechtheum in Athens

Romans dressed formally in togas and high shoes

CLOTHING OF MEN
AND BOYS

ROMAN CLOTHING

The clothing of the Romans was always simple; ordinarily only two or three articles besides shoes were worn. Although these garments varied in material and name from time to time, there was little change in style during the late Republic and early Empire. The mild climate of Italy and the hardiness gained from physical exercise made close-fitting garments like ours unnecessary. Early contact with Greeks on the south and with the Etruscans on the north gave the Romans a taste for beauty which was expressed in the grace of their flowing robes.

Clothing of men and women differed much less than ours. Each article was assigned by Roman writers to one of two classes and was named from the way it was worn: *indutus* (put on), *amictus* (wrapped around). The first class may be called undergarments and the second, outer garments, though these terms do not exactly represent the Latin words.

UNDERWEAR

Next to a man's body was worn a *subligaculum* (a pair of shorts or a loincloth), as shown on statues of athletes. It is said to have been the only undergarment used by Romans in early times. This practice was continued throughout the Republic by the family of the Cethegi, who wore a toga immediately over a subligaculum. Candidates for public office and men who wished to pose as champions of old-fashioned simplicity, like the Younger Cato, also did this. In the best times, however, the subligaculum was worn under the tunic or was replaced by it.

There was no regular underwear corresponding to ours. Men who were old or in poor health sometimes wound strips of woolen cloth like spiral puttees around their legs for warmth, or wore wraps or mufflers, but such things were considered marks of old age or weakness, not to be used by healthy men.

NO TROUSERS

Originally Romans had no trousers, but later they adopted, for riding and hunting, the Gallic *bracae*. These were somewhat like our riding breeches. For warmth, Roman soldiers stationed in the northern provinces sometimes wore bracae. Tacitus tells of the offense given by Caecina on his return from a campaign

Soldiers wearing bracae and short tunics

188

*Bracae and peaked cap indicate a
barbarian prisoner*

A belted tunic

TUNICS

The tunic was adopted in very early times and came to be the chief garment designated as indutus. It was a plain woolen shirt made of two straight pieces, back and front, sewed together at the sides and on the shoulders. Openings were left for head and arms. Sleeves were formed by the cloth extending beyond the shoulders, but these were usually short, not quite covering the upper arm. A tunic reached from the shoulders to the calf of the wearer, who could shorten it by pulling it up through a belt; usually it covered the knees in front and was slightly shorter in the back. Cicero describes some of Catiline's followers as wearing ankle-length tunics, with long sleeves, but such garments were considered an unmanly fad.

in Gaul because he continued to wear bracae even while addressing the toga-clad citizens of Italian towns through which he passed. In classical times *nationes bracatae* (nations who wore pants) was a contemptuous expression for Gauls in particular and for barbarians in general.

A tunic was the informal indoor costume, as a toga was a formal garment. A man at work wore only a tunic, but no Roman of any social or political standing appeared at a social function or in public at Rome without a toga. Even when the tunic was hidden by the toga, good form required it to be belted.

Two tunics were often worn: *tunica interior, tunica exterior* (under and outer tunic). In severe weather persons who suffered from cold, as Augustus did, put on more than two. Woolen tunics were worn all year round, but those intended for winter use were probably thicker and warmer than those for summer.

The tunic of an ordinary citizen was made of plain white wool. Knights and senators had stripes of garnet (the Roman purple), one running from each shoulder to the bottom of the tunic in both back and front. Apparently these stripes were woven in the material. A knight's tunic was called *angusti clavi* (with narrow stripe) and a senator's, *lati clavi* (with wide stripe). Under his official tunic a knight or senator usually wore a plain white one.

Like his father, a boy wore a subligaculum and tunic; children of the poorer classes probably wore nothing else. But in well-to-do families, a boy wore a toga praetexta until he reached manhood and put on a plain white one. The toga praetexta had a border of garnet.

ROMAN TOGAS

The oldest and most important garment that a man wore was the toga. It went back to the earliest times, and for more than a thousand years was the characteristic garment of a Roman citizen. This heavy white woolen robe enveloped the whole figure and fell to the feet. It was cumbersome, yet graceful and dignified

Romans wearing togas and calcei

Two formally dressed Romans attended by a man in a tunic

in appearance; all its associations suggested formality. In the Forum, in assemblies, in the courts, at public games, and wherever social formalities were observed, a Roman had to wear his toga.

The toga was a symbol of citizenship. Wearing a toga, a Roman citizen took his bride from her father's house to his own; in it he received his clients, who were required to wear togas. In a toga he was elected to office and served, governed his province, celebrated a triumph if awarded one, and in a toga he was wrapped when he lay for the last time in his atrium.

No foreign nation had a robe of the same material, color, or style; no foreigner was allowed to wear a toga, even though he lived in Italy or in Rome itself. A banished citizen left his toga behind him, together with his civil rights. Vergil expressed the national feeling about the toga *Romanos, rerum dominos, gentemque togatam"* (Romans, lords of the world, the race that wears the toga).

Slaves were given a tunic, wooden shoes, and for bad weather, a cloak. Very poor citizens of the working classes probably wore similar clothing, since they had little use for togas, even if they could have afforded them.

EARLY TOGAS

The general appearance of the toga is well known, for there are many statues of togaed men. Descriptions of the garment's shape and the way it was worn are given by writers who wore it. As styles changed, the cut and draping of the toga varied somewhat from generation to generation. In its earlier form it was simpler, less bulky, and fitted more closely than in later times. But by the classical period its arrangement was so complicated that a man needed the help of a trained slave to put on his toga.

Augustus wearing toga drawn over his head, for a religious ceremony

In its original form a toga was probably a rectangular blanket worn like that of an American Indian or the plaid of a Scottish Highlander; but it was not colored—a private citizen's toga seems to have been always of undyed wool. Its development into the characteristic Roman style began when one edge of the garment was made curved instead of straight. The statue of the *Arringatore* (orator) shows a toga of this sort, so cut or woven that the two corners are rounded off. For a man five feet six inches tall such a toga would be about four yards long and a yard and three-quarters wide.

The garment was thrown over the left shoulder from the front so that the curved edge fell over the left arm, while the front end hung about halfway between knee and ankle. A few inches of the straight or upper edge were drawn up into folds on the left shoulder. The long portion remaining was then drawn across the back, while the folds passed under the right arm, and across the breast, and were thrown backwards over the left shoulder. The end fell down the back to a point a trifle higher than the corresponding end in front. The right shoulder and arm were free; the left, covered by folds.

TOGAS OF CLASSICAL TIMES

Statues of the third and second centuries B.C. show a larger and longer toga, more loosely draped, drawn around over the right arm and shoulder instead of under the arm. By the end of the Republic the toga was still large, but with some difference in shape and draping. A toga for a man five feet six inches tall would have been about four and a half yards long and two and two-thirds yards broad at the widest part. The lower corners were rounded, and a triangular section was cut off each upper corner.

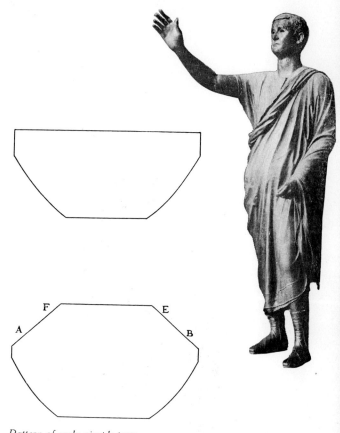

Pattern of early simple toga

Pattern of later toga

Arringatore, wearing early simple toga

The garment was then folded lengthwise so that the lower section was wider than the other. The upper part (AFEB) was called the *sinus* (fold). One end (A) hung from the left shoulder, reaching to the ground in front. The folded edge lay on the left shoulder against the neck. The rest of the folded length was brought across the back under the right arm, across the breast, and over the left shoulder again, as in the earlier toga. The sinus fell in a curve over the right hip, crossing the breast diagonally, in folds deep enough to serve as a pocket for carrying small

Cinctus Gabinus

M. Claudius Marcellus, conqueror of Syracuse, in toga and calcei, with the crescent clasp of a patrician on his ankle

articles. The right arm was left free, but the folds could be drawn over the right shoulder, or over the head from the rear. This seems to have been the kind of toga worn by Caesar and Cicero.

An early toga may well have been woven in one piece, but the larger one must have been woven or cut in two sections, which were then sewed together. Much of the grace of the garment must have been due to the skill of the trained slave who kept it properly creased when not in use and who carefully arranged each fold after it was put on. There is no mention of pins or tapes used to hold the folds. The part falling from the left shoulder over the back kept everything in place by its weight, which was sometimes increased by lead sewed in the hem.

This fashionable toga so confined both arms and legs that rapid or vigorous motion was impossible. Indeed the toga worn by gentlemen of Cicero's time was fit only for the formal, stately ceremonial life of the city. It is easy to see why this garment came to be the emblem of peace, and why Cicero made fun of the fashionable young men of his time for wearing "sails, not togas."

The toga was a burdensome garment in more than one way, for it cost so much that a poor man, especially one of the working class, could hardly afford it. We can understand therefore the eagerness with which Romans welcomed relief from civic and social duties that required wearing it. Juvenal and Martial praise the simple life in country towns, where even city officials might appear publicly in clean white tunics instead of togas. Juvenal sighs for the freedom of the country, where only the dead have to wear the toga, and Pliny the Younger counted it an attraction of his villa that no guest had to wear his toga there.

SPECIAL KINDS OF TOGAS

For certain ceremonial observances the toga, or rather that part of it called the *sinus*, was drawn over the head from the rear. The *cinctus Gabinus* was another manner of arranging the toga for certain sacrifices and official rites. For this the sinus was drawn over the head; then the long end, which usually hung down the back from the left shoulder, was drawn under the left arm and around the waist from back to front, and tucked in there.

The toga of an ordinary citizen, like his tunic, was the natural color of the wool from which it was made, and varied in texture according to the quality of the wool. It was called *toga pura* (plain toga), *toga virilis* (man's toga), or *toga libera* (free toga). A dazzling brilliance could be given to a garment with a preparation of fuller's chalk, and one so treated was called *toga candida* (white toga). Men running for office all wore this toga, and from it they were called *candidati*. Hence, office seekers today are called "candidates."

Curule magistrates, censors, and dictators wore the toga praetexta, with a border of "purple." The toga praetexta was also worn by boys and by the chief officials of free towns and colonies. The border was apparently woven or sewed on the curved edge of the early toga. In later styles it was probably on the edge of the sinus.

The *toga picta* (crimson, embroidered in gold), was worn in triumphal processions by victorious generals, and later by emperors.

A *toga pulla* was a dingy toga worn by men in mourning or threatened with some calamity. Those who wore it were called *sordidati* (shabby) and were said *mutare vestem* (to change their dress). This changing of dress was a common

Front and back views of a toga drawn over the head

form of public demonstration expressing sympathy with a fallen leader. In this case curule magistrates merely changed their bordered togas to plain ones, and only the lower orders wore the toga pulla.

Front and side views of a short paenula

CLOAKS

In Cicero's time there was just coming into fashion a cloak called *lacerna*, which seems to have been used first by soldiers and the lower classes, and then adopted by the upper classes because of its convenience. Men of wealth wore it at first over the toga as a protection against dust and showers. It was a woolen cape, short, light, and open at the side, but fastened with a brooch or buckle on the right shoulder. This was so easily put on and so comfortable that men began to wear it without a toga underneath. This practice became so general that Augustus issued an edict forbidding its use in public assemblies. Under later emperors the lacerna came into fashion again and was the common outer garment at theaters. There were dark shades for poor people, bright ones for gay occasions, and white for formal wear. Sometimes a lacerna had

a hood or cowl, which the wearer could pull over his head as a protection against weather or as a disguise.

The military cape, at first called *trabea*, then *sagum*, was much like a lacerna, but of heavier material. The *paludamentum*, worn by generals, was purple—sometimes with threads of gold.

A *paenula*—an earlier garment than the lacerna—was worn by all sorts and conditions of men as a protection against rain and cold. It was a dark, heavy cloak of coarse wool, leather, or fur. It varied in length—longer ones reaching below the knees. It was usually sleeveless, with a hood or a neck opening through which the wearer thrust his head. Since a paenula was put on over the head and covered the arms, it permitted less freedom of movement than a lacerna. A slit in front from the waist down enabled the wearer to draw the cloak up over one shoulder, leaving one arm free and exposed to the weather. A paenula was worn over either tunic or toga and was the ordinary traveling cloak of citizens of the upper classes. *Paenulae* were also worn by slaves, and were issued regularly to soldiers stationed where the climate was severe.

Of other outer garments we know very little. The *synthesis*—dinner costume—was a garment put on over the tunic by the ultrafashionable. It was worn outdoors only during the Saturnalia and was usually of some bright color. The *trabea* (worn by augurs) seems to have been striped with scarlet and purple.

The *laena* and *abolla* were heavy woolen cloaks. The abolla was a favorite with poor people, who had to make one garment do duty for two or three. It was worn especially by professional philosophers who were often careless in dress. The *endromis* (something like a modern bathrobe) was used by men after exercise.

These hunters wear bracae, tunics, and cloaks—the fringed cloak distinguishes the emperor

Tunics and togas identify the emperor and his attendants; armor, Greek costume, or drapery indicates an allegorical figure

SANDALS

Free men did not appear in public at Rome with bare feet unless they were extremely poor. Two styles of footwear were in use, sandals (*soleae*) and shoes (*calcei*). The former were merely soles of leather or matting attached to the feet by straps. They were worn with a tunic when it was not covered by an outer garment; customarily their use was limited to the house. Sandals were not worn at meals; host and guests wore them into the dining room, but as soon as the men took their places on the couches, slaves removed the sandals and kept them until the meal was over. The phrase *soleas poscere* (ask for one's sandals) came to mean "prepare to leave."

Shoes of different kinds are at the left, a wooden sole at the right

SHOES

A Roman shoe, like a modern one, was made of leather on a last. It covered the upper part of the foot as well as the sole, and was fastened with laces or straps. When a man went outdoors, he wore shoes, though they were heavier and less comfortable than sandals. If he rode to dinner in a litter, he wore sandals; if he walked, he wore shoes, while his sandals were carried by a slave. It was not correct to wear a toga without shoes, since calcei were worn with all garments classed as amicti.

Senators wore thick-soled shoes, open on the inside at the ankle, and fastened by wide straps. These straps ran from the sole and were wrapped around the leg and tied above the instep. The *mulleus* (a patrician shoe) was worn originally by patricians only, but later by all curule magistrates. Red like the *mullus* (mullet) from which it was named, it resembled a senator's shoe, and had an ivory or silver ornament of crescent shape on the outside of the ankle.

Ordinary citizens wore shoes open in front and fastened by a leather strap that ran across the shoe near the top. Some shoes had eyelets and laces. They were not so high as senatorial shoes and were probably of undyed leather. Poor people wore coarse shoes, sometimes of untanned leather, while laborers and soldiers wore wooden shoes or stoutly made half boots (*caligae*).

When the Emperor Gaius was a small boy, living in an army camp with his father Germanicus, his mother Agrippina dressed him as a soldier, and the men called him *Caligula* (Little Boots). He is more generally known in history by this nickname than by his real name, Gaius.

No stockings were worn, but people with tender feet sometimes wrapped them

Pilleus; on a coin commemorating the Ides of March, date of Caesar's assassination

in woolen cloth, to keep their shoes from rubbing. A well-fitting shoe was of great importance for appearance's sake as well as for comfort, and satirists speak of the embarrassment of the poor client who had to appear in patched or broken shoes. Vanity, however, seems to have led to the wearing of tight shoes.

HEAD COVERINGS

A man of the upper classes in Rome ordinarily went bareheaded. In bad weather he wore a lacerna or paenula, sometimes with a hood. If a man was caught without a wrap in a sudden shower, he could pull his toga up over his head. Poorer men, especially those who worked outdoors all day, wore a conical felt cap, called *pilleus*. This may have been in early times a regular part of a Roman citizen's costume, for it was kept

Traveler wearing tunic, high shoes, and felt hat, and carrying musette bag and flask

as part of the insignia of the oldest priesthoods, and was worn by a freed slave as an indication of his new status.

While traveling, a man of the upper classes protected his head against the sun with a broad-brimmed felt hat of foreign origin, called *causia* or *petasus*, which was a sort of sombrero. This kind of hat was also worn in the city by the old and feeble, and in later times by all classes in the theaters. Indoors, men went bareheaded.

STYLES OF HAIR AND BEARDS

In early times Romans wore long hair and full beards. According to Varro, professional barbers first came to Rome in 300 B.C., but razors and shears were used before the beginning of history. Pliny the Elder said that the Younger Scipio, who died in 129 B.C., was the first Roman to shave every day. Citizens of wealth and position had their hair and beards kept in order by their own slaves. Slaves who were skillful barbers brought good prices. Men of the middle class went to public barber shops, which became gathering places for idlers and gossips. The very poor found it cheap and easy to go unshaven and unshorn. But in all periods hair and beard were allowed to grow as a sign of sorrow—as much a part of mourning as mourning clothes.

Styles of wearing hair and beard varied with a man's age and with the period. The hair of children—boys and girls alike—was allowed to grow long and hang around neck and shoulders. When a boy assumed the toga of manhood, his long locks were cut off, sometimes with a great deal of formality; during the Empire they were often made an offering to some god. In the classical period young men wore close-clipped beards. Cicero jeered at some of Catiline's youthful followers for wearing full beards, but declared worse than effeminate their companions who could show no signs of beard on their faces. Mature men were clean-shaven and wore their hair short. Most statues that have survived show beardless men until well into the second century of our era, but when Emperor Hadrian (A.D. 117-138) wore a beard, full beards became fashionable.

JEWELRY

Rings were the only kind of jewelry worn by a Roman citizen, and good taste limited him to a single ring. Although often set with a precious stone and made still more valuable by the carving of the gem, the ring itself was originally of iron. Until late in the Empire, iron rings were generally worn, even when a gold ring was no longer the special privilege of a knight, but merely the badge of freedom. Usually these were seal rings—more for use than ornament. Such a ring bore a

Different styles of haircuts and beards; from the top, *L. Junius Brutus, Lucius Verus, Hadrian, Lepidus, Caracalla*

Romans in togas and baby wearing a tunic

device which the wearer pressed into melted wax when he wished to acknowledge some document as his own or to seal a cabinet or chest.

Of course there were men who violated good taste in the matter of jewelry, as well as in their choice of clothes and the way they wore their hair and beards. It is not surprising, therefore, to read of one man who wore sixteen rings, or of another who had six for each finger. One of Martial's acquaintances had a ring so large that he was advised by the poet to wear it on his leg. More surprising is the fact that a ring was often worn on a joint of the finger—perhaps for convenience in using the seal—and not pushed down as rings are now.

The man standing by the altar is formally dressed

MANUFACTURE AND CLEANING
OF CLOTHING

For centuries wool was spun into thread at home and woven into cloth on the family loom by women slaves, under the supervision of the mistress. This custom was continued throughout the Republic by some of Rome's proudest families. Even Augustus wore garments that had been made at home.

By the end of the Republic, however, home weaving was no longer common. Much native wool was still worked up on farms by slaves, but cloth of any desired quality could be bought in shops. Some articles of clothing came from the loom ready to wear, but most garments required some sewing. Tunics were made of two pieces of cloth sewed together, and togas had to be measured, cut, and sewed to fit. Even a coarse paenula was not woven in one piece. Some ready-made garments, perhaps of cheap quality, were sold in towns as early as the time of Cato, and during the Empire the ready-to-wear business was a flourishing trade.

Romans had no steel sewing needles; they used large needles made of bone or bronze. Their thread was coarse and heavy. With such needles and thread, stitches were long, and fine sewing difficult.

Even with the large number of slaves in the familia urbana, soiled garments were not usually cleaned at home. Woolen garments, especially white ones, required professional handling, and were sent by all who could afford it to fullers to be washed and pressed, bleached or redyed. Shops of fullers and dyers have been found at Pompeii, with their equipment in place. Cleaning must have been expensive, but necessary, for the heavy white garments had to look fresh, as well as be elegantly draped and worn.

Silver hand mirror

Roman women

CLOTHING OF WOMEN
AND GIRLS

WOMEN'S TUNICS

The clothing of Roman women was simple in cut; styles changed little for centuries. The effect varied with the quality of material and the grace with which garments were worn. Ordinarily a matron was dressed in a subligaculum, an under tunic, and an outer tunic (*stola*). She often wore a scarf indoors, and a shawl (*palla*) outdoors. Over or under the inner tunic she usually had a belt or sash to support the breasts.

Her under tunic corresponded to a chemise or slip, although sometimes it had short sleeves. It came to her knees and was not so full as her outer tunic. Neither tunic had colored stripes. Women usually wore both tunics, even in the house.

STOLA AND PALLA

The distinctive dress of Roman matrons was the stola. It usually had sleeves, not set in, but formed by the width of the garment over the shoulders. The early stola apparently was made of two pieces of cloth seamed together over the shoulder and upper arm, with an opening at the neck for the head to slip through. Many statues show a later form of stola made of two pieces, back and front, wide enough to cover the extended arms, but not sewed together over the shoulder and upper arm. In this style, the open edges from the neck to the end of the sleeves were gathered for two or three inches at intervals. (See seated figure, p. 202.) Opposite gatherings were sewed together, and the joinings sometimes covered with buttons or fancy pins.

Since a stola was too long for walking, the extra length was drawn up around the waist through a belt, which was covered by the overhanging folds. On the lower edge of the stola, there was a border of crimson or purple, and there was also a narrow colored border around the neck.

A palla was a large oblong shawl, usually woolen, worn outdoors. There were several ways to put it on. Often one end was thrown over the left shoulder from behind, falling straight in front, the rest drawn around the back and brought forward over or under the right arm. This end was then carried across the breast and thrown back over the left shoulder, or it hung from the left arm. This wrap could also be drawn over the head, although scarves or veils were sometimes worn. For hot weather, shawls, scarves, and veils were made of thin material.

GIRLS' WEARING APPAREL

A young girl sometimes wore only one tunic in the house; outside, she usually wore both inner and outer tunic. A girl's outer tunic was long and belted. One form

Such fibulae are frequently found

Members of the family of Augustus dressed for a religious ceremony

was so long that the top was folded over, front and back, to hang below the waist at the length desired, with a belt holding it in place. The girl in the picture is wearing a toga like that of the two boys beside her, but since they are in a religious procession, there may have been some traditional reason for her costume.

Hairdresses of many styles and periods

FOOTWEAR

Women's street shoes were like men's, but made of finer and softer leather—sometimes white or gilded or dyed a bright color. Shoes for winter often had cork soles, and thick soles were occasionally worn to make a woman look taller. House sandals were of any preferred color—some were beautifully decorated with pearls.

HAIRDRESSING

Women did not wear hats, but their hair was always carefully arranged. Styles of hairdressing varied; at some periods they were elaborate. Statues that have been preserved show almost every imaginable coiffure—puffs, waves, and curls in many combinations. A young girl usually wore her hair in a knot at the back of her neck, but some girls had curls or bangs that were straight or curled.

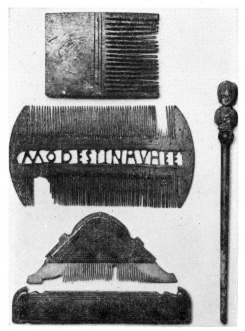

Roman hairpins—above and at the right—were ornamental and quite unlike ours, while combs and comb case resemble modern ones

Women often dyed their hair—occasionally golden-red in imitation of the color of Greek women's hair. They also added false hair—which was used so much during the Empire that it became commercially important. Wreaths of flowers, or flowers and leaves, and coronets of pearls and other precious stones enhanced the natural—or artificial—beauty of the hair. The hairdresser was a female slave, who was skillful in arranging hair in a popular style, as well as in the use of dressings, oils, and tonics to make it soft and lustrous and to encourage its growth.

ACCESSORIES

Parasols were used at Rome as early as the end of the Republic. They were really necessary in that hot climate because women wore no hats. An attendant held the parasol over her mistress' head. Women had fans made of wings of birds, peacock feathers, thin sheets of wood attached to a handle, or linen stretched over a frame. A slave, whose task it was to keep her mistress cool and untroubled by flies, fanned her. Handkerchiefs of fine linen were used by both men and women to wipe perspiration from face and hands. For keeping the palms cool and dry, ladies held balls of amber or glass, just as eighteenth-century ladies in Europe and America used "hand-coolers" of glass.

JEWELRY

Roman women were passionately fond of jewelry, and great sums were spent on rings, brooches, pins, jeweled buttons, and coronets. From the earliest times bracelets, necklaces, earrings, and pendants were worn by all who could afford them. Some were set with precious stones, but goldsmiths made beautiful and elaborate pieces without jewels.

Hairpins were of ivory, silver, or gold, often set with jewels. None was bent in what we call "hairpin" shape; they were straight like a hatpin. Many common toilet articles have been found, including hairpins, combs, boxes—for cream, powder, or rouge—and mirrors—of highly polished metal, not glass—with straight or ring handles.

An engagement ring was often made of iron, so that only its jewel gave it material value; but we know that there were rings of gold because it is said that sometimes an engagement ring was the first bit of gold jewelry a girl possessed.

Most of the precious stones we have, except diamonds, could be found in the jewel box of a woman of wealth. Pearls seem to have been favorites. Suetonius says that Caesar paid nearly three hundred thousand dollars for a single pearl which he gave to Servilia, the mother of Marcus Brutus. According to Pliny the Elder, Lollia Paulina, wife of Emperor Caligula, had a set of pearls and emeralds valued at forty million sesterces, that is, nearly two million dollars.

Gold medallion of a glass ring, showing a girl spinning

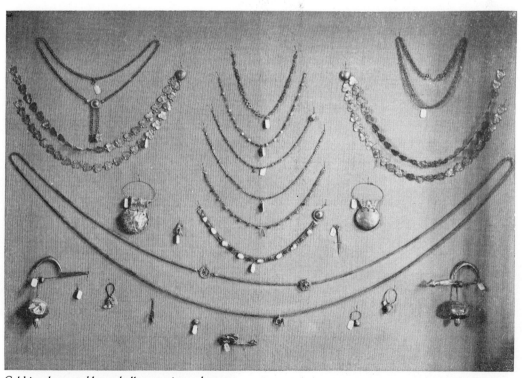

Gold jewelry—necklaces, bullae, earrings, charms

FABRICS

Romans used wool, linen, cotton, and silk for clothing. Woolen garments were worn in ancient days, since the early inhabitants of Latium were shepherds and had wool from their own sheep. During the Republic, wool was used almost exclusively for both men's and women's clothing, but woolen materials varied greatly in weight and fineness. Often undergarments, and sometimes women's tunics, were made of linen. The best native wools were produced in southern Italy, in Calabria and Apulia—the finest coming from the neighborhood of Tarentum. Much wool was imported because the demand was so great.

From very early times, linen goods were made in Italy, but they were not of the best quality. The finest linen came from Egypt and was soft and almost transparent. Cotton was not known in Europe until after the eastern conquests of Alexander the Great. Since the Indian name for cotton (*carbasus*) was also used by Romans for linen, there is often doubt as to which material is meant. Some women wore garments of cloth so sheer that they were reproached for wearing "woven wind."

Silk came from China; early in the Empire it appeared in a mixture with linen. Garments of pure silk were not worn until much later, and were rare and expensive.

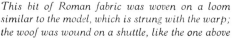

This bit of Roman fabric was woven on a loom similar to the model, which is strung with the warp; the woof was wound on a shuttle, like the one above

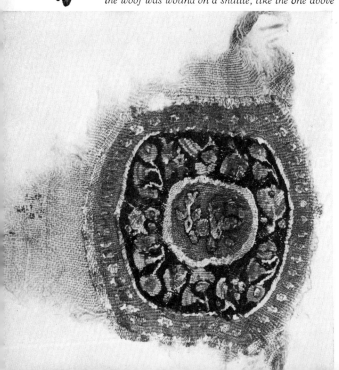

Model of an ancient loom

At the right, women make yarn with distaff and spindle, then wind it into a ball; the central group are marking a design, and the woman at the left is measuring the cloth

Needles, scissors, needles in a case, and thimble

COLORS

Throughout the Republic, white—in most cases the natural color of the wool—was the prevailing color for clothing. The lower classes preferred shades of undyed wool that did not need to be cleaned so often as the white. From Canusium came brown wool with a reddish tinge; from Baetica in Spain, light yellow; from Mutina, gray, or gray mixed with white; and from Liguria, dark gray, used in public mourning. Other shades from red to deep black were found in imported wools.

During the Empire, women wore various colors. Wool was dyed in the fleece before it was spun into thread. Linen, cotton, and silk thread were dyed before being woven into cloth. Almost the only artificial color used for clothing under the Republic was *purpura*, which varied from garnet, obtained from a native mollusk, to true Tyrian ("royal") purple. The Roman shade was brilliant and cheap, but likely to fade. Mixed with the true purple in various proportions, it gave different shades of fast color. Wool dyed violet—a popular shade—was twenty dollars a pound, while cloth of genuine Tyrian purple cost ten times as much.

Even though the costume of women changed little from generation to generation, the general effect could not have been monotonous. Variation in material and color, individuality in draping, the gleam of gold and jewels, gave variety without change of style. A Roman woman, wearing her draperies with graceful dignity, might have laughed or perhaps shuddered at the grotesque styles of many periods since; certainly she would not have envied their wearers.

Mills in a Pompeian bakery

ROMAN FOOD

ITALY'S SOIL AND CLIMATE

Italy is fortunate in natural conditions which produce a large and varied supply of foodstuffs. The fertile soil contains essential chemical elements, rainfall is abundant, and there are many rivers and smaller streams. Although the country's greatest length is from northwest to southeast, the climate does not depend entirely on latitude; it is modified by the surrounding seas, mountain ranges, and prevailing winds. These agencies produce such widely differing conditions that nearly every kind of grain and fruit of the temperate and subtropic zones finds a favorable soil and climate.

FOODS OF EARLY DAYS

The earliest Italic peoples were shepherds rather than farmers. Meat, wild fruits, and nuts must have been the diet of the shepherds who were the traditional founders of Rome. The word used for money, *pecunia* (*pecu*, flock), shows that flocks and herds were the first source of Roman wealth. Many Latin names indicate that Romans had begun cultivating the land in early times: *Fabius* (*faba*, bean), *Cicero* (*cicer*, chickpea), *Piso* (*pistor*, miller), and *Caepio* (*caepe*, onion) are as old as *Porcius* (*porcus*, pig), *Vitellius* (*vitellus*, calf), and *Ovidius* (*ovis*, sheep).

In his *Essay on Old Age*, Cicero attributes to the Elder Cato the statement that a farmer's garden was a second meat supply. But long before Cato's time, meat had ceased to be the principal food. Grapes, olives, and grain gave "wine that maketh glad the heart of man, and oil to make his face to shine, and bread which strengtheneth man's heart." On these three abundant products of the soil the people of Italy lived long ago as they still do today.

FRUITS

Apples, pears, plums, and quinces were either native to Italy or, like olives and grapes, introduced long before history begins. Careful attention was given to their cultivation, and by Cicero's time orchards and vineyards were flourishing. Abundant and cheap in season, their fruits were in common use. In time new fruits were introduced, and native varieties improved. Statesmen and generals gave their names to new and better kinds of apples and pears and, by hothouse culture, competed in the production of fruits out of season.

Every extension of Roman territory brought new varieties of fruits and nuts into Italy. Among nuts gradually intro-

Charred food found in Pompeii

Grapes, pears, pomegranates, and perhaps apples and figs can be recognized in this Roman garland

duced were almonds, filberts, hazelnuts, pistachios, and walnuts. Some new fruits were apricots, peaches, and pomegranates, as well as cherries—brought by Lucullus from the town of Cerasus in Pontus. Lemons were not grown in Italy until the third century of our era, and oranges were not known in Europe in Roman times. Large quantities of fruit, dried or otherwise preserved, were imported, but without rapid transport and refrigeration, fresh fruit could not be brought in.

Even as fruits, grains, and vegetables grown in the provinces were carried to Italy, so the Romans introduced their products wherever they settled. Cherries are said to have been grown in Britain a few years after its conquest.

GARDEN PRODUCE

Gardens gave a wide variety to the Romans' food supply. We read of artichokes, asparagus, beans, beets, cabbage, carrots, chicory, cucumbers, garlic, lentils, melons, onions, peas, poppy seed, pumpkins, radishes, and turnips, as well as others unfamiliar to us. Corn, potatoes, and tomatoes were not grown in Europe until long after Roman times.

The vegetables most used by early Romans seem to have been beans and onions, but later it was considered unrefined to eat onions, and beans were thought too heavy a food for people not doing hard physical work. Cato pronounced cabbage the finest vegetable known. The rich often imported vegetables of larger size or better flavor than could be raised at home, but fresh vegetables, like fresh fruits, could not be brought long distances with the slow transportation.

Roman gardeners gave much attention to greens for salads. Cress and lettuce are often mentioned, and mallows—no longer used for food. Many plants were cultivated for seasoning, including poppies, for poppy seeds were eaten with honey for dessert or sprinkled over bread before baking. Anise, cumin, fennel, mint, and mustard were raised everywhere. Spices, especially pepper, were imported in large quantities from the Orient.

MEATS THE ROMANS ATE

Beef was eaten by the Romans from early times, but until late in the Empire its use was a mark of luxury. During the Republic ordinary citizens ate beef only on special occasions—as when a cow had been sacrificed to the gods. Heart, liver, and lungs were the priest's share, certain portions were burned on the altar, and the flesh furnished a banquet for family and friends. Probably the great size of the carcass had much to do with the rarity of its use at a time when meat could be kept fresh only in the coldest weather. At any rate Romans used cattle for draft and dairy purposes much more than for food.

Pork, the choicest domestic meat, was widely used by rich and poor alike. The Latin language testifies to the importance of the pig—no other animal had so many names. Besides the general term *sus*, we find *porcus*, *porca*, *aper*, and others. In

Some cuts of pork in this Roman meat market are recognizable

Suovetaurilia

A pig driven to sacrifice

the religious ceremony of the *suovetaurilia* (*sus*+*ovis*+*taurus*) the pig had first place, before the sheep and the bull. There are also many words for the parts of the pig used for food. At least six kinds of sausage with pork as their base are mentioned and we read of fifty different ways of cooking pork.

Mutton and veal were also on the Roman menu, but were used less often than beef and pork. Goats' meat was eaten mostly by the lower classes.

FOWL AND GAME

As common domestic fowl, the Romans raised chickens, ducks, geese, and pigeons. Turkeys were not known in Europe until they were brought from America. In

Cicero's time guinea fowls were expensive and peacocks were highly valued—one costing as much as ten dollars. Garnished with their own beautiful feathers, they were served at the banquets of the rich. Wild fowl—cranes, grouse, partridges, snipe, and woodcock—were raised in game preserves on many large estates. Numerous kinds of small birds, such as thrushes also appeared on the table, as they still do in Italy.

Favorite wild animals bred for food were hares and boars. The latter were roasted and served whole much as they were later in feudal times. In contrast, the tiny dormouse was considered a great delicacy.

FISH OF ALL KINDS

In early days fish were not much eaten by the Romans, but before the end of the Republic no article of food brought higher prices than fresh fish of rare kinds. The names of many fish brought to the Roman table mean little to us, but we recognize

Hare, mushrooms, ducks, and baby pig might have been served at the same dinner

A cat with a partridge; ducks, birds, and sea creatures

mullet (*mullus*) and a kind of turbot (*rhombus*). Oysters were as popular a delicacy with the Romans as with modern peoples.

Since fresh fish had to be transported alive, they were more expensive than salt fish. Many rich men built fishponds on their estates where they raised fish for table use. Lucius Licinius Crassus, the orator, set the example for this in 92 B.C.

Salt fish was cheap; it was imported from almost all Mediterranean harbors. A dish made of salt fish, eggs, and cheese —mentioned by Cicero as we speak of hash—seems to have been especially popular.

DAIRY PRODUCTS, HONEY, AND SALT

The Romans used dairy products freely —milk, cream, curds, whey, and cheese. They drank the milk of sheep and goats as well as that of cows, and cheese was made from all three kinds of milk. Cheese made from ewes' milk was thought more digestible, though less palatable, than that made from cows' milk, while goats'-milk cheese was better liked, but less digestible. The Romans occasionally used butter as a salve—never as a food.

Honey was an important farm product, because on the table and in cooking, it took the place of sugar, which was unknown. Salt, used for seasoning and as a preservative, was at first obtained by evaporating sea water, but later it was mined. Its manufacture was a government monopoly, and the price was kept low.

CEREALS

Frumentum was the general term used for any grain grown for food. It occurs fifty-five times in Caesar's *Gallic War*, meaning any kind of edible grain raised in a country where Romans were campaigning. The word "corn," often used to translate *frumentum*, means grain; our corn (maize) was not known to Europeans before 1492. Frumentum was usually wheat, for in classical times wheat, much like that grown today, was the staple grain for food.

In addition to wheat, the Romans had barley, oats, and rye. However, barley was not much used, and rye was not cultivated, while oats served as feed for cattle. In ancient times another grain, *far* (spelt), a hardy kind of wheat, was grown extensively, but it gradually went out of use except for the cake used in the confarreate ceremony of marriage.

Romans used goats' flesh as well as goats' milk

Loaves of bread

A flour mill

PREPARATION OF GRAIN

In the earliest times grain was pounded in a mortar. The resulting meal was mixed with water and made into a sort of porridge (*puls*), which long remained the national dish, as has the oatmeal of Scotland. Plautus (254-184 B.C.) jokingly refers to his countrymen as "pulse-eaters."

Mills for grinding grain were gradually developed. The men who ground the grain were called *pinsitores* or *pistores*. In later times bakers were also called pistores, because they ground the grain as well as baked the bread. Mills beside the ovens have been found in the ruins of bakeries. In a Pompeian bakery there are several mills which were turned by hand.

GRINDING THE GRAIN

A mill consisted of three parts, the lower millstone (*meta*), the upper stone (*catillus*), and the framework surrounding and supporting the latter, which furnished the means to turn the meta. The framework of mills found at Pompeii and other places has disappeared, but the stone and masonry parts which have survived enable archaeologists to rebuild the mills.

The meta was a cone-shaped stone resting on a bed of masonry with a raised rim. Between this rim and the lower edge of the meta the flour collected. In the upper part of the meta a beam was mortised, ending above in an iron pin or pivot, on which hung and turned the framework that supported the catillus. The catillus itself was like two funnels joined at their necks. The upper funnel served as a hopper into which grain was poured; the lower funnel fitted closely over the meta. The distance between the lower funnel and the meta was regulated by the length of the pin, and this controlled the fineness of the flour.

Because of the heavy weight suspended from it, the framework of a mill was strong and massive. The beams used for turning were fitted into holes in the narrow part of the catillus. Power for grinding was furnished by horses or mules that pulled the beams or by slaves who pushed them. Turning a mill was such hard work that slaves were often made to grind as a punishment. Of the same shape but much smaller were hand mills used by soldiers for grinding their rations of grain. Under the Empire, mills operated by water power were introduced, but they are rarely mentioned in literature.

A large hand mill

A meta, and a catillus supported on a meta

PORRIDGE TO BREAD

The link between porridge and bread may have been thin cakes of meal and water baked in front of a fire. We do not know exactly when ovens came into use or when bread was first made with yeast. We read of professional bakers in 171 B.C., but long before that, bread must have been made by the mater familias herself or by a slave under her direction. After public bakeries were established, bread was not usually made in private houses. Only pretentious city mansions were equipped with ovens, and in the country bread continued to be baked at home.

Under Trajan (A.D. 98-117) it became the custom to distribute bread daily to the unemployed, instead of doling out grain once a month. The bakers were organized into a guild that enjoyed certain privileges and immunities.

Bread and grain from Pompeii

BREADMAKING

After the flour which collected about the edge of the meta had been sifted, water, salt, and yeast were added; then the dough was kneaded in a trough or in a simple machine. Bread was baked in an oven much like those still found in parts of Europe, or the brick ovens used in this country before cookstoves were introduced. Such ovens were found in Pompeii. In the oven proper, a fire was built; the draft was furnished by an opening. The surrounding chamber was intended to retain the heat after the fire (usually of charcoal) had been raked out into the ash pit and the vent closed. There was a receptacle for water, which may have been used for moistening bread while it was baking, to produce a hard crust. After the oven had been heated and the fire raked out, loaves were put in, vent closed, and the bread left to bake.

KINDS OF BREAD

There were several qualities of bread, depending on the flour, which varied with the kind of grain, the setting of the millstones, and the fineness of the sieves. The very best bread was made of fine wheat flour. Breads of coarse wheat flour, of flour and bran, or of bran alone were called *panis plebeius, castrensis, sordidus,* or *rusticus,* (common, army, dark, or country bread). In the first century of our era, people preferred fine white bread, though then as now, whole-wheat bread was considered more nutritious.

Loaves were circular in form and rather flat, like some of our coffee cakes, and were divided by lines through the center into four or more parts. Such loaves have survived in Pompeii. In some bakeries, cakes and confections were also made and sold.

Oil works in North Africa

Reconstruction of an oil press

THE USEFUL OLIVE

Among foods, olives were next in importance to wheat. It is because olives have so many uses that their cultivation is still so general in southern Europe. Introduced into Italy from Greece, the olive tree spread westward through the Mediterranean countries. In ancient times the best olives came from Italy. Olives were most valuable for their oil. The best oil was made from fruit not fully ripe, but the largest quantity was yielded by ripe fruit. Olive oil was used as we

Grapes beside a Pompeian house

use butter or other fats in cooking and in relishes and dressings. Olives were also an important food as fruit and were eaten both fresh and preserved.

They were preserved in a number of ways. Ripe olives were sprinkled with salt and left undisturbed for five days; the salt was then shaken off and the fruit dried in the sun. They were also kept sweet in boiled grape juice. Half-ripe olives were picked with stems, placed in jars, and covered with the best quality of oil. They are said to have retained the flavor of fresh fruit for more than a year.

Green olives were pickled in strong brine, as they still are, or crushed and preserved with spices and vinegar, as a relish. Another relish was made by stoning the fruit—green, half-ripe, or ripe—chopping up the pulp, seasoning it with vinegar, coriander seeds, cumin, fennel, and mint, and placing the mixture in jars with oil enough to exclude the air. This was served with cheese.

ROMAN BEVERAGES

Although grapes were eaten both fresh and dried (raisins), their chief importance was for winemaking. Next to water and milk, wine was the most common drink of all classes, but the Romans almost always mixed it with water, using more water than wine. Pliny the Elder mentions a wine that could be mixed with eight times as much water. Only the dissipated drank wine straight; to drink it undiluted was not considered civilized.

Grove of olive trees

Under the Empire ordinary wines were cheap enough to be sold at a few cents a quart. Choicer kinds were expensive, entirely beyond the reach—Horace gives us to understand—of a man in his circumstances.

More rarely used than wine were other beverages mentioned in Latin literature.

A favorite drink was *mulsum*—four parts of wine and one of honey. A combination of water and honey fermented together was called *mulsa* (mead). The Romans also made cider from apples, wines from mulberries and dates, and various cordials from aromatic plants. Tea and coffee were unknown.

MEALS OF THE DAY

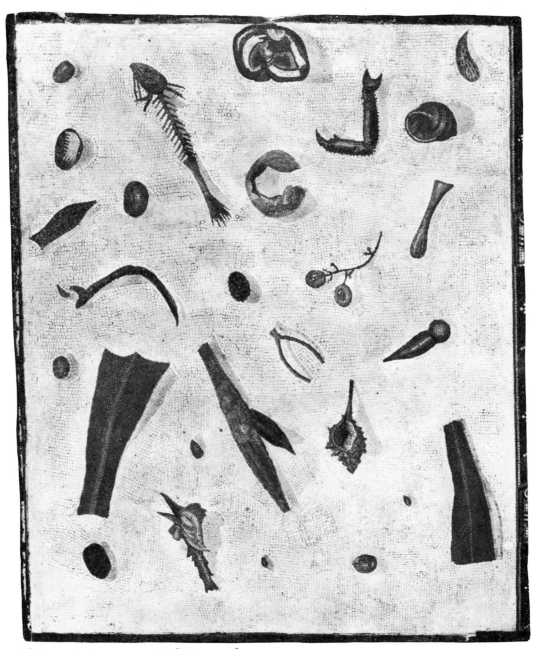

This mosaic shows an unswept dining-room floor

SIMPLE FARE

As with any people, the meals and table customs of the Romans varied with the degree of their civilization, and with the means and tastes of classes and individuals. During the Republic—perhaps almost through the second century B.C.—Romans cared little for pleasures of the table. They lived frugally and ate sparingly. Almost strict vegetarians, they ate much of their food cold; cooking and table service were extremely simple. All meals were prepared by the mother or by female slaves under her direction.

The table was set in the atrium. Father, mother, and children all sat around it on stools or benches, waiting on one another and on their guests. Dependents ate the same food but apart from the family.

Dishes were of common crockery or even wood, though a silver saltcellar was often a cherished ornament. Table knives and forks were unknown, but the Romans had spoons like ours. Before it was served, food was cut into convenient portions, and spoons were used as well as fingers.

During the early Republic there was little difference between the fare of a patrician and his poorest client. The Samnite envoys found Manius Curius, conqueror of Pyrrhus (275 B.C.), eating his simple dinner of vegetables from an earthen bowl. A century later Plautus says that even the wealthiest Romans had no specially trained cooks. When a dinner out of the ordinary was given, a professional cook was hired, who brought with him his own utensils and helpers, just as a caterer does today.

In the country the Roman custom of reclining at meals was not always followed

A Pompeian cookstove

LUXURIOUS LIVING

In the last two centuries of the Republic the simple style of life changed. Wars and travel in Greece and Asia Minor, as well as the Punic Wars, had given many Romans contact with luxurious living, and there were gradual changes in their ways of eating. Poor and rich no longer had the same simple table customs. Naturally the lower classes continued to live frugally, on dark bread, vegetables, an occasional bit of meat, and a little cheap wine mixed with water. The rations of Caesar's soldiers, who won his battles for him, were measures of grain, which they ground in their hand mills and baked at their campfires. But some of the very rich, aping Greek luxury without Greek refinement, became gluttons instead of

Pottery from Roman Britain

gourmets. They ransacked the world for rare and expensive foods, rather than contenting themselves with really palatable and delicate dishes. Petronius, in the *Banquet of Trimalchio*, burlesques this style of living.

A separate dining room was introduced, and great houses had two or more such rooms. In place of benches or stools there were dining couches; slaves served a meal to reclining diners, and a special dinner costume was worn. Every rich man's household in the city included a high-priced chef with a staff of trained assistants.

Some wealthy men—like Cicero's friend Atticus—clung to the simpler customs of early days, but they could make little headway against general dissipation and extravagance. A fawning, needy client preferred the rich food of an ostentatious patron to the plain fare of honest independence. Between these two extremes was the middle class of well-to-do citizens whose ordinary meals are sometimes mentioned in literature.

HOURS FOR MEALS

Three meals a day were customary with the Romans, though there were some who considered two meals more healthful than three, while others indulged in an extra meal late at night. Hours for meals were fixed by custom, though they varied with the period and with the occupations and inclinations of individuals.

In early times in the city, and always on the farm, the chief meal (*cena*) was eaten in the middle of the day, breakfast (*jentaculum*) in the early morning, and

Silver plate showing Minerva

Silver plate with mythological figures

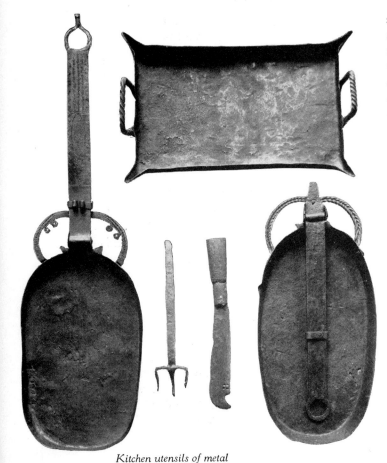

Kitchen utensils of metal

*Metal ladles, strainers, and spoon were handmade
with decorative detail*

supper (*vesperna*) in the evening. In classical times in Rome, cena was postponed until the work of the day was finished, thus crowding out vesperna, while luncheon (*prandium*) took the place of the old-fashioned noon dinner. Late dinner came to be a social function, since guests were often present, and food and service were the best the house could afford.

BREAKFAST

Breakfast and luncheon were simple, informal meals. Usually breakfast was merely bread, dry or dipped in wine or sprinkled with salt, though raisins, olives, and cheese were sometimes added. Workmen pressed for time seem to have eaten breakfast on the way to work, and schoolboys often stopped at a bakery to buy a pancake for a hasty meal. More rarely breakfast was a regular meal at which eggs were served and mulsum or milk drunk. Probably this was eaten at a later hour by people who ate no lunch.

LUNCHEON

Luncheon, usually a cold meal served about eleven o'clock, consisted of bread, salad, olives, cheese, fruit, nuts, and cold meat from dinner of the day before. Sometimes hot meat and vegetables were served, but the meal was never elaborate. Writers occasionally mention it as a morning meal, but in this case it must have followed a very early breakfast, or have been a late breakfast, if the usual early meal was omitted.

After luncheon came the midday rest, or siesta, when all work was laid aside for two or three hours, except in law courts and senate. In summer, at least, everybody took a nap, and even in Rome streets were almost as deserted as at midnight.

SUPPER

On the farm the day closed with an early supper—a meal unknown in city life. It consisted of food left over from the noon dinner, with the addition of uncooked vegetables or fruit raised on the farm. The word *merenda* seems to have been applied in early times only to this evening meal, while later it was used for refreshments eaten at any time in the day.

FORMAL DINNERS

After the busy life of Rome crowded dinner from the middle of the day to midafternoon, this custom spread to towns and cities. Naturally it was observed by city people on their country estates, so that in classical times a late cena was the practice of all persons of any social standing. Dinner was even more of a function with the Romans than it is with us, because they knew no other form of purely social intercourse. There were no receptions, balls, theater parties, or other occasions when they could entertain their friends or be entertained by them. Probably when a wealthy Roman was in town, he was host or guest at a dinner every afternoon, unless urgent business or some unusual circumstance prevented his being there.

On country estates dinner guests were neighbors, or friends who stopped unexpectedly for a night as they were passing by. These dinners, though formal, were not the extravagant banquets of the ostentatious rich, but were a wholesome expression of genuine hospitality. The guests were friends of the host, their number was limited, his wife and children were present at the table, and the occasion was one of pleasant social enjoyment.

Pottery jug with decorations of applied clay

Silver cup and shell-shaped dish

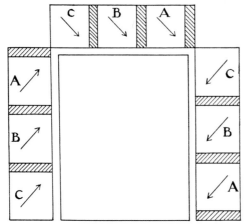

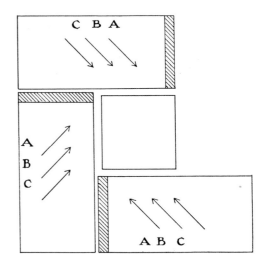

Two arrangements of table and couches

DINING COUCHES

By classical times, dining couches had replaced stools or benches. A dining couch, broader and lower than the common one, had no back, sloped from front to rear, and had an arm at one end. Here a cushion, or bolster was placed. Parallel with it, two other bolsters divided a couch into three parts. Each division accommodated one person, so that a single couch held three people. The dining room was planned to hold three of these couches, each at one side of the table, the fourth side of which was open.

The three couches were equidistant from the table, which was served from the fourth side. There was so little space between table and couches that guests could help themselves.

The arrangement varied a little with the size of the room. In a large room couches were set as in the left diagram, but in a smaller space they were placed as in the one on the right. Probably the latter arrangement was more common. Nine may be taken as the limit of the number at an ordinary table.

SEATING GUESTS

If the diners all belonged to the same family—especially if one was a child—or when guests were intimate friends, a fourth person might find room on a couch, but this was not usual. Probably when an unexpected guest arrived, some member of the family gave him his place. Often the host reserved one or more places for friends that guests might bring without notice. Such uninvited persons were called *umbrae* (shadows). When guests were present, the host's wife sat on the edge of the couch instead of reclining, and children usually sat on stools.

On special occasions a larger room was used, which held two or more tables, each accommodating nine persons.

PLACES OF HONOR

A diner approached the couch from the rear and took his place on it, facing the table and lying on his left side, supported by his left elbow, which rested on the cushion. Each couch and each place on the couch had its own name, according to its position: highest, middle, lowest. Diners reclining on the middle couch had the highest couch on their left, and the lowest on their right. Etiquette assigned the highest and the middle couches to guests, while the lowest was reserved for the host, his wife, and some other member of his family. If the host alone of the family was present, he gave the two places beside him to the least important guests.

In the same way the places on each couch were called high, middle, and low positions. The person in place A was said to be above the person on his right, while the diner in the middle of a couch was above the person on his right and below the one on his left. The place of honor on the highest couch was that marked A, and the corresponding place on the lowest couch was taken by the host. To the most distinguished guest was given the place on the middle couch marked C; if a consul was present, it was assigned to him, and hence was called the consul's place. It was beside the seat of the host, and was very convenient for

a public official; if he had to receive or send a message during dinner, he could speak to the messenger without even turning on his elbow.

THE CURVED COUCH

In the early years of the Empire a new type of couch was designed to be used with a round table. Because of its shape, this couch was called *sigma*, from one form of the Greek letter. Its one cushion, which curved around the inner side of the couch, apparently accommodated all guests, whose number varied with the size of the table and couch. The places of honor were at the ends; the one at the right end of the couch, as a diner stood behind it and faced the table, was that of the consul.

FURNITURE AND TABLEWARE

In addition to couches and table, a sideboard was usually the only article of furniture in a dining room. Sideboards varied from a simple shelf to tables of

Roman glassware

Dishes of Roman glass

Elaborately decorated silver bowl

different shapes and sizes, and open cabinets set against the walls. Like our buffets and china cabinets, they were used to display silver and other tableware.

Individual plates were not placed on the table; it was used to hold serving dishes and certain formal articles, such as a silver saltcellar and things necessary for offerings to the gods. The table was never very large, though often beautiful and expensive. Its top was not hidden by a covering; not until about the end of the first century of our era were tablecloths used.

In the time of Augustus ordinary dishes were of Arretine ware, an attractive but inexpensive red-glazed pottery with designs in relief. Graceful glassware and beautiful silver services have been found

Cooking utensils and jars

—pitchers, serving dishes, bowls, cups, and spoons. The cost and beauty of the tableware were limited only by the means and taste of the owner.

FROM EGG TO APPLES

In classical times even the simplest dinner was divided into three parts: *gustus* (appetizers), *cena* (dinner proper), *secunda mensa* (dessert). At elaborate dinners each part was served in several courses. The gustus consisted of fresh oysters and other shellfish, salted or pickled salt-water fish, and uncooked vegetables, especially onions and lettuce. Almost invariably there were eggs, and piquant sauces for these appetizers. Mulsum was drunk with the gustus, because

Silver urn of delicate workmanship

The shape of this silver dish suggests its use for eggs

wine was considered too heavy for an empty stomach. From *mulsum* this course was sometimes called *promulsis;* it was also called *antecena*.

The main part of the dinner consisted of fish, meat, fowls, and vegetables, often served in several courses. Three was considered a moderate number; it is said that Augustus often dined on three courses and never went beyond six. With this part of the meal wine (mixed with water) was drunk, but in moderation, so as not to dull the sense of taste.

Secunda mensa—pastry, sweets, nuts, and fruit, fresh or preserved—closed the meal. With dessert, wine was drunk freely; after dinner was over, the real drinking began.

From the fact that eggs were eaten at the beginning of the meal and apples at the end came the saying *ab ovo ad mala* (from egg to apples)—like our "from soup to nuts."

BILLS OF FARE

Literature gives us menus of a few meals, which may be taken as typical of simple, abundant, and sumptuous dinners. The simplest menu is supplied by Juvenal: for gustus, asparagus and eggs; for cena, young kid and chicken; for secunda mensa, fruit. Martial describes two dinners. The first consisted of lettuce, onions, tuna, and sliced eggs; sausages with porridge, fresh cauliflower, bacon, and beans; pears and chestnuts, and with the wine, olives, parched peas, and lupines (as we serve salted nuts). The second dinner included mallows, onions, mint, elecampane, anchovies with sliced eggs, and sow's udder in tuna sauce for gustus; cena served in a single course—kid, chicken, cold ham, green beans, and young cabbage sprouts. Fresh fruit with wine made the dessert.

We have also a bill of fare which Macrobius (fifth century of our era), assigns to a banquet of the *pontifices* in the late Republic. Such banquets were proverbial for their magnificence. Antecena was served in two courses: first, raw sea urchins, oysters, and three kinds of salt-water mussels, cooked thrush on asparagus, a fat hen, panned oysters and mussels; second, mussels again, shellfish, jellyfish, figpeckers (small birds), loin of goat, loin of pork, fricasseed chicken, figpeckers again, and two kinds of salt-water snails. The cena included sow's udder, boar's head, panned fish, panned sow's udder, domestic duck, wild duck, hare, roast chicken, starch pudding, and bread. Neither vegetables nor dessert are mentioned by Macrobius, but undoubtedly they were served on the same lavish scale. The wine which the pontifices drank at these feasts was famous for its high quality.

LATE DINNER

Since the dinner hour marked the close of the day's work, it varied with the season of the year and the social position of the family. In general the time may

235

be said to have been between the ninth and tenth hours—that is, about the middle of the afternoon. Dinner usually lasted until bedtime—at least for three or four hours. Romans usually went to bed early because they rose early, but sometimes even an ordinary dinner lasted until midnight. When a banquet was expected to be unusually long, it was begun earlier, so that the guests might still get needed rest. Banquets beginning before the ninth hour were called *tempestiva convivia* (early dinners)—the word *tempestiva* carrying with it some reproach.

At ordinary family dinners the time was spent in conversation, though in some good houses (notably that of Atticus) a trained slave read aloud. At "gentlemen's dinners" other forms of entertainment were provided, such as music, dancing, and juggling by professionals. At elaborate dinners souvenirs were sometimes distributed—Book xiv of Martial's *Epigrams* consists of couplets to be attached to such gifts.

Large bronze jug

Two bowls of multicolored glass

236

Bowl of Arretine pottery

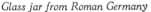

Glass jar from Roman Germany

SERVING THE DINNER

When the guests had been ushered into the dining room, the gods were solemnly invoked, a custom to which "saying grace" corresponds. Then the guests took their places on the couches as assigned. Their sandals were removed by their own attendants, and water and towels were carried around for washing their hands. Each guest brought his own napkin.

The meal then began. Each course was placed upon the table on a tray, from which dishes were passed in regular order to the guests. As each course was finished, the dishes were placed on the tray and removed. Between the chief parts of the meal, too, the table was cleared and wiped with a cloth or sponge. Water and towels were passed to the guests—since fingers were used for forks. Between the dinner course (or courses) and dessert there was a long pause, and silence was kept while wine, salt, and meal—perhaps also other ordinary articles of food—were offered to the lares. Dessert was then brought on in the same way as other courses. When ready to leave, the guests called for their sandals and departed.

COMISSATIO

Cicero tells of Cato the Elder and his Sabine neighbors lingering over their dessert and wine until late at night, finding the chief charm of the long evening in conversation. For this reason Cato is said to have declared the Latin word *convivium* (living together) a better word for such social intercourse than the one the Greeks used—*symposium* (drinking together).

The younger men in the gay circles of the capital inclined rather to the Greek view and followed the cena proper with a drinking bout, or wine supper, called *comissatio* or *compotatio*. This differed from the supper Cato approved, not merely in the amount of wine consumed, the lower tone of the occasion, and the questionable amusements, but also in the adoption of certain Greek customs unknown among the Romans until after the Second Punic War and never adopted in such conventional dinner parties as those described. The new customs included the use of perfumes and flowers, the selection of a master of the revels, and a different method of drinking.

Perfumes and flowers were used not so much for their fragrance—although the Romans enjoyed it—as because the ancients believed that the scent of flowers prevented, or at least delayed, intoxication. This is shown by the fact that the diners waited to anoint their heads with perfumes and crown them with flowers until after the dessert and wine had been brought on. Various flowers and leaves were used for garlands according to individual tastes, but roses were the most popular and came to be generally associated with wine drinking.

MASTER OF THE REVELS

After guests had put on their floral crowns—sometimes they also wore garlands around their necks—each man threw dice, usually calling as he did so on his sweetheart or some god to help his throw. The one whose throw was highest was forthwith declared *rex (magister, arbiter) bibendi* (master of the revels). Just what his duties and privileges were is not definitely known, but probably he determined the proportion of water to be added to the wine, laid down rules for drinking (*leges insanae*, Horace calls them), decided what each guest should do to entertain the others, and imposed penalties and forfeits for breaking the rules.

DRINKING HEALTHS

Under the direction of the master of the revels, the wine was mixed in a large bowl and then ladled by slaves into goblets for the guests. The ladle held about a twelfth of a pint or perhaps was gradu-

Two glass bowls and a pitcher with elaborate patterns in color

Silver drinking cup

Bronze pitcher

Cast of a bronze pitcher

ated by twelfths. At ordinary dinners each person mixed wine and water to suit himself, and drank as little or as much as he pleased, but at the comissatio all had to drink alike. The wine seems to have been drunk in "healths," but an odd custom controlled the amount of each drink. A person might propose the health of anyone he pleased to name. Immediately slaves ladled into the goblet of each guest as many twelfths from the bowl as there were letters in the name mentioned, and the goblets had to be emptied with one swallow.

The rest of the entertainment was often wild enough. Gambling was common, and Cicero speaks of even more scandalous practices. Sometimes guests spent the evening roaming from house to house, playing host in turn, staggering through the streets and making the night hideous, still wearing their garlands.

BANQUETS OF THE VULGAR RICH

In the last century of the Republic and the time of the early emperors, banquets of vulgar nobles and the newly rich were arranged much like the dinners described above, but they differed in ostentatious display of furniture, tableware, and food. Judged by today's standards, these dinners were grotesque and revolting rather than magnificent. Couches made of silver, wine instead of water for the hands, twenty-two courses to a single cena, seven thousand birds served at another, a dish of livers of fish, tongues of flamingos, brains of peacocks and pheasants mixed together—such ostentation strikes us as extreme vulgarity. Banquets of this kind were not typical of the life of the average citizen.

The sums spent on these banquets do not seem so fabulous now as they did then. Every season in our great capitals

Pompeian fresco showing the end of a Roman banquet

there are social functions that surpass—in cost as far as they do in taste and refinement—even the feasts of Lucullus, who entertained extravagantly, spending ten thousand dollars on a single dinner. As signs of the times, however, and as indications of changed ideals and of degeneracy and decay, these extravagant banquets deserved the notice that Roman historians and satirists gave them.

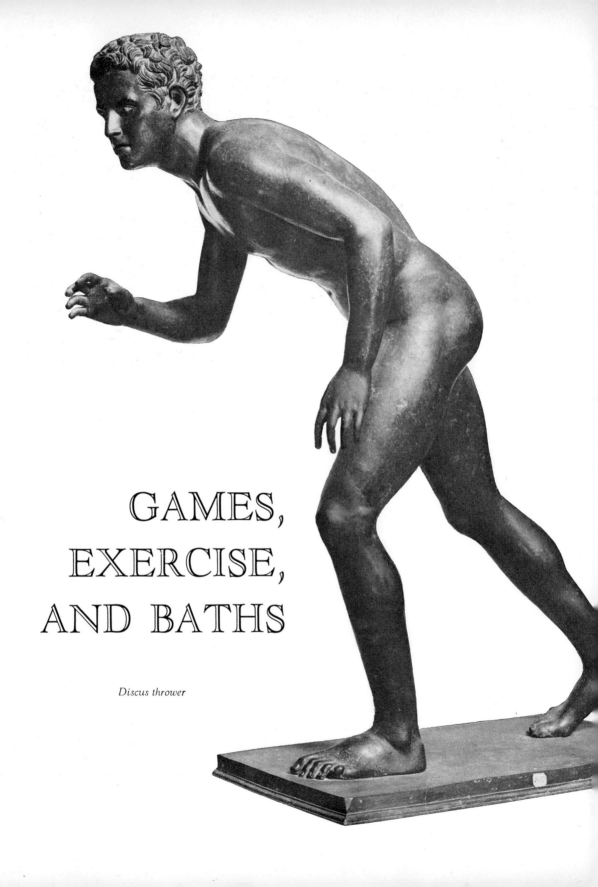

GAMES,
EXERCISE,
AND BATHS

Discus thrower

Fighters

SPORTS OF THE CAMPUS MARTIUS

While we are inclined to think of the great spectacles of the theater, circus, and amphitheater as the chief amusements of the Romans, it must not be forgotten that there were others in which they took active part. There were indoor games and outdoor sports, among them, of course, swimming; and the great public baths of Imperial Rome made all these available under one roof, along with the bath for cleanliness' sake.

After the games of childhood, Romans did not enter into competitive sports as we do. There was no national game for young men, such as baseball or football. Of such sports Romans knew nothing. Men practiced riding, fencing, wrestling, throwing the discus, and swimming—sports which were useful training for a soldier. In the country, men went hunting

Wrestlers

Formerly called a stadium, this space on the Palatine Hill may have been a garden

and fishing. Often they played ball before dinner for exercise, and sometimes engaged in a few games of chance for excitement. There were no social amusements, like dancing or card parties, in which men and women took part together, nor did women join in the outdoor sports of men.

The Campus Martius, which was often called simply the *Campus*, included all the level ground between the Tiber and the Capitoline and Quirinal Hills. The northwestern portion of this plain, bounded on two sides by the river, was the old drill ground for soldiers, and for centuries the playground of Rome. Here in the cooler hours of the day young men gathered for athletic games. After lunch and siesta, older men sometimes went to the Campus for exercise before visiting the baths and dining. Younger men often preferred a plunge in the convenient river to one in the baths. Even men of high position, such as Caesar, Maecenas, and Augustus often exercised on the Campus.

The sports on the Campus Martius were those now grouped together as track and field athletics. They included foot racing, jumping, throwing the discus, archery, wrestling, and boxing. Judging by Vergil's description in the *Aeneid*, these sports were carried on much as they are now, with the exception of the ball games. In comparison with modern games of baseball, football, basketball, and tennis, Roman ball games seem very dull, but Romans played games more for healthful exercise than for the joy of playing.

BALL GAMES

The basis of all ball games was throwing and catching; rarely was a bat used. Balls of different sizes, filled with hair, feathers, or air, were used. In the simplest game a player threw a ball as high as he could and tried to catch it before it struck the ground. In a variation of this sport, a player juggled two or more balls in the air, throwing and catching them by turns with another player, who was doing the same.

In a game resembling handball, a ball was struck with the open hand against a wall, and after it had bounced on the ground, was again struck against the wall. The aim of a player was to keep the ball in motion longer than his opponent could. In many private houses and public baths there were courts especially for this amusement.

Another game, called *trigon*, was played by three persons, each stationed at one angle of an equilateral triangle. Two balls were used, and a player tried to throw his ball at the opponent who would be less likely to catch it. Two players might throw at the third at the same moment, or the thrower of one ball might have to receive the second ball at the very moment of throwing. Since both hands had to be used, skill with each hand was required. Other games of ball are mentioned in Latin literature.

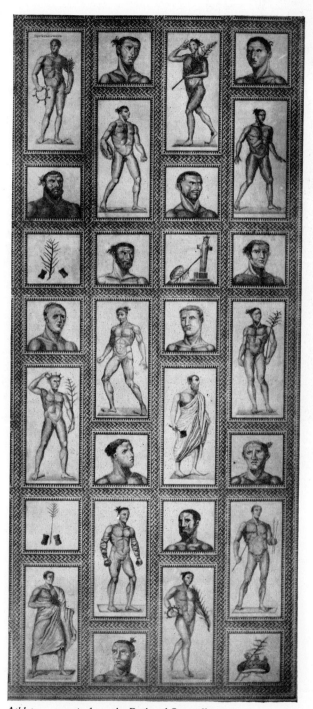

Athletes—mosaic from the Baths of Caracalla

GAMES OF CHANCE

The Romans were passionately fond of games of chance, but there was so much gambling in connection with these games that they were forbidden by law, even when not played for stakes. These laws were hard to enforce—as such laws usually are—and large sums were won and lost at gambling resorts as well as in private houses. During the Saturnalia in December, gambling was unrestricted; and public opinion allowed old men to play at any time.

Playing for high stakes was one of the greatest attractions at men's dinners. The most common form of gambling was like our "Heads or Tails," in which coins were used. In another common game, like our "Odd or Even," each player guessed whether the number of counters held by another was odd or even. Then he in turn

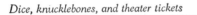

Dice, knucklebones, and theater tickets

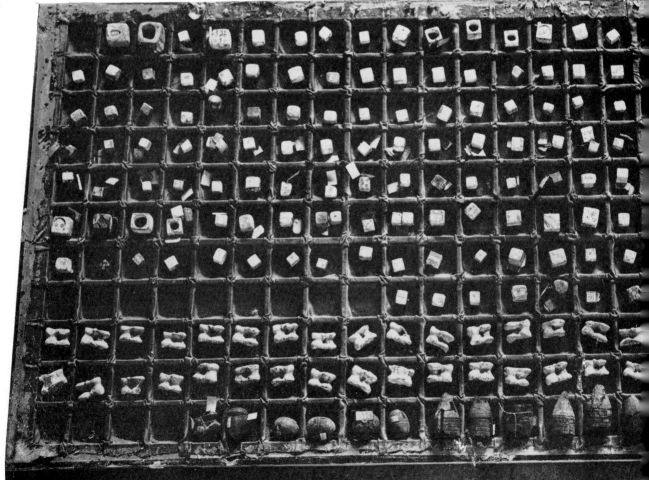

held counters concealed in his outstretched hand for his opponent to guess. The stake was usually the contents of the hand, but side bets were not unusual. In a variation of this game, players guessed the exact number of counters held in a hand.

KNUCKLEBONES

Some games were played with knucklebones (*tali*) and dice. Knucklebones of sheep and goats and imitations of them in ivory, bronze, and stone were used by men in gambling, and also by children as toys. The latter played a game like jackstones. They threw five tali into the air at once and caught as many as possible on the back of one hand. Since tali were longer than they were wide, each had four long sides and two short ones. The ends were rounded off or pointed, so that a *talus* could not stand on end. Two of the four long sides were broader than the others. One broad side was concave, the other convex; one narrow side was flat, the other indented.

In gambling, four tali were used at once, thrown either from a hand or from a dicebox. The side on which a bone rested was counted, not the side which came up. Since no two sides had the same shape, tali did not require marking as do dice, but for convenience they were sometimes numbered 1, 3, 4, 6 (2 and 5 being omitted). Thirty-five different throws were counted, each of which had its individual name and value. Four aces were the

lowest throw (Vulture), while the highest (Venus) occurred when all the tali lay differently. It was this throw that designated the master of the revels at a drinking party.

DICE

The Romans also had dice (*tesserae*) made of ivory, stone, or close-grained wood. Each side was marked with dots, from one to six in number, just as ours are. Three dice were thrown at one time from a dicebox. In this game, the side of the die that came up was counted, not the side on which it rested, as with tali. The highest possible throw was three sixes, the lowest three aces. In ordinary gambling the aim of every player was to throw a higher number than his opponent. Dice games were also played on boards with counters, somewhat like backgammon, in which skill was united with chance.

BATHING

Romans of early times washed for health and cleanliness. They bathed at home in a primitive sort of washroom near the kitchen, so that water might be heated there and brought in easily. It was customary to take a full bath only once a week; but arms and legs were washed every day, because ordinary clothing left them exposed.

By the last century of the Republic,

A bronze bathtub from a villa near Pompeii

bathing had become a part of the daily routine, as important as the dinner which it regularly preceded. Although there were still bathrooms in some private houses, most Romans preferred a public establishment. Public baths were operated on a large scale, not only in all parts of Rome, but also in the smaller towns of Italy and even in the provinces. Baths were often built where there were hot or mineral springs—as at Baiae on the Gulf of Naples and at Bath, England. The pools at Bath are fed by the same springs the Romans used; the buildings are an eighteenth-century restoration.

PUBLIC BATHS

Ruins of public and private baths all over the Roman world, together with an account by Vitruvius, make clear their general construction and arrangement, but show wide variation in details. Countless allusions in Latin literature help to complete the picture. Public establishments offered all sorts of baths—plain, plunge, hot and cold—as well as massage by trained men, who were nearly always slaves.

Often baths provided exercise grounds, gymnastic apparatus, courts for games,

(Left) *Remains of the baths at Bath, England*

Dressing room of a large public bath—the Stabian—with niches for clothing

Remains of the Baths of Caracalla

rooms for reading and conversation, libraries—nearly everything that modern athletic clubs have. These features eventually became more important than the bathing itself, so that going to the bath was a popular recreation.

The simple bathhouse of earlier times and the bath itself were called *balneum* or *balnea*. The more complex establishments of later times were called *balneae*, and to the very largest the name *thermae* was finally given. These names were used loosely and interchangeably.

Public baths are first heard of after the Second Punic War—when many changes in living came about—but their number increased rapidly. At least one hundred seventy were operated in Rome in the year 33 B.C., and later there were more than eight hundred. These were public in the sense of being open to all citizens who could pay a small fee. Free baths did not exist.

Occasionally there was a magistrate, public-spirited citizen, or candidate for office who himself paid the charges for a definite time. Agrippa in the year 33 B.C. kept one hundred seventy public baths in Rome open free of charge. Sometimes rich men in their wills provided free baths for the people, but always for a limited time.

MANAGEMENT

Some of the first public baths were opened by individuals for speculative purposes. Others were built by wealthy men as gifts to their native towns. The administration of these baths was in the hands of the town authorities, who kept the buildings in repair and the baths open. These were supported by fees. Some baths were built by towns from public funds, and others were credited to some of the later emperors. Management of all was practically the same. They were leased for a definite time and for a fixed amount to a manager, who paid his expenses and made his profits out of the fees which he collected.

The fees were very low; the regular price at Rome for men seems to have been *quadrans* (a quarter of a cent). The bather furnished his own towels, oil, and anything else he wanted.

Women were required to pay more, perhaps twice as much, while children paid nothing. Prices varied in different places. It is likely that higher prices were charged in some baths than in others of the same city—perhaps because they were more luxuriously equipped or more fashionable and exclusive.

ESSENTIALS OF THE BATH

For a luxurious bath in classical times four things were necessary: a warm anteroom, a hot bath, a cold bath, and rubbing and anointing with oil. All these could have been provided in one room, but even in modest private houses, at least three rooms, and often five or six, were set apart for bathing. In public establishments this number was sometimes multiplied several times. The better equipped baths provided a dressing room (*apodyterium*), usually unheated, but furnished with benches and often with compartments for clothes; a warm anteroom (*tepidarium*), in which bathers waited until perspiration started, in order to avoid the danger of passing too suddenly into the high temperature of the next room; a hot room (*caldarium*) for the hot bath; a cold room (*frigidarium*) for the cold bath; a room for rubbing and anointing with oil to complete the bath (*unctorium*). Sometimes there was an additional hot room without water (*laconicum*) for a sweat bath.

Some bathers went through all the rooms in order; others omitted the hot bath and took a sweat in the laconicum. If there was no laconicum, they went to the hot room. Then after having the perspiration removed with a scraper (*strigilis*) they took a cold bath and were rubbed with linen towels and anointed with oil.

In less elaborate baths, space was saved by using one room for several purposes. A separate dressing room might be omitted, since the bather could undress and dress in the cold or warm room, according to the weather. The unctorium also might be left out, and the warm room used for the rubdown. In this way the number of rooms in the bath was reduced to two or three.

A public bathhouse usually had an exercise ground of its own, with a pool at one side for a cold plunge. In a room nearby, the sweat and dirt of exercise were scraped off, before the bath. Young men who deserted the Campus and the Tiber for the palaestra and the bath could remove the effects of exercise with a strigil and then take a plunge in the pool, followed by a second scraping and anointing with oil. Much depended on an individual's time and tastes. Physicians, too, laid down strict rules for their patients to follow.

Hypocaust at Verulamium

HEATING THE BATHHOUSE

The arrangement of rooms in a bath-house, regardless of their number, depended on the method of heating. In early times they were heated by charcoal stoves but later, a furnace (*hypocaust*) was used to heat both rooms and water.

Hot air from the furnace, instead of being conducted directly into the rooms, circulated under the floors and through spaces in the walls. The temperature of a room naturally depended on its nearness to the furnace. If there was a laconicum, it was put directly over the furnace, with the hot room next to it, and then the warm room. Since the cold room and dressing room had no need of heat, they were farthest from the fire and had no connection with it. If there were two sets of baths in one building for the use of men and women at the same time, the two hot rooms were on opposite sides of the furnace, the other rooms connecting with them in the usual order. The two entrances were as far apart as possible.

A bath had two floors—the first even with the top of the firebox, the second even with the top of the furnace. Between them was a space of about two feet, through which hot air passed. Over the furnace, just above the level of the upper floor, were two tanks for heating water. One, containing water that was kept merely warm, was placed where the fire was only moderately hot. Water from this tank flowed into the other, which was placed directly over the fire; the water in it was kept intensely hot. A tank of cold water was nearby. From these tanks water was piped to the different rooms.

CALDARIUM

The hot-water bath was taken in the hot room, which was rectangular, with one rounded end. At the other end was a large shallow pool filled with hot water, in which several persons bathed at one time. Built up two steps from the floor, this pool was as long as the width of the room, and at least six feet wide. At the bottom it was narrower, and the back sloped inward, so that bathers could recline against it. The front had a long broad step inside for convenience in going down into the pool, or for a seat.

The water, which was piped into the bath from the hot-water tank over the furnace, circulated through a metal heater, which kept it hot. The heater, semicylindrical in shape, was placed directly over a large hot-air chamber under the floor and opened into the bath. Since the bottom of the heater was a little lower than that of the bath, the water circulated from the bath into the heater, was warmed, and returned. Near the top of the pool was an overflow pipe, and near the bottom an escape pipe, which could be opened to allow water to run out on the floor for scrubbing. In the rounded end of the room was a large basin of metal, which probably contained cool water. In private baths, where this room was usually rectangular, the basin was placed in a corner. For those who used the room as a sweat bath only, there were benches along the wall. Since the air in the caldarium was very moist and that of the laconicum perfectly dry, the effect would not be precisely the same.

FRIGIDARIUM

The frigidarium usually contained only a cold plunge bath. If it was also used as a dressing room, there were compartments in the walls for clothes, and benches for slaves, who watched the clothes. Those who found this bath too cold would use the open swimming pool in the court, which was warmed by the sun. In a public bath at Pompeii there seems to have been a cold bath in the warm room, perhaps for invalids who found even the swimming pool too cool.

UNCTORIUM

The final process of scraping, rubbing, and oiling was exceedingly important. Often the bather was treated twice—before the warm bath and after the cold. The first treatment might be omitted; the second, never. The special room for this, called the *unctorium*, was furnished with benches and couches. Each bather brought his own strigils—carried by a slave, along with towels and oil flask. A bather might scrape and oil himself, or he might have a slave apply the strigil and the oil. Trained slaves also gave massage. When there was no unctorium, the warm room or dressing room was used.

BATHING HOURS

A bath was regularly taken before dinner. The hour varied in different seasons and for different classes. In general it was about the eighth hour—two or three o'clock—and at this time managers were bound by their contracts to have the baths open and everything ready. Since many persons preferred to bathe before lunch, some baths must have been open then. All were regularly open until sunset, and in small towns where there were fewer baths, they may have been open later. The many lamps found in Pompeian baths indicate evening hours. Managers probably kept the doors open as long as they found it profitable to do so.

ACCOMMODATIONS FOR WOMEN

Respectable women bathed in public baths only with other women, enjoying the opportunity to meet their friends. In cities there were some baths which served only women. In large towns, rooms in public baths were set apart for them, but these were smaller than those for men. In villages, the same baths were open to men and women, but at different hours. Late in the Empire we read of men and women bathing together, but women who did this had no claim to respectability.

An oil flask and two strigils

THERMAE

The plan of the Stabian Baths at Pompeii gives an idea of one of the smaller thermae and illustrates the combination of baths for men and women under the same roof. The rooms in the plan which opened on surrounding streets were used for shops and stores independent of the baths. Some of those opening within were for the use of attendants. The main entrance (A), on the south, opened on the exercise court (B), which was enclosed on three sides by colonnades and on the west by a bowling alley (C), where large stone balls were found. Behind the bowling alley was a pool (F) open to the sun, with a room on either side for shower baths (E, G), and a room (D) for the use of the athletes while scraping and rubbing down.

There were two side entrances (H) at the northwest, with a passage (I) leading to the toilet (L); the porter's room (west of J) and the manager's office (K) were conveniently near. The room (J) at the head of the bowling alley was for the use of the players.

On the east were the baths themselves, with the one for men to the south. There were two dressing rooms (V, W), and waiting rooms for the slaves, one with a door on the street (X). Then came the cold room (T), the warm room (U), and the hot room (S). The warm room, contrary to custom, had a cold bath. There

Plan of the Stabian Baths

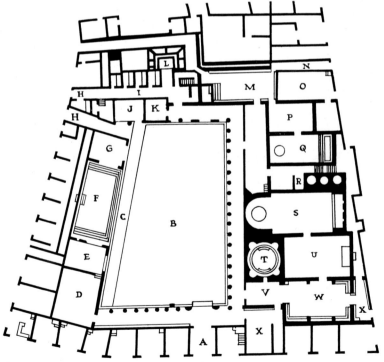

Frigidarium of the Stabian Baths at Pompeii

was no laconicum. Perhaps V or W was used for a rubbing room.

The main entrance (N) to the women's bath was at the northeast, but there was also an entrance from the northwest through a long corridor. Both doors opened into the dressing room (M), which had a cold bath in one corner, since women had no separate cold room. Then in the regular position were the warm (P) and the hot (Q) rooms. The furnace (R) was between the two hot rooms, and beside it, were three tanks for hot, warm, and cold water.

The rooms were artistically decorated, and probably luxuriously furnished. Ample space was given by the colonnades and the large waiting rooms for a stroll and talk with friends and acquaintances, which the Romans enjoyed after the bath.

A PRIVATE BATHHOUSE

While public baths were popular because of their varied features and social atmosphere, private baths are found occasionally in Italy and the provinces.

The private bathhouse found in Caerwent, England, dating from about the time of Constantine (A.D. 306–337), is small (34 by 31 feet) but shows the arrangement of rooms. The entrance (A) leads into the cold room (B), with a plunge bath (I) at the left. To the right is the dressing room (C), which had a curved end such as the hot room often had. The warm room (D) is the largest rather than the smallest of the four main rooms. Then comes the hot room (E) with a bathing pool (F) six feet long.

Plan of bath at Caerwent

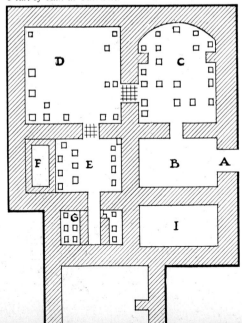

There is no sign of the basin, perhaps because it was small and had no special foundation. Finally there is the rare laconicum (G), located over one end of the furnace, which was in the basement. Hot air passed between the floors, escaping with the smoke through openings near the roof in the outside walls of the dressing room. There is no direct passage from the hot room to the cold room and no special entrance to the laconicum. The warm room must have served for the rubdown.

THE BATHS OF DIOCLETIAN

The irregular plan and waste of space in the Pompeian thermae described are due to the fact that the baths were built at various times with all sorts of alterations and additions. Nothing can be more symmetrical than the thermae of the later emperors. One of these was the Baths of Diocletian, dedicated in A.D. 305. They were in the northeastern part of Rome, and in magnificence were second only to the Baths of Caracalla. The main rooms, in a line through the center of the building, were the open pool, the combined dressing room and cold room, the warm room, and the hot bath, which projected beyond the other rooms for the sake of sunshine.

The uses of all the halls and courts in the building cannot be determined, but evidently no luxury known to the time was omitted. In the sixteenth century Michelangelo restored the warm room as the Church of *S. Maria degli Angeli* (St. Mary of the Angels), one of the largest in Rome. The cloisters that he built in the east part of the building became a museum. One of the corner domed halls of the Baths is now a church, and a number of other institutions occupy parts of the site of the ruins.

Arches of the Baths of Caracalla

An opera is being given with the remains of the Baths of Caracalla as a background

Theatrical masks—each one representing a type of character

THEATERS AND PLAYS

A writer of comedies, looking at masks; the woman originally held a stylus, symbolizing writing

PUBLIC SPECTACLES

The great public games, or shows (*ludi*), were free entertainments, given at first in honor of some god, at the expense of the State. They consisted of *ludi scaenici* (dramatic entertainments in a theater), *munera gladiatoria* (combats between gladiators, usually in an amphitheater), *ludi circenses* (chariot races and other exhibitions in a circus). Entertaining the Roman people was difficult and expensive, for only highly exciting sights appealed to them. Romans took their greatest pleasure in watching elaborate shows that involved danger to life or limb of the participants. Races and gladiatorial combats were more popular than plays.

Because of their popularity, public games increased in number and became

A soldier and a buffoon act their roles in a comedy, while officials watch

(Right) *Comic actors winking*

great spectacles, which were exploited for political purposes until all original religious significance was lost. By the end of the Republic they had become the chief pleasure of the lower classes. Juvenal declares that free bread and shows in the circus were the people's sole desire. When great free entertainments were given, all public business stopped and every citizen took a holiday. By the end of the Republic, holidays had become so numerous that there were sixty-six in a year; in the reign of Marcus Aurelius (A.D. 161-180) one hundred thirty-five days out of each year were holidays.

Besides established games, there were frequent spectacles for outstanding events. When a prominent man died, a funeral show was often provided by relatives. These were called private games because, although open to the public, they were paid for by private citizens and the days on which they were given were not legal holidays.

DRAMATIC PERFORMANCES

In classical times dramatic performances consisted of comedies, tragedies, farces, and pantomimes. The last two, used chiefly as interludes and afterpieces, were most popular with the general public

and outlived other kinds of drama. Tragedies never appealed strongly to Romans, and only the liveliest comedies gained their favor. We have no complete Roman comedies except those of Plautus and Terence, which were adapted from Greek plays, dealt with Greek life, and were given in Greek costumes. These plays were more like modern comic operas than straight comedies. Large sections were recited to music, and other parts were sung while the actors danced.

Since Roman theaters had no lighting facilities, plays were presented only in the daytime. At first they were given after the noon meal, but by Plautus' time they took place in the morning. An average comedy must have required about two hours for its performance, including occasional music between scenes.

STAGING A PLAY

There were no commercial theaters, and plays were presented in public only when games, public or private, were given. All plays, as well as other shows, were supervised by state officials in charge of the games. These men contracted for the production of a play with some recognized manager—usually a famous actor with a troupe of capable actors, all slaves.

Above, the remains of the stage of a theater at Sabratha, North Africa; below, a model of the stage

As in Shakespeare's time, men played women's parts. There was no fixed number of actors in a company, but to save money, a manager produced a play with the smallest possible number. Often two or more parts were assigned to one actor. Sometimes a wealthy man maintained his own troupe of players to give private performances for himself and his guests.

Characters in comedies wore inexpensive costumes representing ordinary Greek dress. Almost the only make-up required in the days of Plautus and Terence was paint for the face, especially for those who took women's parts. Later, masks came into use. Wigs conventionally represented different characters: gray for old men, black for young men, red for slaves. Actors' clothing and make-up, as well as the few stage properties, were furnished by the manager. It was also customary for him to give a complimentary dinner for the actors when a performance was unusually successful.

THE EARLY THEATER

During the period (200-160 B.C.) when the best comedies were being written by Plautus and Terence, very little was done to accommodate either actors or audience. The stage was a crude temporary platform, much wider than deep, built at the foot of a hill or grass-covered slope. There were few of the devices now commonly associated with a stage—no curtains, no scenery that could be shifted, no sounding board to amplify an actor's voice, no lighting for effect, no way to show an interior. For a comedy the stage always represented a street, with an entrance at each end. Usually the fronts of two or three houses with doors that opened were shown at the back of the stage. Entrances and exits were through the doors or at either end of the street.

An ancient dramatist was forced to place action and conversation on the street—even when they would normally take place indoors. In the later theater, changes of scenery were possible, although extant Roman plays seldom required them. An altar stood on the stage to remind the audience of the religious origin of the festival.

Spectators gathered on the slope in front of a stage, some sitting or reclining on the grass, some standing. Others probably sat on stools brought from home. With crowds pushing, men and women disputing and quarreling, and children wailing, there was always noise and confusion to try the actors' voices. In the middle of a play the report of some livelier entertainment elsewhere sometimes drew the whole audience away.

THE LATER THEATER

Beginning about 145 B.C., efforts were made to improve the theater, in spite of opposition from those who considered playgoing harmful to morals. A wooden

Terra-cotta statuette of a masked actor

Fresco in a Pompeian house, showing a scene from a tragedy

theater with seats in Greek style was erected, but the senate had it pulled down as soon as the games were over. It became the custom to build a temporary theater whenever plays were given, with special seats in a separate section for senators and, much later, there was also a section for knights.

In 55 B.C. Pompey erected the first permanent theater at Rome in the Campus Martius. It was built of stone and patterned after a theater which Pompey had seen at Mytilene, on the island of Lesbos. Probably it seated about ten thousand people, although Pliny the Elder says forty thousand. Its site is now covered with later buildings.

Pompey's theater differed in several ways from its Greek model. Greek theaters were excavated out of the side of a hill, while Roman theaters were erected on level ground. The flat site allowed an architect to create a magnificent exterior. In a Greek theater a space, usually circular, in front of the stage was called the *orchestra* (dancing place). Here choruses and actors performed. Since there was rarely a chorus in a Roman play, the orchestra was not needed and became a semicircle in front of the stage.

At Rome the seats nearest the orchestra were assigned to senators; in country towns, to city officials and members of the council. From 67 B.C., the first fourteen rows of seats behind those of the senators were reserved by law for knights. Martial tells us with malicious glee that ushers firmly removed from these anyone not qualified to sit there. Upper rows were occupied by the rest of the audience, apparently without reservations.

Theatrical masks as a wall decoration

Pompey's theater was the only permanent one at Rome until 13 B.C., when two others were constructed. The larger, erected in honor of Augustus' nephew Marcellus, is said to have seated from ten to fourteen thousand spectators; and the smaller, the Theater of Balbus, about seventy-seven hundred.

These improved theaters permitted spectacular effects that had been impossible on temporary stages. A letter from Cicero describes some of the shows with which Pompey celebrated the opening of his theater. To make scenes representing the looting of a conquered city realistic, he furnished troops of cavalry, bodies of infantry, hundreds of mules loaded with

Gigantic mask, used as an architectural detail

spoils of war, and three thousand bowls for mixing wine. Such exaggerated spectacles proved the ruin of legitimate drama, which could no longer satisfy an audience.

PLAN OF A THEATER

A plan of such a theater—the type of many erected later throughout the Roman world—is given by the architect Vitruvius. GH represents the back of the stage (*proscaenium*); between GH and CD is the *scaena*, where the actors performed; beyond CD is the *cavea*, with seats for spectators. Opposite IKL are three doors, indicating three houses. The first four rows of seats, in the semicircular orchestra (M) in front of the stage, are those reserved for senators. The seats behind these front rows are divided by five passageways into six sections or wedges (*cunei*). Similarly, the seats above the semicircular passage are divided by eleven aisles into twelve sections.

Senators reached their seats by passageways under the seats at the right and left of the stage. The best seats (E, F), which were somewhat like theater boxes of modern times, were over the vaulted passageway. On one side these were reserved for the emperor, if he was present, or for officials who superintended the games. Those on the other side were for the Vestals. These reserved seats were reached by private stairways on the stage side of the auditorium.

Access to the upper tiers of the cavea was by way of passages constructed under the seats and stairs running up to the aisles between the *cunei* (sections). The picture on page 264 shows part of the Theater of Marcellus. Within the arches may be seen the outer passageways leading to the seats. Above the highest seats were broad colonnades for shelter in case of rain, and above these were tall masts from which awnings (*vela*) were spread to protect the audience from the sun.

(Left) Theater of Marcellus, built by Augustus in honor of his adopted son

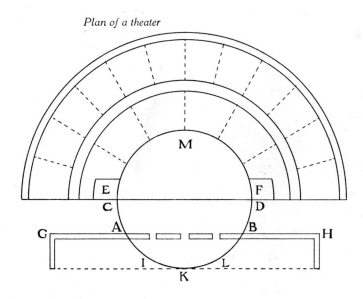

Plan of a theater

An idea of the appearance of the wall of the stage end may be obtained from the picture which shows the remains of a Roman theater still in existence. The great width of the Roman stage—sometimes one hundred twenty or one hundred eighty feet—made possible the use of dramatic devices that would seem unnatural on a modern stage—such as asides and dialogues on one part of the stage unheard on another, and the length of time allowed for an actor to cross the stage.

The stage was connected with the auditorium by seats over the vaulted passages to the orchestra. To hide the stage, a curtain was raised from the bottom, not lowered from the top as is done today. The slot through which the curtain was dropped can still be seen in some theaters, as in the ones at Pompeii. Vitruvius suggested that rooms and porticoes be built behind the stage to provide space for actors and properties and shelter for the audience in case of rain. Such a portico—an open square surrounded by colonnades—is seen behind the theater at Ostia and the one at Minturnae.

Remains of theaters are found in many cities of the Roman world. Some have been restored and are now used for open-air productions, including revivals of Roman plays.

Great theater of Pompeii, with stage (unfloored) and curtain slot on the left

Small theater at Pompeii, with stage entrance at left

Roman theater at Sagunto, Spain

Chariot racing—in which accidents were expected—is represented by cupids

CIRCUSES AND RACES

Relief showing a chariot race

A charioteer, holding the palm of victory

ROMAN CIRCUSES

The games in the circus were the oldest of the great free shows at Rome and were always the most popular. The word *circus* means simply "ring"; *ludi circenses* were, therefore, shows given in a ring. There were different kinds of shows, but chariot races are always meant when no other show is specifically mentioned.

For these races the first and only requirement was a long level piece of ground. Such a place was the valley between the Aventine and Palatine Hills, and here in prehistoric times the first Roman racecourse was established. This remained *the* circus, the one always meant when no descriptive term was added. After others had been built, it was sometimes called the *Circus Maximus*. None of the others ever approached it in size, magnificence, or popularity.

The second one at Rome was the *Circus Flaminius*, erected in 221 B.C. by Gaius Flaminius, who also built the Flaminian Road. It was located in the

Restoration of the Circus of Maxentius

southern part of the Campus Martius and, like the Circus Maximus, was exposed to frequent overflowing of the Tiber. Its site—near the Capitoline Hill —is known, but actual remains are very scanty, so that little is known of its size or appearance. A third circus was named after Gaius (Caligula) and Nero, the two emperors responsible for its construction. It was built at the foot of what is now called the Vatican Hill, about where St. Peter's stands, but we know little more of it than that it was the smallest of the three.

These were the only circuses within the city, but in the immediate neighborhood there were three others. Five miles out on the Via Portuensis was the Circus of the Arval Brothers. About three miles out on the Appian Way was the Circus of Maxentius, erected A.D. 309, which is the best preserved of all. On the same road, about twelve miles from the city, in the old town of Bovillae, was another circus, making six within easy reach of the people of Rome.

PLAN OF A CIRCUS

All the Roman circuses known to us had the same general arrangement. As in the reconstruction on page 271, the long, narrow stretch of ground which formed the racecourse was almost surrounded by tiers of seats, running in two long parallel lines that united in a semicircle at one end. In the middle of this semicircle was the triumphal gate by which the winner left the circus.

Opposite this gate at the other end of the arena were stations for chariots (CC), called *carceres* (barriers), flanked by a tower at each corner. The barriers were divided into two equal sections by the gate (D) through which processions entered the circus. There were also gates between the towers and the seats. Because the towers and barriers—seen from the outside—looked like a walled town, they were called the *oppidum*.

The arena was divided for about two-thirds of its length by a fence, or wall (KK) called the *spina* (backbone). Be-

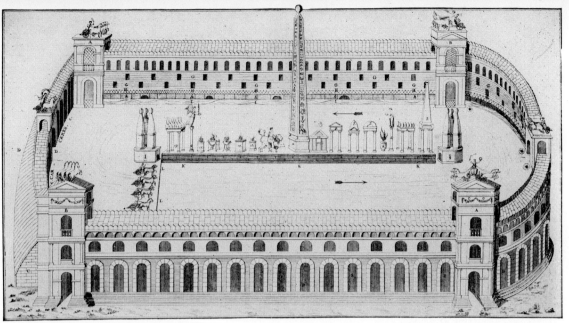

Imaginative reconstruction of the Circus Maximus

yond the ends of this wall were *metae* (II), goal posts marking the ends of the course. Once around the spina was a lap (*spatium, curriculum*); an established number of laps, usually seven to a race, was called a *missus*. The last lap had only one turn—the one at the goal post nearest the triumphal gate.

The finish was a straightaway dash to the *calx*, a chalk line drawn on the arena. This line was far enough from the second goal post to keep it from being destroyed by the hoofs of the horses as they made the turn, and far enough from the barriers to enable the driver to stop his team before dashing into them.

ARENAS

An arena was a level space surrounded by seats and barriers. The name was derived from the sand (*harena*) used to cover its surface as protection for the unshod feet of the horses.

Speed was not of great importance in a race. The sand, the shortness of the stretches, and the sharp turns between them were all against great speed. A Roman found his enjoyment in the danger of a race. In most representations of a racecourse that have come down to us, there are broken chariots, fallen horses, and drivers under wheels and hoofs.

There has been an accident at the left

Remains of the Circus of Maxentius

The length of the course varied in different circuses. The Circus Maximus was fully three hundred feet longer than the Circus of Maxentius. All circuses seem to have had the same number of laps—seven to the race (more evidence that danger was the chief element in the popularity of the contests).

The distance traveled in the Circus of Maxentius has been closely estimated. The length of the spina was about nine hundred fifty feet, and if fifty feet is allowed for the turn at each meta, a lap makes a distance of two thousand feet; six laps, twelve thousand feet. The seventh lap had only one turn in it, but the final stretch to the calx made it perhaps three hundred feet longer than any other one—about twenty-three hundred feet. This gives a total of fourteen thousand, three hundred feet for the whole missus, or about two and seven-tenths miles.

CARCERES

The *carceres* (barriers), were the stations of the chariots and teams when ready for the races to begin. They were a row of strongly built stalls separated by solid walls, and closed at the back by doors through which the chariots entered. The front of each stall was formed by double doors of iron bars, which admitted the only light. Because of the barred doors, the stalls were called *carceres* (prisons).

Each stall was just large enough to hold a chariot with its team. Since a team was sometimes composed of as many as ten horses, a "prison" must have been nearly square. Up to the time of Emperor Domitian (A.D. 81–96) the highest number of chariots was eight. Later, when as many as twelve sometimes entered the same race, twelve stalls had to be provided. The usual number of chariots had originally been four—one from each racing company—though each company might enter more than one. Half of these stalls lay to the right, half to the left of the processional gate.

STALLS

The stalls were arranged in a curved line, so that all the chariots would travel the same distance to reach the beginning of the course. There was no advantage in position, therefore, at the start, and places were assigned by lot. In later times a starting line was drawn with chalk between the second goal post and the seats to the right, but the line of stalls remained curved as before.

At the end of the row of stalls stood a tower, which was apparently a musicians' stand. Over the processional gate was the box of the chief state official of the games (*dator ludorum*), and between his box and the towers were seats for his friends and persons connected with the games. This official gave the signal for the start with a white cloth, and after a race, awarded the prize to the victor, who then drove in triumph around the arena to leave by the triumphal gate.

SPINA AND METAE

The *spina* (wall) divided the racecourse into two parts, and thus measured a minimum distance to be run. Its length was about two-thirds that of the arena, but at its beginning it was only the width of the track (plus the goal posts) away from the triumphal gate. A much larger space at the end near the processional gate was left vacant. Although perfectly straight, the spina did not run exactly parallel to the rows of seats. The end of the spina near the stalls was closer to the seats at the left of the starting line than to those at the right, in order to allow more room at the start, where the chariots would be side by side, than farther along the course, where they would be scattered.

The goal posts were called *metae* because their shape was conical like a lower millstone. Although erected beyond the spina with a space between, these pillars were architecturally related to it. They are represented as built of stone or concrete—a group of three pillars on a heavy foundation—but in Republican times spina and metae must have been made of wood and movable, in order to provide

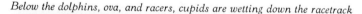
Below the dolphins, ova, and racers, cupids are wetting down the racetrack

Charioteer about to round the spina

space for the shows of wild beasts and exhibitions of cavalry originally given in a circus.

After amphitheaters were built, circuses came to be used primarily for races, and spinae were made permanent. A spina was built solidly on a foundation of concrete and was usually decorated with magnificent works of art. These must have concealed the horses and chariots from the spectators when they were running on the opposite side of the arena.

A representation of a circus has been preserved in a board game found at Bovillae, which gives an excellent idea of a spina. Reliefs and mosaics show that the spina of the Circus Maximus bore a series of statues and ornamental structures, such as obelisks, small temples or shrines, columns surmounted by statues, altars, trophies, and fountains.

In the reconstruction on page 271, the goddess of Fortune is on a pillar near one end of the spina, and Victory with a laurel branch near the other. There is an imposing obelisk in the center with shrines and altars on either side. A smaller obelisk is at one end.

Augustus was the first to erect an obelisk in the Circus Maximus. This obelisk—which was restored in A.D. 1589 —is about seventy-eight feet in height without the base, and now stands in the Piazza del Popolo. In the same circus

Constantius erected another obelisk, more than one hundred feet high, which now stands before the Lateran Church. The one from the Circus of Maxentius is now in the Piazza Navona.

Besides these purely ornamental features, every circus had on each end of its spina a pedestal—one supporting seven large eggs (*ova*) of marble, the other seven dolphins. One egg and one dolphin were taken down at the end of each lap, in order that spectators might know just how many laps were still to be run.

Another and very different spina is shown in a mosaic from Lyons. This is a canal filled with water, with an obelisk in the middle. The goal posts in their developed form are shown clearly—three conical pillars of stone set on a semi-circular base, all of the most massive construction.

SEATS IN THE CIRCUS

The seats around the arena in the Circus Maximus were originally of wood, but by the time of the Empire, losses due to decay and fire had led to their reconstruction in marble, except perhaps in the uppermost rows. In later circuses the seats were apparently made of stone from the beginning. At the foot of the tiers of seats a marble platform (*podium*) ran along both sides and the curved end. On this podium were erected boxes for the more important magistrates and officials of Rome, and here Augustus placed the seats of the senators. He also assigned seats to various classes and organizations, separating the women from the men, though up to his time they had sat together.

Between the podium and the track was a screen of metal openwork. When Caesar exhibited wild beasts in the circus, he had a canal ten feet wide and ten feet deep dug next to the podium and filled with water as an additional protection for the spectators.

Numerous broad stairways ran up to the horizontal aisles (*praecinctiones*), of which there were probably three in the Circus Maximus. The horizontal sections between the aisles were each divided by stairways into several *cunei* (wedges). The rows of seats in the cunei were called *gradus* (steps). The sittings in a row seem to have been unmarked, as they now are in baseball bleachers. Seats reserved for a number of persons were described as so many feet in a certain row of a certain wedge of a certain section. The seats were reached from the rear.

The number of seats testifies to the popularity of the races. The little circus at Bovillae seated at least eight thousand people; the Circus of Maxentius seated about twenty-three thousand. The Circus Maximus, which accommodated sixty thousand in the time of Augustus, was enlarged to a capacity of nearly two hundred thousand in the time of Constantius. The seats were supported by arches of massive masonry. (An idea of their appearance from the outside may be obtained from the exterior view of the Colosseum.) Every third vaulted chamber under the seats seems to have been used for a staircase. The other rooms were shops and booths, and in the upper parts there were rooms for employees of the circus, who must have been numerous.

Galleries seem to have been built above the seats, as in theaters, and a balcony for the emperor was always located in a conspicuous place. It is not possible from the ruins to fix these positions exactly. Although details are uncertain, a general idea of the appearance of the seats from within the arena may be derived from a reconstruction of the Circus Maximus.

RACING COMPANIES

There must have been a time when races in the circus were open to all who wished to show their horses or their skill in driving. By the end of the Republic, however, no reputable persons took part in the games—teams and drivers were furnished by racing companies (*factiones*). These practically controlled the supply of trained men and horses. With them a giver of games contracted for teams and drivers in the number of races that he wanted—ten or twelve a day in Caesar's time, later twice as many, and on special occasions, even more.

The racing companies were named from the colors worn by their drivers. At first there were only two, red and white; the blue company probably was organized in the time of Augustus, the green, soon after his reign. Finally Domitian added two more, purple and gold. The site of the stables of the green company has been identified in Rome.

Great rivalry existed between these organizations. They spent immense sums of money on horses, importing them from Greece, Spain, and Mauretania, and even larger amounts on drivers. They also maintained training stables on a grand scale. A mosaic found in an establishment in Algeria shows blanketed horses in their stalls, and, among the attendants, jockeys, grooms, stableboys, saddlers, doctors, trainers, coaches, and messengers. This rivalry spread throughout Rome. Each company had its partisans, and vast sums of money were lost and won on every race. All the tricks of the ring were skillfully practiced. Horses were drugged, and drivers were hired from rival companies, bribed, or even poisoned when they refused bribes. Further, magicians were paid to curse a team to prevent its winning.

RIVAL TEAMS

A racing chariot was low and light, closed in front and open behind, with long axles and low wheels to lessen the risk of overturning. The driver stood well forward in the car—in fact, there was no standing place behind the axle. The teams consisted of two, three, four, and in later times, six or even seven horses, but the four-horse team was most common and may be considered typical. Two of the horses were yoked together, one on each side of the tongue. The others were attached to the car by traces. Of the four, the horse to the extreme left was the most important. The goal post lay always on the left, and the highest skill of the driver was shown in turning it as closely as possible. Failure of the horse nearest it to respond promptly to the rein or the word might mean the wreck of the car (by going too close) or the loss of the inside track (by going too wide). In either case it meant the loss of the race.

Inscriptions sometimes give the names of all the horses in a team. In other instances only the horse on the left is mentioned. Before a race, a list of horses and drivers was posted for the benefit of

Racing chariot

Charioteers wearing the colors of four companies

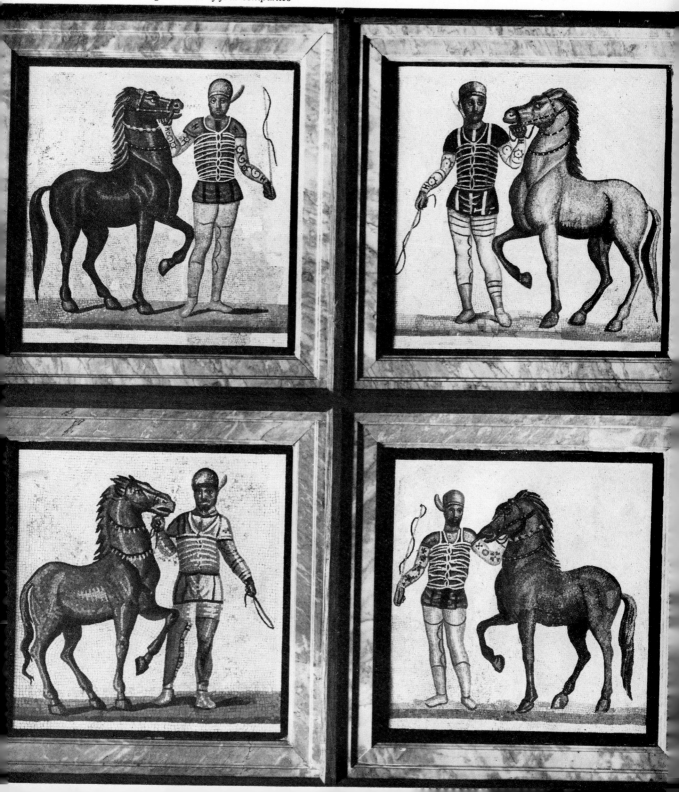

Ornamented racing chariot

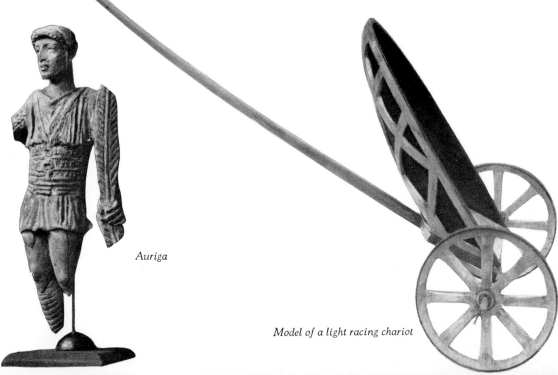

Auriga

Model of a light racing chariot

those who wished to bet. Though no time was kept, the records of horses and men were eagerly followed. From the nature of the course, with its short stretches and long turns, it is evident that strength, courage, and above all, endurance were more essential than speed. The horses were almost always stallions (mares are rarely mentioned), and were never raced under five years of age. Considering the length of the course and the great risk of accidents, it is surprising how long horses lasted. It was not unusual for a horse to figure in a hundred victories, when he was called a *centenarius*. Diocles, a famous driver, owned a *ducenarius* (horse that had won two hundred races).

RACING DRIVERS

The drivers (*agitatores, aurigae*) were slaves or freedmen, some of whom had won their freedom by their skill and daring in the course. Only in the most corrupt days of the Empire did citizens of any social position take an active part in the races.

The clothes of the driver were somewhat like those of our football players. Especially noticeable are the close-fitting cap, the short tunic (always the color of his company), laced around the body with leather thongs, the straps of leather around the thighs, the shoulder pads, and the heavy leather protectors for the legs. The reins were knotted together and passed around the driver's body. In his belt he carried a knife to cut the reins if he was thrown from the car, or to cut the traces if a horse fell and became entangled in them.

The races gave many opportunities for skillful driving, and required strength and daring. What we should call "fouling" was encouraged. One driver would turn his team against another, or upset the car of a rival if he could. Having gained the inside track, he might drive out of the straight course to keep a swifter team from passing his.

Rewards for winning races were proportionately great. A successful driver, even though his social station was low, was the pet and pride of the race-mad crowd. Under the Empire, at least, he was courted and feted by high and low alike. His pay was extravagant, since rival companies bid against one another for the services of the most popular drivers. Rich presents were given to a winning driver by his company, and also by outsiders who had bet on him and won.

FAMOUS AURIGAE

We know the names of some winners from inscriptions composed in their honor or to their memory by their friends. Among them were Publius Aelius Gutta Calpurnianus of the late Empire (1127 victories); Caius Apuleius Diocles, a Spaniard (in twenty-four years, 4257 races, 1462 victories, with winnings amounting to 35,863,120 sesterces [about $1,800,000]); Flavius Scorpus (2048 victories by the age of twenty-seven); Marcus Aurelius Liber (3000 victories); Pompeius Muscosus (3559 victories). To these may be added Crescens, honored in an inscription found at Rome in 1878.

"Crescens, a driver of the blue company, of the Moorish nation, twenty-two years old. He won his first victory as a driver of a four-horse chariot in the consulship of Lucius Vipsanius Messalla, on the birthday of the deified Nerva, in the twenty-fourth race, with these horses —Circius, Acceptor, Delicatus, and Cotynus. From Messalla's consulship to the birthday of the deified Claudius in the consulship of Glabrio he was sent

Men fighting with animals in the circus

from the barriers six hundred eighty-six times and was victorious forty-seven times. In races between chariots with one from each company, he won nineteen times; with two from each, twenty-three times; with three from each, five times. He held back purposely once, took first place at the start eight times, took it from others thirty-eight times. He won second place one hundred thirty times; third place, one hundred eleven times. His winnings amounted to 1,558,346 sesterces (about $78,000)."

OTHER SHOWS IN THE CIRCUS

Circuses were used at times for other shows, among them the performances of the *desultores*, men who rode two horses and leaped from one to the other while they were going at full speed. There were also trained horses that performed tricks while standing on a sort of wheeled platform which gave a very unstable footing. Citizens of good standing gave exhibitions of horsemanship, riding under leaders in squadrons, to show evolutions of the cavalry. The Game of Troy (*ludus Trojae*) was performed by young nobles on fine horses, executing such elaborate cavalry maneuvers as Ascanius and his friends performed in the Aeneid, Book V.

More to the taste of the crowd were the hunts, when wild beasts were turned loose in the circus to slaughter one another or be slaughtered by men trained for the purpose. We read of exhibitions, during the Republic, of panthers, bears, bulls, lions, elephants, hippopotami, and even of crocodiles swimming in lakes in the arena. In a circus, too, combats of gladiators sometimes took place, although these were more frequently held in an amphitheater.

One of the most brilliant holiday spectacles was the procession (*pompa circensis*) which formally opened certain public games. It started from the Capitol and wound its way down to the Circus Maximus, entering by the processional gate, and passing entirely around the arena. In a car at the head rode the presiding magistrate, wearing the garb of a triumphant general and attended by a slave who held a wreath of gold over his head. Next came a crowd of im-

Lion's head—an architectural carving

portant persons on horseback and on foot, then drivers in their chariots and horsemen who were to take part in the games. Priests followed, marching by colleges, as well as bearers of incense and instruments used in sacrifices. Then came statues of deities on low cars drawn by mules, horses, or elephants, or carried in litters on the shoulders of men. Bands of musicians headed each division of the procession. This brilliant display provided a spectacle for many persons who saw it from their homes, but it was merely preliminary to the show of the day.

Cupids racing, with deer instead of horses

The Colosseum by night

AMPHITHEATERS AND GLADIATORS

GLADIATORIAL COMBATS

From very early times gladiatorial combats were held in Italy. We first hear of them in Campania and Etruria. In Campania wealthy and dissipated nobles made slaves fight to the death at banquets and revels, to entertain the guests. In Etruria the combats probably go back to the offering of human sacrifices at the burials of distinguished men. The victims were captives taken in war, and it gradually became the custom to give them a chance for their lives by supplying them with weapons and allowing them to fight one another at the grave. A victor was spared, at least for the time.

The Romans were slow to adopt this custom of their Italian neighbors. The first exhibition in Rome was given in 264 B.C., almost five centuries after the traditional date of the founding of the city. That gladiatorial combats were introduced from Etruria rather than from Campania is shown by the fact that they were funeral games. The earliest ones were held at the funeral games of Brutus Pera (264 B.C.), M. Aemilius Lepidus (216 B.C.), M. Valerius Laevinus (200 B.C.), and P. Licinius (183 B.C.).

For the first hundred years after their introduction the exhibitions were rare, as these dates show. The games mentioned are all that we know of during this period. But later they were given more and more frequently and became increasingly elaborate. During the Republic they remained, in theory at least, private games —not celebrated annually on fixed days and not paid for by the State. The givers of these *munera* had to find some pretext for them in the deaths of relatives or friends, and to pay the expenses themselves. In fact we know of only one case in which magistrates (consuls P. Rutilius Rufus and C. Manlius, 105 B.C.) gave such an exhibition, and we know too little of the circumstances to assume that they acted in their official capacity.

Even under the Empire, gladiators did not fight on the days of regular public games. Augustus provided funds for "extraordinary shows" under the direction of the praetors. Under Domitian the aediles-elect were put in charge of the regular December shows—the only instance known of fixed dates for gladiatorial games. All others were free public entertainment provided by emperors, magistrates, or private citizens.

Bronze statuettes of gladiators

Gallery inside the outer arches of the Colosseum

Gallery of the amphitheater at Pozzuoli (Puteoli)

POPULARITY OF THE COMBATS

Because of the Romans' love of excitement, gladiatorial shows became immensely popular. At the exhibition in honor of Brutus Pera, only three pairs of gladiators fought, but in the three following shows, the number of pairs were twenty-two, twenty-five, and sixty. By the time of Sulla, politicians had found the munera a most effective means to win popular favor and competed with their rivals in the frequency of shows and number of combatants.

Some politicians also made these shows a pretext for surrounding themselves with bands of professional fighters—called gladiators whether they fought in the arena or not. They were used to start

Entrance to the amphitheater at Puteoli; and a view of the interior

Gladiators, from a Roman villa in Libya

street riots, break up public meetings, overawe courts, and even control or interfere with elections. Caesar's preparations for a large-scale exhibition when he was canvassing for the aedileship (65 B.C.) caused such general fear that the senate passed a law limiting the number of gladiators a private citizen might employ to 320 pairs. The gangs of Clodius and Milo—political enemies—made the city a slaughterhouse in 54 B.C., and order was not restored until late the following year when Pompey, who had been appointed "sole consul," made use of his soldiers to put an end to the battles of the gangs in the streets.

During the Empire the number of gladiators exhibited is almost beyond belief. During his reign, Augustus gave eight munera, in which no less than ten thousand men fought. In celebration of his conquest of the Dacians, Trajan exhibited as many gladiators in only four months of the year A.D. 107. Gordian I, emperor in A.D. 238, gave munera monthly in the year of his aedileship, the number of pairs ranging from 150 to 300. Under the different emperors, gladiatorial shows continued to be given until the fifth century A.D.

SOURCES OF SUPPLY

Originally, gladiators were captives taken in war—experienced fighters—who usually preferred death by the sword to slavery. Captives remained the chief source of supply for gladiators, though it became inadequate as the demand increased.

From the time of Sulla, there were gladiatorial schools in which slaves of the most intractable and desperate character were trained, whether or not they had previous experience in fighting.

From the time of Augustus, criminals—in all cases noncitizens—were sentenced to combat fighting—later "to the lions"—for such crimes as treason, murder, and arson. Finally, in the late Empire, the arena became the last desperate resort of dissipated and prodigal men. These, as volunteers, were numerous enough to receive as a class the name *auctorati*.

As the number of shows increased, it became harder to supply gladiators, for in addition to those at Rome, there were exhibitions in many cities of the provinces and in smaller towns of Italy. In order to meet the growing demand, thousands of men died miserably in the arena who only through glaring injustice could be considered criminals. In Cicero's time provincial governors were accused of sending unoffending thousands to be slaughtered in Rome, and of forcing obscure and friendless Roman citizens to fight in provincial shows.

When the supply of criminals ran short, it was common to send to the arena men sentenced for petty offenses. Charges were even brought against innocent persons to secure more victims. The persecution of Christians was largely due to the demand for more gladiators; their refusal to worship the gods of the Roman State was regarded as treasonable. After the fall of Jerusalem (A.D. 70), all captive Jews over seventeen years of age were condemned by Titus to work in the mines or fight in the arena. Wars on the border were sometimes waged to capture men who could be made gladiators. When no men were available, even women and children were occasionally made to fight.

A gladiator's tombstone

SCHOOLS FOR GLADIATORS

Cicero speaks of a training school for gladiators at Rome during his consulship (63 B.C.); before his time there were schools at Capua and Praeneste. Some of them were set up by wealthy nobles to prepare their own gladiators for munera they expected to give; others were the property of regular dealers in gladiators,

The pillars of the gladiators' barracks still stand in Pompeii

who trained them for hire. During the Empire, training schools were maintained at public expense and under the direction of State officials. In Rome there were at least four such schools, and there were also schools in other cities in Italy where shows were frequently given, as well as in the provinces. The purpose of all these training schools was to make the men effective fighting machines. The gladiators, in charge of competent teachers, were strictly disciplined; their food was carefully looked after, and a special diet provided. They had regular gymnastic exercises and lessons by experts in using various weapons. In their fencing bouts wooden swords were used. The gladiators in a training school were called a familia.

BARRACKS

These schools served also as barracks— or rather as prisons—for gladiators between engagements. It was from the school of Lentulus at Capua that Spartacus escaped to lead the great slave uprising (73-71 B.C.), and the Romans needed no second lesson. The general arrangement of these barracks may be understood from the ruins of one uncovered at Pompeii. Since this building, however, had originally been planned as a portico behind a theater, its plan may not be typical in all respects.

A central court (D), used as an exercise ground, was surrounded by a wide colonnade, and this in turn by buildings two stories in height, so that the general effect

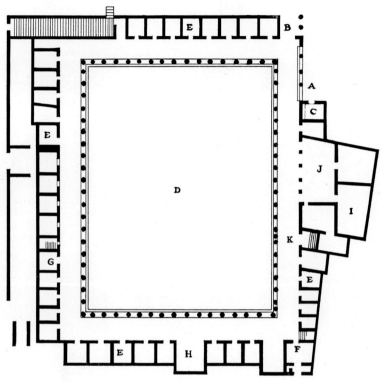

Plan of the gladiators' barracks

was not unlike that of a peristyle of a house. The court was nearly one hundred twenty by one hundred fifty feet. The buildings were cut up into rooms (E), nearly all small (about twelve feet square), unconnected and opening on the court. Those in the first story were reached from the colonnade; those in the second from a balcony served by several stairways. These small rooms—assumed to be sleeping rooms of the gladiators— each accommodated two persons. There are seventy-one of them, providing space for one hundred forty-two men. The uses of the other rooms are largely conjectural.

The pillared entrance (A) had beside it a room (C) for the watchman, or sentinel. The old entrance (B) from the theater had been walled up. There was an exedra (H) where gladiators may have waited in full panoply for their turn in the exercise ground. The guard-room (G) is identified by the remains of stocks, in which unmanageable fighters were fastened for punishment or safekeeping. The stocks permitted culprits only to lie on their backs or to sit in a very uncomfortable position.

There was an armory (F), or property room, judging from articles found in it. Near it in the corner were steps leading to the balcony on which the rooms of the second story opened. The large room (J) was the messroom, with the kitchen (I) opening into it. A stairway (K) gave access to the rooms above the kitchen and messroom, which may have been the apartments of trainers and their assistants.

Roman amphitheater at Verona

PLACES OF EXHIBITION

During the Republic, combats sometimes took place at a grave or in the circus, but usually in the Forum. None of these places was well adapted to the purpose—a grave least of all. The circus had seats enough, but the spina was in the way, and the arena was too long to give all spectators a good view of a struggle going on in any one spot. In the Forum, temporary seats could be conveniently arranged. They ran parallel with the sides, could be curved around the corners, and left only enough space for the combatants. The difficulty here was due to the fact that the seats had to be erected before each performance and removed after it, delaying business if the seats were constructed carefully and threatening life if they were put up hastily.

These considerations finally led the Romans, as they had led the Campanians half a century before, to provide permanent seats for the munera, arranged as they had been in the Forum, but in a place where they would not interfere with public or private business. Such a structure came to be called *amphitheatrum*, a word previously given in its general sense to any arena in which seats ran all the way around, as in the circus, as opposed to the theater, where the rows of seats were cut off by the stage.

Remains of the Roman amphitheater at Italica, Spain

Amphitheater at Capua

Roman amphitheater at Arles, France, now used for bullfights

AMPHITHEATERS AT ROME

Just when the first amphitheaters for gladiatorial combats were built at Rome we do not know. Caesar is said to have erected a wooden amphitheater in 46 B.C., but there is no detailed description of it, and it was probably only a temporary structure. In 29 B.C. an amphitheater was built by Statilius Taurus, at least partly of stone, that lasted until the great fire in the reign of Nero (A.D. 64). Nero himself built one of wood in the Campus Martius.

Finally, by A.D. 80, an immense structure was completed, known at first as the *Amphitheatrum Flavium*, later as the Colosseum. It was large enough and durable enough to make unnecessary the erection of any more amphitheaters in the city.

In many cities throughout the Roman world, remains of amphitheaters have been found. Those at Nîmes and Arles, France, have been cleared and partly restored in modern times and are still in use. Bullfights, however, have taken the place of gladiatorial combats. The amphitheater at Verona, too, in northern Italy, has been partly restored. The famous Buffalo Bill gave his Wild West Show there. Concerts and operas are also given in these arenas.

THE AMPHITHEATER AT POMPEII

The essential features of an amphitheater may be most easily understood from the ruins of the one at Pompeii, which was erected about 75 B.C., almost half a century before the first permanent one at Rome. Built and donated by two Pompeians, it is the earliest amphitheater known to us from either literary or archaeological sources.

Since the arena and most of the seats lie in a great hollow excavated for the purpose, the outside wall must originally have been not more than ten to thirteen feet above ground. Even this wall was necessary on only two sides, since the amphitheater was built in the southeast corner of the city and its south and east sides were bounded by the city walls. Its shape is elliptical; the major axis 444 feet long, the minor 342; the seating capacity may have been twenty thousand.

The arena occupies the middle space. It was encircled by thirty-five rows of seats arranged in three divisions. The lowest division had five rows, the second twelve, and the highest eighteen. A broad terrace ran around the amphitheater at the height of the topmost row of seats. Access to this terrace was from outside, by a double stairway on the west, and by single stairways next to the city walls on the east and south. Between the terrace and the top seats was a balcony, or row of boxes, each about four feet square, probably for women. Beneath the boxes persons could pass from the terrace to the seats.

The arena itself formed an ellipse with axes of 228 and 121 feet. Around it ran a wall a little more than six feet high, and here, on a level with the top of the wall, were the lowest seats. For the protection of spectators when wild animals were shown, a grating of iron bars was put up on top of the arena wall.

The arena and the seats of the lowest and middle sections were reached by two underground passages, one of which turned at right angles because of the city wall on the south. From the arena a third passage, low and narrow, led to the Death Gate, through which bodies of the dead were dragged with ropes and hooks. Near the entrances to these passages were small chambers or dens, the purpose of which is unknown. As in the circus, sand covered the floor of the arena but here its purpose was to soak up blood as well as to give a firm footing to the gladiators.

Of the part of this amphitheater set aside for the spectators, only the lowest division was supported on artificial foundations. In the middle and upper divisions, the seats were of stone, and rested on the bank of earth. All the other seats were constructed in sections by various donors at different times. Mean-

Amphitheater at Pompeii

time, the spectators found places for themselves on the sloping banks as in early theaters. The lowest division was not supplied with seats all the way around. A section on the east and west sides was arranged with four low, broad ledges of stone, rising one above the other, on which the members of the city council could occupy the seats of honor to which their rank entitled them.

In the middle of the section on the east, the lowest ledge is double in width for about ten feet. This was the place set apart for the giver of the games and his friends. Probably all places in the lowest section were reserved for people of distinction, and seats in the middle section for the well-to-do. It is likely that admission to the less desirable seats of the highest section was free.

THE COLOSSEUM

The Flavian Amphitheater, or Colosseum, is the best known of all the buildings of ancient Rome, because so much of it has survived to the present day and because of the nature of the entertainment provided there. It lay near the center of Rome, and was easily reached from all directions. Built on street level, its walls rose to a height of nearly one hundred sixty feet. This permitted the architectural magnificence that had always distinguished the Roman theater from that of the Greeks.

The Colosseum covers nearly six acres of ground. Its interior is an ellipse with axes of 620 and 513 feet. Its arena is also an ellipse, with axes measuring 287 and 180 feet. The width of the space allotted to the spectators is, therefore, $166\frac{1}{2}$ feet all around the arena. Subterranean chambers were constructed under the whole structure, including the arena; and part of the floor of the arena has been

An imaginative reconstruction of a section of the interior of the Colosseum

removed to show them. These compartments were for the regiments of gladiators, for dens of wild beasts, beast elevators, and machinery used in transformation scenes such as are described by Gibbon in Chapter XII of *The Decline and Fall of the Roman Empire*. Above all, these chambers provided space for a vast number of water and drainage pipes, which could flood the arena and turn it into a lake at a moment's notice or drain it quickly.

The wall that surrounded the arena was fifteen feet high. It was faced with

Most of the floor of the Colosseum has been removed, to show the substructure

The Colosseum—now in the heart of modern Rome

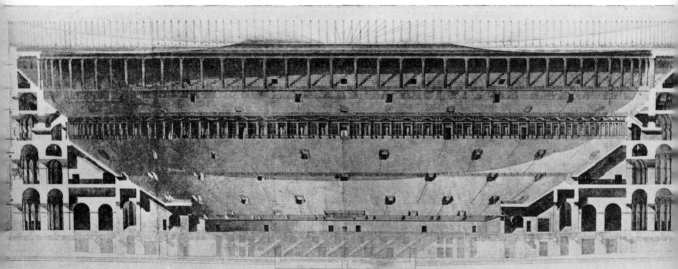

Reconstructions of the exterior and interior of the Colosseum

marble and reënforced by a grating or network of metal above it. Rollers hung on this wall to keep the beasts in the arena from climbing it. The top of the wall was level with the podium—a marble platform, as in the circus—which had room for two, or at the most, three rows of marble chairs. These seats were for the emperor and his family, the man who gave the games, magistrates, senators, vestal virgins, ambassadors of foreign states, and other important persons.

The Roman crowds easily found their places through eighty numbered entrances. The seats were arranged in three tiers, one above the other, separated by broad passages. The farther they were from the arena, the more steeply they rose. Above them was an open balcony. Twelve feet above the podium the first bank of seats began, with fourteen rows of seats reserved for the knights. Then came a broad horizontal passage, and after it the second bank of seats, intended for ordinary citizens. Back of this was a wall, above which was the third bank, with rough wooden benches for the lowest classes, foreigners, slaves, and others. The row of pillars in front of this highest section made the view all the worse.

In the open balcony above this section women were allowed to sit. They were not encouraged to attend the entertainments of the amphitheater, and no other seats were open to them unless they were distinguished enough to claim a place on the podium. At the very top of the outside wall was a terrace, in which masts were fixed to support the awnings used to protect sections lying in the sun.

The seating capacity of the Colosseum has been estimated as high as eighty thousand, with standing room for twenty thousand more, but later authorities think it could have provided seats for no more than forty or fifty thousand.

STYLES OF FIGHTING

Gladiators usually fought in pairs, man against man, but sometimes in masses. When they were actually soldiers taken captive in war, they naturally fought with the weapons and equipment to which they were accustomed. When professionally trained gladiators began to fight, they were called either "Samnites" —heavy-armed—or "Thracians"—light-armed—according to their weapons and method of fighting. In later times, victories over peoples of distant lands were celebrated with combats in which the actual weapons and methods of war of the conquered were shown to the people of Rome. After the conquest of Britain, chariot fighters demonstrated in the arena the kind of warfare Caesar had encountered in his first invasion of Britain and which he described in his *Gallic War*.

Since people enjoyed seeing different arms and tactics tried by gladiators, a Samnite was matched against a Thracian, a man with heavy arms against a light-armed one. Under the Empire these uneven matches were favorite kinds of combat. Finally, when people had tired of the regular shows, grotesque novelties were introduced. Men fought blindfold or armed with two swords or with a lasso or a heavy net. There were also battles between dwarfs and between women.

Dress helmet

Net-men in combat

WEAPONS AND ARMOR

The armor and weapons used in these combats are known from pieces found in various places and from paintings and sculpture, but it is not always possible to assign them to definite classes of gladiators. The oldest class, the Samnites, were named from that warlike Italian people, who were ancient enemies of Rome. A Samnite wore a helmet with a visor, a thick sleeve on his right arm, a greave on his left leg, a belt, a short sword, and carried a long shield. Under the Empire the name Samnite was gradually lost, and gladiators with similar equipment were called *hoplomachi* (heavy-armed) when matched against the lighter-armed Thracians, and *secutores* when they fought with the net-men.

A Thracian was armed in much the same manner as a Samnite but had a small shield and carried a curved sword. He wore greaves on both legs, instead of on only one. Gauls, also, were heavy-armed, but there is no record of how they differed from the Samnites. The same man might of course appear at different times as a Samnite, Thracian, or other fighter, if he was skilled in the use of the various weapons.

The net-fighters had no defensive armor except a leather protection for the shoulders. A net-man carried a huge net in which he tried to entangle his opponent, who was always heavily armed. If his throw was successful, the thrower killed his opponent with a dagger; if not, he got his net ready for another throw. If he lost his net, he tried to keep his opponent off with a heavy spear, which was his only other weapon.

Samnite gladiator

The Colchester vase

ANNOUNCEMENTS OF SHOWS

Games were advertised in advance by notices painted on walls of public buildings and private houses, and even on tombstones that lined the approaches to towns and cities. Some are worded in general terms, merely announcing the name of the giver of the games with the date.

A · SVETTI · CERTI
AEDILIS · FAMILIA · GLADIATORIA · PUGNAB · POMPEIS
PR · K · IVNIAS · VENATIO · ET · VELA · ERUNT

"On the last day of May gladiators of the aedile Aulus Suettius Certus will fight at Pompeii. There will also be a hunt, and awnings will be used."

Other notices promise that not only awnings will be provided, but also the dust will be kept down in the arena by sprinkling. Sometimes when a troop of gladiators was particularly good, their names were announced in pairs as they would fight together. Details of their equipment were also given, the name of their training school, the number of combats in which each had fought, together with other information. On such a notice on a wall in Pompeii someone added after the show the result of each combat. Part of this notice is given below.

MVNUS · N... · IV · III
PRID · IDUS · IDIBUS · MAIS

	T		M		O		T
v.	PUGNAX · NER · III			*v.*	CYCNVS · IVL · VIII		
p.	MVRRANVS · NER · III			*m.*	ATTICVS · IVL · XIV		

"The games of N . . . from the twelfth to the fifteenth of May. The Thracian Pugnax, of the gladiatorial school of Nero, who has fought three times, will be matched against Murranus, of the same school and the same number of fights. Cycnus, from the school of Julius Caesar, who has fought eight times, will be matched with the Thracian Atticus of the same school, who has been in fourteen fights."

The letters in italics before the names of the gladiators were added after the exhibition by some interested spectator, and stand for *vicit*, he won, *periit*, he was killed, and *missus*, he was let off. Sometimes, to arouse interest, announcements stated that additional pairs would fight.

Interior of the amphitheater at Verona, the exterior of which is shown on page 290

THE FIGHT ITSELF

The day before the exhibition a banquet was given to the fighters, and they received visits from friends and admirers. The games took place in the afternoon. After the presiding official took his place, the gladiators marched in procession around the arena, halting before him to give the famous greeting, *Morituri te salutant* (Those about to die salute you). All then left the arena, returning in pairs according to the program.

In preliminary fights, blunt weapons were used. When the people had had enough of this, trumpets gave the signal for the real fighting to begin. Those whose courage gave way at the last moment were driven into the arena with whips or hot iron bars. If a fighter was not killed but clearly outmatched, he might appeal for mercy by holding up a finger to the official in charge. The custom was to refer the plea to the people, who signaled in some way if they were in favor of granting mercy, or gesticulated *pollice verso*, apparently with the arm out and thumb down as a signal for death. In the latter case the defeated man received the death blow without resisting. His body was dragged away through the Death Gate, sand was sprinkled or raked over the blood, and the show went on until all had fought. Combats where all must fight to the death were forbidden by Augustus.

THE REWARDS

At his first public appearance, a gladiator was called a *tiro* (beginner). When after many victories he had proved himself to be the best, or second best, in his class, he gained the title of *primus palus* or *secundus palus* (first or second sword). When he had won his freedom, he received a wooden sword (*rudis*). From this the titles *prima rudis* and *secunda rudis* seem to have been given to those afterwards employed as training masters (*doctores*) in the schools.

Valuable prizes and gifts of money were bestowed on famous gladiators by their masters and backers. If not so generous as gifts made to racing drivers, they were enough to enable fighters to live in luxury the rest of their lives.

The men, however, who became professional gladiators probably found their greatest reward in the immediate and lasting notoriety that their strength, skill, and courage brought them. Their tomb-stones record their classes and the number of their victories, and often have cut upon them their likenesses, showing the wooden sword in their hands.

D · M · ET · MEMORIAE
AETERNAE · HYLATIS
DYMACHAERO · SIVE
ASSIDARIO · P · VII · RV · I
ERMAIS · CONIVX
CONIVGI · KARISSIMO
P · C · ET · S · AS · D

"To the gods Manes and the eternal memory of Hylas, a *dimachaerus* (two-sword man) or an *essedarius* (charioteer) of seven victories and head trainer. His wife Ermais erected this monument to her beloved husband and dedicated it, reserving the usual rights."

OTHER SHOWS IN THE AMPHITHEATER

Of other games sometimes held in amphitheaters the most spectacular were the fights of wild beasts. They were sometimes killed by men trained to hunt them, and sometimes forced to kill one another. Since the amphitheater was primarily intended for the slaughter of men, these hunts gradually became fights of men against beasts. The victims were condemned criminals, some guilty of crimes that deserved death, others sentenced on trumped-up charges. Still others, including women and children, were condemned "to the lions" for political or religious convictions. Sometimes victims were supplied with weapons; sometimes they were exposed unarmed, or even fettered or bound to stakes.

By flooding an arena with water, it could be adapted for the maneuvering of

Remains of a Roman amphitheater in Tunisia

boats. Naval battles (*naumachiae*) were often fought, as desperate and as bloody as many of those that have had an effect on world history. The very earliest exhibitions of this sort—also called naumachiae—were given on artificial lakes. The first one was dug by Caesar for a single exhibition in 46 B.C. Augustus had a permanent basin constructed in 2 B.C., measuring 1800 by 1200 feet, and at least four others were built by emperors who came later.

While the amusements of the Romans seem to us unnecessarily cruel, it is possible that some of our customs may seem inexcusable to future generations.

The Roman Empire

TRAVEL AND
CORRESPONDENCE

INTEREST IN TRAVEL

If any books of travel were written by Romans, they have not come down to us. For knowledge of their travels, we have to rely on indirect sources. While no distance was too great for them, no hardship too severe, Romans, in general, did not travel for pleasure or for mere sightseeing. This was partly due to their lack of enjoyment of wild, romantic scenery, but even more perhaps to their feeling that to be out of Rome was to be forgotten.

Once in his lifetime, perhaps, a Roman citizen made a long tour, visiting famous cities and strange or historic sites. Sometimes a man spent a year abroad in the retinue of a general or governor. After that, only the most urgent private affairs or public duties could draw him from Italy.

And to him Italy usually meant only Rome and his country estates, which he visited when the hot months closed the courts and caused the senate to adjourn. Restlessly he roamed from one estate to another, enjoying the beauty of trees and fountains, but impatient for his real life in Rome to begin again.

CORRESPONDENCE

When public or private business called him away from the city, a Roman kept in touch with affairs by correspondence. He expected his friends to write him long letters, and was ready to return the favor when their positions were reversed. Letters from Cicero to Caesar and to others in his camp indicate that couriers were carrying letters from Rome to Caesar at least once a month. So, too, a proconsul usually kept as near Rome as the boundaries of his province permitted. Cicero's letters from Cilicia when he was proconsul show his intense interest in news from home.

Seaside villas—fresco on a Pompeian wall

Tombstone of a boat builder

TRAVEL BY WATER

Roman means of travel were much like those of our immediate ancestors before railways and steamships were invented. When traveling by water, Romans used sailing vessels, and occasionally canal boats. There were few transportation companies, with boats running on a regular schedule between certain places and carrying passengers at a fixed price. A traveler by sea who could not afford to buy or charter a ship for his exclusive use often had to wait at a port until he found one sailing in the desired direction, and then make arrangements for his passage.

There were other inconveniences, too. Boats were small, and uncomfortable in rough weather; lack of a compass compelled sailors to follow the coast. This often increased the distance and sometimes the danger of the journey. In bad weather, few ships sailed.

Because of these difficulties, travel by water was avoided as much as possible. Rather than sail to Athens from Ostia or Naples, a traveler would go by land to Brundisium, by sea across to Dyrrhachium, and continue his journey by land. Between Brundisium and Dyrrhachium, boats were constantly passing, and the only delay to be feared was that caused by bad weather. This short voyage of only one hundred miles usually took twenty-four hours or less. An account of an ancient voyage is given in Acts 27-28, where St. Paul describes his voyage from Caesarea to Rome as a prisoner of state.

TRAVEL BY LAND

Romans who journeyed by land had more advantages than American travelers at the time of the Revolution. Roman inns were not so good as our Colonial ones, but the Romans' vehicles and horses were fully equal to those of the early Americans, and Roman roads surpassed any that have been built until recent times.

Horseback riding was not a recognized mode of traveling; riding was hard work because the Romans had no saddles. For short distances sedan chairs or litters carried by slaves were used, and for longer trips, vehicles drawn by horses or mules. There were both open and covered wagons, some with two wheels and some with four, drawn by one horse or by two or more. It was possible to rent these outside the gates of all important towns. To save the trouble of loading and unloading baggage, travelers going long distances probably took their own vehicles and merely hired fresh horses from time to time. For short or unhurried journeys, travelers would naturally use their own horses as well as their own carriages.

Couriers and government officials, especially in the provinces, used post routes with changes of horses at regular stages, but for ordinary travelers there were no such arrangements.

Four-wheeled covered carriage

Two-wheeled cart; four-wheeled carriage, probably used for fast transportation; and an ancient cart— similar to some still used in Italy

VEHICLES IN ROME

The streets of Rome were so narrow that wagons and carriages were not allowed on them at hours when crowds of people were abroad. Through many years of the Republic, and for at least two centuries afterwards, streets were closed to all vehicles from sunrise until past the middle of the afternoon. Only four classes were excepted: market wagons, which brought produce into the city by night and left empty the next morning; trucks carrying material for public buildings; carriages used by the Vestals, *flamines* (priests of special gods), and *rex sacrorum* (high priest), in their priestly functions; and chariots driven in triumphal or circus processions. Similar regulations were in force in most Italian towns, and still are today.

LITTERS

In imperial times these restrictions brought about the general use of litters in the city. Besides litters in which a passenger reclined, a sedan chair in which he sat erect was common. Both were covered and curtained. Litters were sometimes used for short journeys, when in place of six or eight bearers, mules were put between the shafts—one before and one behind. This was not done, however, until late in the Empire. Such a litter was called *basterna*.

Litters continued in use so long that in 1785, when Benjamin Franklin, old and ill, left Paris for Philadelphia, friends lent him one for his comfort on the journey to the French coast. This was swung between two tall Spanish mules, and was much like a Roman basterna.

In this scene of travel, two four-wheeled carriages dash along, while children play—one boy has a scooter

CARRIAGES

Some carriages of ancient design were kept almost entirely for use as state vehicles in processions. Such were the *pilentum*, which had four wheels, and the *carpentum*, which had two. Both were covered and drawn by two horses, and both were used by Vestals and priests. The carpentum is rarely spoken of as a traveling carriage; its use for such a purpose was a mark of luxury. According to Livy, the first Tarquin came from Etruria to Rome in a carpentum.

The *petoritum* also was used in triumphal processions, but only for spoils of war. Essentially a baggage wagon, it was occupied by a traveler's servants. The *carruca* was a luxurious traveling coach, first used during the late Empire. It was furnished with a bed on which the traveler reclined during the day and on which he slept at night.

RAEDAE AND CISIA

The common traveling vehicles were *raedae* and *cisia*. A *raeda* was a large, heavy covered wagon, with four wheels, drawn by two or four horses. It was regularly used by family groups and other travelers with baggage, and could be rented for this purpose.

For a rapid journey, when a man traveled alone with little baggage, a two-wheeled, uncovered *cisium* was a favorite vehicle. This was a light cart, drawn by two horses, one between the shafts and the other attached by traces; possibly three horses were sometimes used. A cisium had a single seat, broad enough to accommodate a driver and passenger. Cicero says such a cart had made fifty-six miles in ten hours, probably with one or more changes of horses.

Other vehicles of the cart type came into use during the Empire. Since these

Model of a carruca, similar to a Conestoga wagon

carts had no springs, a traveler needed plenty of cushions. None of these carts had a Latin name. Their names, with perhaps one exception (*pilentum*), are Celtic—just as French terms are sometimes given to automobiles and some of their parts.

Monuments show crude representations of several kinds of vehicles, and the names of at least eight are known. We are not able positively to connect representations and names; so we have only general ideas of the style and construction of even the commonest.

ANCIENT INNS

There were numerous inns, lodging-houses, and restaurants in the cities and towns of Italy. At inns people found food and beds, and their horses were cared for under the same roof in unpleasant proximity. All such inns were of poor quality, and were avoided by respectable travelers. Either they had stopping places of their own on roads they used frequently, or they stayed with friends or hospites, whom they were ready to entertain in their turn and were

The two wheels indicate a carpentum

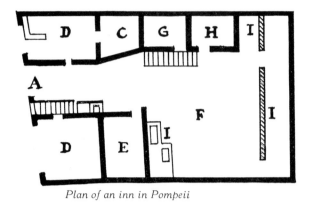

Plan of an inn in Pompeii

sure to have everywhere. Only accident, bad weather, or unusual haste could drive a traveler to an inn or a tavern. At such places the guests were of the lowest class, and innkeepers and inns had most unsavory reputations.

An inn at Pompeii may be taken as an example of such houses. The entrance (A) was broad enough to admit wagons to the wagon room (F), behind which was the stable (I). In one corner was a water-

Shop in Ostia where beverages were sold

ing trough, in another a toilet. On each side of the entrance was a wineroom (D), with the proprietor's room (C) opening off one of them. The small rooms were bedrooms (E, G, H), and other bedrooms on the second floor over the wagon room were reached by a back stairway. The front stairway had an entrance of its own from the street, and the rooms reached by it probably had no connection with the inn. Behind this stairway on the lower floor was a water heater.

An idea of the moderate prices charged in such places is given by a bill which has come down to us in an inscription preserved in the museum at Naples: a pint of wine with bread, one cent; other food, two cents; hay for a mule, two cents.

The corners of streets, especially at points close to the city walls, were favorite sites for inns. They displayed individual signs, such as an elephant or eagle, as many inns in England and a few in the United States still do.

SPEED OF TRAVEL

Since there were no public conveyances running on regular schedules, it is impossible to know the speed ordinarily made by travelers. The time depended on the total distance to be covered, the degree of comfort demanded by the traveler, the urgency of his business, and the facilities at his command. When Cicero spoke of fifty-six miles in ten hours by cart he considered that speed unusual, but on Roman roads it must have been possible to go much faster, if fresh horses were provided at proper distances.

SENDING LETTERS

The sending of letters gives the best basis for comparison. There was no public postal service, but every important

Roman had among his slaves special messengers (*tabellarii*), who delivered important letters for him. In a day these slaves covered twenty-six or twenty-seven miles on foot, and forty or fifty miles in carts. Letters were sent from Rome to Brundisium—three hundred seventy Roman miles—in six days, and on to Athens in fifteen more. A letter from Sicily would reach Rome on the seventh day after it was sent; one from Africa on the twenty-first day; one from Britain on the thirty-third day; and one from Syria on the fiftieth day. In George Washington's time, it was not unusual for a letter to take a month to go from the eastern to the southern states in winter, for there were no paved roads and travel was slow and difficult.

For long distances, especially overseas, sending letters by special messengers was so expensive that except for very urgent

Milestone

(Left) *A paved street in Ostia*

messages, letters were sent by traders and travelers going in the desired direction. People about to send a messenger or who intended to go on a journey made it a point of courtesy to notify friends in time for them to prepare letters. Travelers sometimes carried letters for strangers.

There was danger, of course, that letters sent in this way might fall into the wrong hands or be lost. It was customary therefore to send a copy of an important letter, or at least an abstract of its contents, by another person, and if possible, by a different route. In order to disguise the meaning, fictitious names known only to the correspondents and cipher codes were used. Suetonius says that Caesar simply substituted for each

letter the one three places lower in the alphabet (*D* for *A*, *E* for *B*, etc.), but more complicated systems were also in use.

WRITING LETTERS

The extensive correspondence carried on by every Roman of wealth or high position made it impossible for him to write with his own hand any but the most important of his letters or those to dear friends. Instead of stenographers and typists there were slaves or freedmen, often highly educated, who wrote at dictation. Such slaves were in general called *librarii* or, more accurately, *servi ab epistulis*, *servi a manu*, or *amanuenses*.

Instead of notepaper the Romans had tablets (*tabellae*) of various sizes, made of fir wood or ivory, often fastened together in sets of two or more by wire

Much traffic went through the Stabian Gate at Pompeii

Pens and inkwell

Wax tablet

Page of Latin in cursive writing

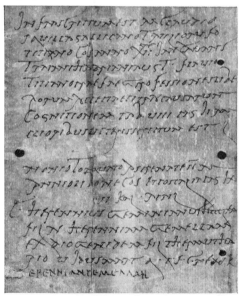

Letter on papyrus

hinges. The inner faces were slightly hollowed out, and the depression nearly filled with wax. This left a raised rim around the edges, much like the frame of an old-fashioned slate. Upon the wax, letters were traced with an ivory, bone, or metal tool (*stilus, graphium*), which had one end pointed, like a pencil, for writing, and the other broad and flat, for smoothing the wax. With the flat end mistakes could be corrected or the whole letter erased and the tablets used again—often for a reply to the letter itself. Such tablets were used not only for letters, but also for written schoolwork and business documents.

For longer communications Romans used a coarse "paper" (*papyrus*). Writing was done with pens made of split reeds and thick ink made of soot (lampblack) mixed with resinous gums. Since paper, pens, and ink were poor and papyrus expensive, the bulky tablets, which could be used again, were preferred for all but the longest letters. Parchment did not come into general use until the fourth or fifth century of our era.

SEALING AND OPENING OF LETTERS

For sealing a letter, thread (*linum*), wax (*cera*), and a seal (*signum*) were used. The seal not only secured a letter against improper inspection, but also attested the genuineness of letters written by librarii. It seems not to have occurred to the Romans to use autograph signatures, but every gentleman wore a seal ring for use in sealing his letters.

The tablets were put together face to face with the writing on the inside, the thread was passed around them and through small holes in them, and securely tied. Softened wax was dropped on the knot, and the seal pressed down on the wax. A letter written on a sheet of papyrus was rolled lengthwise and secured in the same way. Sealing a letter was necessary because, as Cicero once said, a messenger might make the burden of a heavy letter lighter by reading it. On the outside was written the name of the person addressed, with perhaps the place where he was to be found, if the letter was not sent by a special messenger.

When the thread was cut, the letter was open. Care was taken not to break the seal; if the letter was kept, the seal was left on it to prove that it was authentic. In the *Third Oration Against Catiline*, Cicero describes the opening of a letter, and mentions the distinctive seal.

So while there was little travel for pleasure in ancient times, necessary journeys could always be accomplished. Without planes or railroads, telegraph or telephone lines, messages were sent—even secret ones—and it was possible to get word from any part of the Empire to its heart—the city of Rome.

The larger pictures are raised impressions made by the intaglio gems in the seal rings—the head at the left is probably that of Mark Antony

BOOKS
AND
LIBRARIES

Erato, Muse of lyric poetry

Papyrus growing

PAPYRUS ROLLS

Almost all the materials that ancient people wrote on were used by the Romans. For the publication of works of literature, however, during the period when the great classics were produced, the material was "paper" (papyrus); the form, the roll (*volumen*).

The Romans adopted the papyrus roll from the Greeks, who had received it from the Egyptians. In museums there are Egyptian papyrus rolls that were written at least twenty-five hundred years B.C. The oldest Roman books of this type that have been preserved were found in Herculaneum, badly charred and broken. Those that have been deciphered are by obscure authors. At the time when these books were buried, rolls in the handwriting of the Gracchi may still have existed, and autograph copies of works of Cicero, Vergil, and Horace were undoubtedly common. All these rolls must long since have been lost or destroyed.

Scribe writing on a tablet

ROMAN PAPER

The papyrus reed has a triangular stem which grows at most fourteen feet high and four or five inches thick. Roman paper was made from the pith in the stem.

After the bark was removed, the pith was carefully cut into thin lengthwise strips. These strips were then arranged side by side until they reached the required width, thus forming a layer. Across them another layer of strips was laid at right angles, with perhaps a coating of glue between them. The mat-like sheet that resulted was then soaked in water and pressed or hammered into a substance similar to our paper.

This was called *charta*. After these sheets (*schedae*) had been dried and bleached in the sun, rough places were removed by scraping. The sheets were then trimmed to uniform sizes, depending on the length of the strips of pith.

The fewer the strips in a sheet, that is, the wider each strip of pith, the better the quality of the charta, because of its closer texture. It was possible, therefore, to grade paper by its size, with the width of the sheet rather than the length as the standard. The best quality was sold in sheets about ten inches wide, the poorest in sheets about six inches wide. In each case a sheet was perhaps one or two inches longer than it was wide. It has been calculated that about twenty sheets could be made from a single papyrus plant. This number seems to have been the commercial unit of measure by which paper was sold—a unit corresponding roughly to our quire.

PENS AND INK

Usually only the upper surface of the sheet—formed by the horizontal layer of strips—was used for writing. The strips, which showed even after the paper was finished, guided the pen of the writer. In books where it was important to have the same number of lines on each page, sheets were ruled with a round piece of lead. A pen was made of a sharpened reed, split like a quill pen.

Black ink was made of soot and resinous gums; occasionally the liquid of the cuttlefish was substituted. Red ink was much used for headings and ornaments. In pictures an inkstand is generally represented with two compartments, one presumably for black ink and the other for red. Roman ink was more like paint than modern ink, and when fresh, could be wiped off the paper with a damp sponge. Even when it had become dry and hard, it could be washed off. To wash sheets in order to use them a second time was a mark of poverty or stinginess, but the backs of used schedae often served as scratch paper, especially in schools.

MAKING THE ROLL

While a single sheet might be enough for a letter or a brief document, many sheets were required for literary purposes. These were not fastened side by side in a binding, as are the separate leaves in modern books. Nor were they numbered and laid loosely together, as pages of letters and manuscripts are now arranged. Instead, the sheets were glued together at the sides (not at the tops and bottoms) into a long, unwieldy strip, with the lines on each sheet running parallel with its length, and the writing on each sheet in a column perpendicular to the length of the strip. On each side of a sheet a margin was left as the writing was done, and these margins, overlapping and glued together made a thick blank space—a double thickness of paper—between every two sheets in the roll. Broad margins were also left at the top and bottom of each page, where the paper got much more wear than in our bound books.

When the sheets had been securely fastened together in the proper order, a thin strip of wood was glued to the left (outer) margin of the first sheet, and a second piece (*umbilicus*) to the right (also outer) margin of the last sheet. When not in use, a volume was kept tightly rolled about the umbilicus. Some authorities think that *umbilici* were not always attached to the rolls, but might be slipped in when the books were in use.

The first sheet was used for the dedication—if there was one—and on the back of it a few words giving a clue to the contents of the roll were frequently written. Sometimes a pen-and-ink portrait of the author was sketched on this page. In many books the full title and name of the author were written only at the end of the roll on the last sheet. In any case a strip of parchment (*titulus*) with the title and author's name on it was glued to the top of this sheet. This strip extended above the edge of the roll like a tag.

Roman holding a manuscript roll

Polyhymnia, Muse of sacred song

CARE OF ROLLS

A roll intended for permanent use was always finished with great care. Top and bottom were trimmed perfectly smooth, polished with pumice stone, and often painted black. The back of the roll was rubbed with cedar oil to protect it from moths and mice. To the ends of the umbilicus were added knobs (*cornua*), which were sometimes gilded or painted a bright color.

Every roll had a cylindrical parchment cover, into which it was slipped from the top, so that only the titulus was visible. If a work was divided into several volumes, the rolls were put together in a bundle and kept in a wooden box, somewhat like our round hat boxes. When the cover was off, the tags were visible, and one roll could be taken out without disturbing the others. Sometimes rolls were kept in cabinets, where they were laid on shelves with tags to the front.

Boy reading from a roll; other rolls are stored in the cabinet

SIZE OF THE ROLLS

Since there was theoretically no limit to the number of sheets that could be glued together, a roll might be of any size or length. Early ones were always long and heavy. Often one was made long enough for an entire book. In ancient Egypt, there were rolls a hundred fifty feet long, and some as long were used in Greece and Rome in early times.

A reader held a strip in both hands and unrolled it column by column with his right hand. With his left he rolled up the part he had read. When he had finished reading, he rolled the volume back on the umbilicus, usually holding it under his chin and turning the cornua with both hands. In the case of a long roll, this turning backward and forward took much time and patience and undoubtedly soiled and damaged the papyrus.

In the third century B.C., it became customary to divide long works into two or more volumes. At first the division was arbitrarily made wherever it was convenient to end a roll, no matter how much the unity of thought was interrupted. A little later, authors began to divide their works into convenient parts, each having a unity of its own, as do the five books of Cicero's *De Finibus*. Each of these books had a separate roll. An innovation so convenient and sensible quickly became the practice. Even some ancient works which had not been divided by their authors—Herodotus, Thucydides, and Naevius—were divided into books.

At the same time it became the custom to sell sheets already glued together in rolls. It was, of course, much easier to glue two or three of these together, or to cut off the unused part of one, than to work with separate sheets. The ready-made rolls were well put together. Since

Vergil and Homer

even sheets of the same quality varied slightly in toughness or finish, the manufacturers were careful to put the best sheets at the beginning, where they would get the most wear. The less perfect sheets were kept for the end, where they might not be needed and so could be cut off.

MAKING BOOKS AT HOME

The process of publishing a long book at Rome differed little from that of writing a short letter. Every copy was made individually, the hundredth or the thousandth taking just as much time and effort as the first. If the author was a man of wealth—a Caesar or a Sallust—his manuscript was distributed for reproduction among his own copyists. If he was a poor man—a Terence or a Vergil—his patron's copyists did the work. Each amanuensis would write and rewrite the portions assigned him, until the required number of copies had been made.

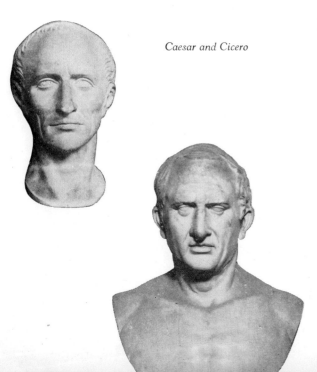

Caesar and Cicero

Then if ready-made rolls were not used, the sheets were assembled in the proper order and the rolls mounted. Finally the books had to be read to correct errors sure to be there—a process much more tedious than modern proofreading. Each copy had to be corrected separately, since no two copies would show exactly the same errors. Books made in this way were used mostly for gifts, although friends exchanged them with one another, and a few found their way into the market.

Up to the last century of the Republic there was no organized book trade, and no such thing as commercial publication. When a man wanted a certain book, instead of buying it at a bookstore, he borrowed a roll from a friend and had his slaves make him as many copies as he desired. In this way Atticus had many Greek and Latin books made for himself and Cicero as well as distributing Cicero's own writings.

COMMERCIAL PUBLICATION

The publication of books at Rome as a business began in the time of Cicero. There was no copyright law and no protection for author or publisher. An author had no royalties, although he sometimes received gifts or grants from those who admired him for his genius. The name of Maecenas—generous patron of Vergil and Horace—has become proverbial. In the case of new books, publishers depended on meeting the demand before rivals could market their editions. With standard books, publishers depended on the accuracy, elegance, and cheapness of the copies.

The process of commercial publication was essentially the same as the private method, except that larger numbers of copyists were employed. A publisher estimated the demand for any new work, and put as many slaves to work as possible. No copies left his establishment until the whole edition was ready. After copies were on sale, they could be reproduced by anyone.

The best houses took great care to have their books free from errors; they had competent correctors read them copy by copy. In spite of their efforts, however, there were many blunders. With their own hands authors sometimes corrected books intended for their friends. In the case of standard works, purchasers often engaged noted scholars to revise the work of the amanuenses, while copies of known excellence were borrowed or rented at high prices for comparison.

RAPIDITY AND COST OF PUBLICATION

Cicero tells of Roman senators who wrote fast enough to take evidence verbatim, and trained copyists must have been much faster. Martial said that his second book could be copied in an hour. Since it contains 540 lines, the copyist must have written nine lines per minute. It is evident that a small edition, consisting of not more than two or three times as many books as there were copyists, could be put on the market more quickly than a printed edition can be produced now.

The cost of books varied with their size and the style of their mounting. Martial's first book, containing 820 lines and covering 39 pages in Teubner's text, sold for what would be thirty cents, fifty cents, and one dollar. His *Xenia*, containing 274 lines and covering 14 pages in Teubner's text, sold for twenty cents, but cost the publisher less than ten. Such prices would be surprising now. Much depended on the reputation of the author and the consequent demand. High prices were put on certain books. Autograph copies and copies whose correctness was guaranteed by some recognized authority

A fragment of manuscript from Sallust, a Roman historian

commanded extraordinary prices. According to Gellius (late second century A.D.), an autograph copy of one of Vergil's books cost the owner the equivalent of $100.

LIBRARIES

Toward the end of the Republic the assembling of large private libraries began to be general, and soon every town house had its library. Cicero had libraries not only in his home at Rome, but also at his country houses. Probably when Lucullus and Sulla brought to Rome whole libraries from the East and from Greece, they started the fashion of collecting books. At any rate collections were made by many persons who knew and cared nothing about the contents of the rolls; soon every town house had its library. In these rooms busts of great writers and statues of the Muses were often displayed.

Public libraries date from the time of Augustus. Asinius Pollio (75 B.C.-A.D. 4) opened the first one in Rome, in the *Atrium Libertatis*. Augustus himself founded two others, and the number was increased to twenty-eight by his successors. The most magnificent of these was the *Bibliotheca Ulpia*, begun by Trajan. Smaller cities had their libraries, too. Even the little town of Comum boasted one started by Pliny the Younger and supported by an endowment that produced thirty thousand sesterces ($1500) annually. Often there were libraries and reading rooms in public baths.

Vergil with a Muse on each side

Augustus

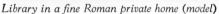
Library in a fine Roman private home (model)

Trajan

Inconvenient as papyrus rolls were, they remained in use through the period when the great Latin classics were written and published. Gradually books of parchment or vellum came into use, and by the fourth century A.D. papyrus rolls were discarded. A book made—as ours are—of folded sheets was much more convenient to handle. Parchment lasts longer than papyrus, and gives a better writing surface. With it a finer pen could be used, permitting more letters to a line, and both sides of the sheets could be written on. It is on parchment, then, that Latin literature has come down to us. No papyrus rolls that have survived contain any Latin work of importance. A thousand years later, the invention of printing and the manufacture of paper made mass production of books possible.

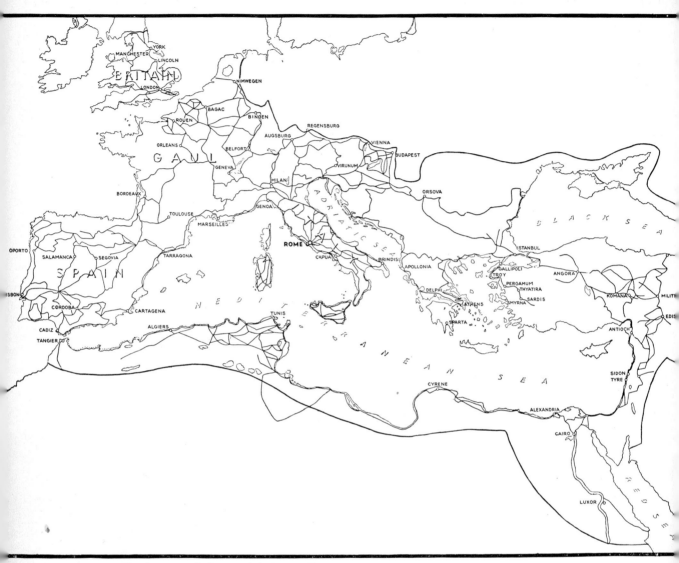

Roads connected all parts of the Roman Empire

ROADS, AQUEDUCTS, AND SEWERS

EXTENT OF ROMAN HIGHWAYS

The engineering skill of the Romans and their lavish expenditures made their highways the best roads the world had ever known until recent times. Although these roads, especially the earlier ones in Italy and those in the provinces, were built primarily for military purposes—to facilitate the moving of supplies and the massing of troops in the shortest possible time—they also encouraged commerce and travel.

Beginning with *Via Appia*, built in 312 B.C. after Rome's first important acquisition of territory in Italy, the construction of roads kept pace with the expansion of Roman boundaries, until a great network of highways—estimated at nearly fifty thousand miles—covered the Roman world, all leading to Rome, as the saying was. It is said that in the fourth century A.D. nineteen great roads entered Rome through the fifteen gates of the Wall of Aurelian.

In Britain a network of main and subsidiary roads—some of which are still in use—connected towns in the interior with one another and with towns on the coast. The main highways converged at *Londinium* (London), linking this important trading town with other parts of the island. Even beyond Hadrian's Wall, which extended from Newcastle to Carlisle, roads ran north as far as the wall of Antoninus Pius, sixty miles farther on. And the roads of Britain extended to the Channel, across which the highways of Gaul connected with those of Italy, and led eventually to Rome.

In Italy roads were built at the expense of the State; in the provinces conquered communities paid for their construction and maintenance, but the actual work

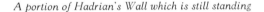

A portion of Hadrian's Wall which is still standing

Mattock—such tools were used in road-building

Milestone

was done under the direction of Roman engineers, often by soldiers between campaigns.

Roads ran as straight as possible between towns they connected, with frequent crossroads and branch roads, which, like our side roads, were not so carefully constructed as the main highways. The grade was always easy—hills were cut through, gorges and rivers crossed on substantial bridges of stone, and valleys and marshes spanned by viaducts.

Milestones showed the distance from the starting point of a road and often the distance to important places in the opposite direction, as well as the names of the consuls or emperor under whom the road was built or repaired. A milestone found on the *Via Salaria* bears the inscription *L. Caecili Q. F. Metel cos CXIX Roma.* "Erected by the consul [117 B.C.] Lucius Caecilius Metellus, son of Quintus. One hundred nineteen [miles] from Rome."

The road itself was wide enough to permit the meeting and passing of large wagons. For pedestrians there was a footpath on either side, sometimes paved, and often there were seats beside the milestones, where tired travelers could rest. Horsemen found blocks of stone set here and there along the way, for convenience in mounting and dismounting. Where there were springs, wayside fountains for men and watering troughs for stock were provided.

A Roman arch in Italy supports a road still in use

A Roman wagon (model)

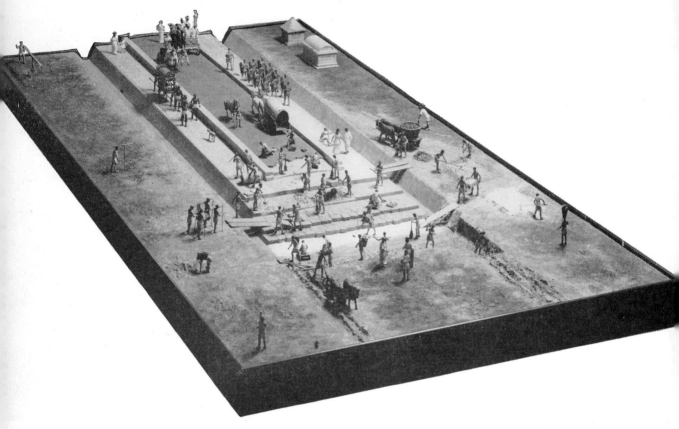

Building the Appian Way (model)

HIGHWAY ENGINEERING

Our knowledge of the construction of military roads comes from a treatise by Vitruvius on pavements and from remains of the roads themselves. The Latin phrase for building a road, *munire viam*, sums up the process exactly, for *munire* means "to build a wall" (*moenia*); and throughout its full length, whether carried above the level of the surrounding country or in a cut below it, a Roman road was really a solid wall, on the average, fifteen feet wide and perhaps three feet high.

First a cut (*fossa*) was made the width of the planned road and deep enough to hold the filling, which varied with the nature of the soil. The earth at the bottom of the cut was leveled and made solid with heavy rammers. On this base was spread a foundation layer of stones small enough to be held in the hand— its thickness varying with the porousness of the soil. On a rocky subsoil the foundation course or even the first and second courses might be unnecessary. Over this came a nine-inch layer of coarse concrete or rubble made of broken stones and lime. Next was laid a six-inch bedding

of fine concrete—made of broken pot-
sherds and lime—in which was set the
final course of blocks of lava or other
hard stone found in the surrounding
country.

This last course formed the roadway
itself and was laid with great care, so
that there were no seams or cracks that
would admit water or jar the wheels of
vehicles. The stone blocks were commonly cut to a point or edge, so that
they might hold firm in the concrete
bedding. The surface of the road was
slightly rounded, with gutters at the
sides to carry off rain and melted snow.

The roadway was bounded on the sides
by curbstones, beyond which lay foot-
paths. On less traveled branch roads,
the roadway seems to have consisted of
a thick course of gravel, well rounded
and rammed down, instead of blocks of
stone, while the crossroads may have
been even less solidly constructed.

These solid roads of the Romans often
went a hundred years without needing
repairs; some sections, after enduring the

Carrying stone (detail of model)

Rolling the surface (detail of model)

traffic of centuries, are still in good
condition.

While the roads were originally built
for moving troops with their equipment
and supplies, they naturally aided commerce wherever the cheaper transportation by sea was impossible. Rapid
communication throughout Italy and the
provinces was furthered by the spider
web of roads. Even without a regular
postal system, letters came and went in
all directions. And when Christianity had
once reached Rome, it spread easily over
the western world by way of the Roman
roads.

Roman pavement nearly two thousand years old

WATER SUPPLY

In early days the city of Rome was well supplied with water. Springs were abundant, wells did not have to be sunk far to find water, water from the Tiber could be used, and rain water was collected in cisterns. But these sources became inadequate, and in 312 B.C. the first of the great aqueducts (*aquae*) was built by the famous *censor* (official), Appius Claudius, and named for him, *Aqua Appia*. It was eleven miles long, and except for three hundred feet, ran underground. This and the *Anio Vetus*, built forty years later, supplied the lower levels of the city.

The first high-level aqueduct, *Aqua Marcia*, was built in 140 B.C. by Quintus Marcius Rex, to bring water to the top of the Capitoline Hill. Its water was and still is particularly cold and good. *Aqua*

The Aqua Claudia can still be seen in the Campagna, which until a few years ago was an open plain

The Acqua Paola, the great fountain on the Janiculum, is fed by the restored Aqua Trajana

336

Street fountain in Pompeii

Today water gushes from the animal's head of a fountain that served the Pompeians

Pipes used in Roman plumbing

Tepula (named from the temperature of its waters), completed in 125 B.C., was the last aqueduct built during the Republic.

Under Augustus three more were constructed, *Aqua Julia* and *Aqua Virgo* by Agrippa, and *Alsietina* by Augustus to supply his artificial lake. *Aqua Claudia*, whose ruined arches are still a magnificent sight near Rome, and *Anio Novus* were begun by Caligula and finished by Claudius. *Trajana* was built by Trajan in A.D. 109, and the last, *Alexandrina*, by Alexander Severus. Eleven aqueducts then served ancient Rome. Modern Rome is considered unusually well supplied with water from four, using the sources and occasionally the channels of ancient ones. *Virgo*, now *Acqua Vergine*, appears in the Fountain of Trevi. It was first restored by Pius V in 1570. The springs of *Alexandrina* supply *Acqua*

Felice, built in 1585. *Aqua Trajana* was restored as *Acqua Paola* in 1611. The famous *Marcia* was reconstructed in 1870 as *Acqua Pia*, or *Marcia-Pia* and provides excellent drinking water.

The remains of aqueducts found in France, Spain, Africa, and other regions once Roman provinces, as well as in Italy, show how important the Romans considered a good water supply. Probably all important towns in Italy—as well as many cities in the provinces—were supplied with water brought by carefully planned and constructed aqueducts.

The channels of aqueducts were usually built of masonry because the Romans had no pipes strong enough to carry so much water. They did not have cast-iron pipes; lead was rarely used for large pipes,

Until recently, this ancient aqueduct carried water to Segovia, Spain

Aqueduct of the ancient city of Mactaris, which stood in what is now a waste of North Africa

and bronze was too expensive. It was because of this lack, and not because the Romans did not understand the principle of the siphon, that high-pressure aqueducts were not commonly constructed. To avoid high pressure, the aqueducts that supplied Rome with water—and many others—were built at an easy slope and frequently carried around hills and valleys, though tunnels and bridges were sometimes used to save distance. The great arches, so impressive in their ruins, like those of Aqua Claudia, were used for comparatively short distances, since most channels were underground.

In the city, water flowed into distributing reservoirs, from which ran street mains. It was carried into houses by pipes made of strips of sheet lead with edges folded together and welded at the joining. This made them pear-shaped rather than round. Many of these pipes have been found in Rome, and since each is stamped with the name of the owner and user, they have helped locate sites of residences of many distinguished men. In Pompeii the water pipes can easily be seen, for in that mild climate they were often laid on the surface of the ground close to the house, not buried as they are in most parts of this country.

The poor carried the water they needed from the public fountains that stood at frequent intervals in the streets, and whose waters ran constantly for all comers. A reminder of this is seen in the many large and beautiful fountains that play in the streets of Rome today.

Cistern on the Palatine, part of Rome's early water supply

Remains of the Cloaca Maxima, the sewer of ancient Rome

DRAINS AND SEWERS

The need of drains and sewers in Rome was recognized in early times. The famous *Cloaca Maxima* (main sewer) is said to have been built by King Tarquinius Superbus to drain the marshy valley where the Forum was situated, but it probably was of later origin. At first an open, stone-lined channel, it was later vaulted over and served as a central collector for a number of other drains. It was still in use in the last century, and its opening into the Tiber may yet be seen.

Eventually there was a network of sewers in Rome which tended to follow natural lines of drainage. Sewers were not metal or tile pipes, but were built of masonry like the channels of the aqueducts. Some sewers were so large that a wagon could be driven through them.

This network of sewers was used chiefly to collect sewage from the baths, from the ground floors of buildings, and from public latrines. It is unlikely that many private homes—except perhaps those of the very rich—were connected with sewers, for the drainage system of the Roman house was really not as modern as is often believed. If insulae had any running water or drainage, it must have been on the ground floor only. Slaves carried water to the upper stories, and tenants often emptied their slop jars into the streets. In Shakespeare's time sanitary conditions in London were not very different, though without the frequent fountains, well-paved streets, and good drainage of Rome.

ROMAN RELIGION

The Pantheon in Rome, dedicated to the great gods—now a church containing the tombs of the kings of Italy

EARLY RELIGION

The religion of the Romans was originally a simple animism—a belief in spirits or powers (*numina*) associated with everything surrounding man and with all his acts. These spirits were not personified and not imagined as human in form. There were no temples and no statues of gods. Rites were clean and simple and performed with a scrupulous exactness believed pleasing to the gods. When thus carefully worshiped, gods were friendly. This was the religion of a simple agricultural people. In calendars that have come down to us, old festivals are indicated by larger letters than later ones. These were rural festivals, marking the year of country people.

THE COMING OF FOREIGN GODS

As the Romans developed from a small Italian community to an imperialistic nation—as they came in contact with other peoples and their religions—their own religion inevitably changed. Divinities of conquered communities were brought into the pantheon of Roman gods, and in times of stress gods were imported to meet emergencies. It is believed that Etruscan kings built the first temples in Italy and set up the first statues of gods. Contact with Greeks led to the introduction of Greek gods and Greek ritual and to the identification of the old Roman gods with the Greek gods that seemed most like them. However,

Venus, goddess of love and beauty

Juno, queen of the gods

much of the primitive Roman religion remained, and the worship of Greek gods was influenced by it.

Exactness in the performance of rites led naturally to a deadening formalism. Before the end of the Republic, the educated classes were turning from religion to philosophy. As the native stock was more and more displaced by people from the East, mystical or orgiastic cults of Greece and the Orient were adopted. Under the Empire, Oriental religions became firmly established, while worship of the emperors came to be the distinguishing feature of the State religion. In the end Christianity replaced all the cults.

THE RELIGION OF NUMA

To Numa, second of the seven kings, Roman tradition ascribed the organization of worship and the assignment to the calendar of the proper festivals in due order. Whether or not we believe that a great priest-king left his personal impress on ritual and calendar, "the religion of Numa" is a convenient designation for the religion of the early State. Numa is said to have organized the first priestly colleges and to have appointed the first flamines. Most important of these were the priest of Jupiter and the priests of Mars and Quirinus (the deified Romulus).

(Left) *A sacrifice*

Mars, god of war

Fortuna with a cornucopia of fruits, wearing the headdress of Isis

Columns of a Temple of Diana, still standing in Jerash, Syria

When the monarchy was abolished, the office of king of rites was instituted to carry on religious ceremonies formerly in charge of the king. The rex sacrorum, the three flamines, and the college of high priests, with the Pontifex Maximus at its head, controlled and guided the State religion. Under the Empire the emperor was regularly Pontifex Maximus.

PRIESTLY COLLEGES

Priestly colleges were groups of priests organized to perpetuate certain rites. *Salii* (dancing priests) made up an old and famous college that worshiped Mars, god of war. A similar college, *Salii Collini*, was in charge of the worship of Quirinus.

Unofficial associations carried on the worship of various gods. The pontifices took care of the calendar, assigning dates for festivals. The *augures* interpreted the will of the gods as shown when auspices were taken by magistrates before any public occasion or action. Among official colleges was the Commission of Fifteen, in charge of the famous Sibylline books, which foretold the history of Rome. Burial societies were ostensibly organized as colleges to promote the worship of some god.

One of the oldest and most famous colleges was that of Vesta, goddess of the hearth, whose worship was directed by the six Virgines Vestales. The sacred fire on the altar of *Aedes Vestae* (temple of Vesta) symbolized the continuity of the life of the State. The temple of Vesta was round, with a pointed roof.

Caesar and Cicero would have seen these temples, which date from the first century B.C.

Temple of Vesta

Even in its latest development of marble and bronze, it had not changed much in shape and size from the original round hut of poles, clay, and thatch. There was no statue of the goddess in the temple.

In a simple round temple, village girls had tended the fire whose maintenance was necessary for a primitive community. To light a fire had then been a toilsome business of rubbing wood on wood, or later, of striking flint on steel to get the precious spark. But to rekindle the sacred fire, flint and steel were never used; ritual demanded the traditional use of friction.

Each vestal served for thirty years. A vacancy in the order had to be filled promptly by the appointment of a girl of suitable family, not less than six years old nor more than ten, physically perfect, of good character, and having both parents living. On appointment a girl was freed at once from her father's authority, and went to live in the House of the Vestals (*Atrium Vestae*) beside the Temple of Vesta in the Forum.

Vestals spent ten years in learning their duties, ten in performing them, and ten in training younger vestals. In addition to caring for the sacred fire, the vestals took part in most festivals of the old calendar. At the end of her service, a vestal might return to private life if she wished, but the privileges and the dignity of her position were so attractive that this rarely occurred.

RELIGION OF THE FAMILY

In each family the pater familias was the household priest and as such was in charge of family worship. He was assisted by his wife and children. In both town and country the *Lar Familiaris*

was the protecting spirit of the household. In the country the lares were also guardian spirits of fields and were worshiped at crossroads by owners and tenants of the lands that met there. In town, the Lares of the Crossroads were worshiped at street-corner shrines in different precincts.

Instead of the single lar of the Republican period, we later find two lares. Pompeian household shrines show frequent examples of this. A lar is represented as a boy dressed in a belted tunic, stepping lightly as if dancing, sometimes with a bowl in his right hand, and a jug upraised in his left. In place of the old penates—protecting spirits of the storeroom—these shrines show images of such of the great gods as each family chose to honor in its private devotions.

The genius of the pater familias is sometimes represented in such shrines as a man with a toga drawn over his head as for worship. Often a genius is

A vestal virgin

Figure of a goddess on a candelabrum

Behind Minerva, Jupiter, and Juno are Hercules, Bacchus, Ceres, and Mercury

represented by a serpent. In such shrines we find two figures, a bearded one standing for the genius of the father, the other for the Juno of his wife.

Vesta, spirit of the fire essential to man's existence, was worshiped at the hearth. Originally, when the atrium was the one room where the household lived

Diana, goddess of the moon and of hunting

Venus

and worked, the shrine was there. When a separate kitchen was established, the shrine followed the hearth. In addition, shrines are often found in garden or peristyle, and occasionally in the atrium and other rooms.

FAMILY DEVOTIONS

Devout Romans prayed and sacrificed every morning, but the usual time for family devotions was the pause at dinner before dessert, when offerings to household gods were made. Kalends, nones, and ides were sacred to the lares. On these days garlands were hung over the hearth, the lares were crowned with flowers, and simple offerings were made. Incense and wine were the usual offerings, but when possible a pig was sacrificed. Horace gives us a pretty picture of the "rustic Phidyle" who crowns her little lares with rosemary and myrtle, and offers incense, new grain, and a "greedy pig."

All family occasions from birth to death were accompanied by proper ceremonies. Strong religious feeling clung to family rites and country festivals even when the State religion had stiffened into formalism and many Romans were reaching after strange gods.

The gens of which each family formed a part had its own rites (*sacra*). The maintenance of these was considered necessary not merely for the welfare of the clan itself, but also for that of the State. It was believed that the State might suffer from the gods' displeasure if rites were neglected.

THE RELIGION OF THE STATE

Of the early gods of the Roman State, Jupiter was the greatest. He was the light-father, worshiped on hilltops and called on by men to witness their agreements. He was king of the gods, as Juno, his wife, was queen. Saturn was god of the crops, and Venus was concerned with gardens. Mars was worshiped in connection with agriculture and war, for the farmer was a fighter, too. Vesta was the spirit of the hearth.

The first temple at Rome was built on the Capitoline Hill by the Etruscans for the worship of Jupiter, Juno, and Minerva. The latter, patron of craftsmen and their guilds, had her own temple on the Aventine. Diana was a wood spirit from Aricia in Latium. Hercules came from

Apollo with a quiver of arrows

Cybele, enthroned between her lions

nearby Tibur as god of commerce; Castor and Pollux were from Tusculum. Mercury, god of commerce, came from Cumae. The last four were of Greek origin, naturalized in Italy. Because of the famine in 493 B.C., the Sibylline oracle at Cumae advised bringing in the Greek Bacchus, Ceres, and Proserpina. Apollo came early from Cumae as god of healing; his temple was built in 432 B.C. In 293 B.C., a time of pestilence, the worship of Aesculapius, god of medicine, was brought from Epidaurus to the island in the Tiber—still the site of a hospital.

The Asiatic *Magna Mater* (Cybele) was brought by the State from Phrygia in 205 B.C., during the Second Punic War, but after the orgiastic nature of her worship became known, it was ordained that Romans should never be her priests. The adoption of her cult was the beginning of the movement toward Oriental religions.

Naturally, with new gods came new modes of worship. More and more Greek gods were introduced, only to become gradually identified with Roman gods. Greek craftsmen built temples, and artists made statues of gods like those of Greece. Acquaintance with Greek mythology, literature, and art finally made the identification complete.

A RELIGIOUS REVIVAL

In time the study of Greek philosophy supplanted the old religious beliefs among the upper classes. As interest in religion waned, some forms and ceremonies and even priesthoods were discarded, especially during the troubled times of the Civil Wars. When Augustus restored order in the State, he stressed a religious revival as part of his constructive policy of repairing and rebuilding temples and reviving old rites and priesthoods.

Minerva, goddess of wisdom

RELIGION IN THE IMPERIAL AGE

The introduction of Eastern rites and the spread of their influence was naturally encouraged by the weakening of the old Roman stock, the constantly increasing number of Orientals in the West, and the campaigns of Roman armies in the East. The cult of Magna Mater found a reviving interest among people from places where she was worshiped.

Apollo, god of music and poetry

With their rites of purification and assurance of happiness after death, the mystery religions also gained strength. Among them the worship of Isis, brought by Egyptians from Alexandria, spread among the lower classes. Mithraism came in with captives from the Eastern campaigns, and later with troops that had served or had been enlisted in the East. It was established in Rome and other cities and was carried by the army from camp to camp.

There were many Jews in Rome, and their religion also made some progress. The first appearance of Christianity at Rome was among the lower classes— particularly Orientals, since it came to Rome from the East. Gradually the upper classes adopted it, and from Rome it spread over the West.

In the Imperial Age, worship of the emperors developed naturally from the time of the deification of Julius Caesar. The movement for this deification was of Oriental origin, because in Oriental countries the ruler was thought to be divine. The genius of the emperor was worshiped in the State as the genius of the father had been worshiped in the household. Beginning in the East, this worship was then established in the western provinces, and finally in Italy. In each of the municipalities it was under the care of the Augustales.

The worship of the emperor in his lifetime was not permitted at Rome, but it spread through the provinces and took the place there of the old State religion. To this emperor worship Christianity was opposed. The refusal of Christians to take part in it was regarded as treasonable, but their offense was political, not religious. Gradually as Christianity spread and increased, older religions diminished, and it became the religion of Rome and the Empire.

Columns of the Temple of Jupiter, Baalbek, Lebanon

Isis, with a lotus on her forehead and a
rattle in her hand

Body of a Roman woman lying in state

THE ROMANS
AND THEIR DEAD

IMPORTANCE OF CEREMONIAL RITES

The Romans' view of the future life explains why it was so important that their dead should have a ceremonial burial. The soul, they thought, could find rest only when the body had been duly laid in the grave; until this was done, the spirit haunted its home—unhappy itself, and bringing unhappiness to others. Thus observance of appropriate funeral rites was the solemn religious duty of surviving members of the family. The Latin term for such rites, *justa facere* (to do the right things), shows that these marks of respect were considered the dues of the dead.

If a body was lost at sea, or for any other reason unrecovered, burial ceremonies were still piously performed; an empty tomb (*cenotaphium*, cenotaph) was sometimes erected in honor of those lost. If a Roman happened on the unburied corpse of a citizen, he was bound to perform such rites as were possible, since all Romans were members of the great family of the commonwealth. If for any reason a body could not actually be interred, the scattering of three handfuls of dust over it was sufficient for ceremonial burial and also assured happiness to the troubled spirits.

BURIAL AND CREMATION

Burial was used in the most ancient times by the Romans, and even after cremation came into general use, it was ceremonially necessary that some small part of the remains, usually the bone of a finger, should be buried in the earth. Cremation was practiced before the time of the Twelve Tables (traditional date, 451 B.C.), for it is mentioned in them, together with burial. Hygienic reasons had probably something to do with the

To the family of the Haterii, this relief represented the building of their tomb

general adoption of cremation after Rome had become a city of some size.

By the time of Augustus cremation was practiced throughout the Roman world, but even in Rome burial was never entirely discontinued. Cremation was too costly for very poor people, and some wealthy and aristocratic families held fast to the more ancient custom. The Cornelii, for example, always buried their dead until the great dictator, Lucius Cornelius Sulla, directed that his body be burned, lest his bones be dug up and dishonored by his enemies, as he, himself, had dishonored those of Marius. Children less than forty days old were always buried, and so, usually, were slaves, whose funeral expenses were paid by their masters. After the introduction of Christianity, burial again became the custom.

Castel Sant' Angelo on the bank of the Tiber—originally the tomb of Emperor Hadrian

HADRIAN'S MAUSOLEUM

Most imposing of all Roman tombs was the Mausoleum of Hadrian. The emperor built it and the bridge that leads to it. Through the centuries this enormous tomb has been put to various uses. It has been in turn fortress, castle, and a home of popes. Battered in sieges, often flooded by the overflowing river, shaken by earthquakes, and changed by man, it is still a splendid monument to the glories of the past.

PLACES OF BURIAL

The Twelve Tables forbade burying or even burning bodies of the dead within the city walls. For the very poor, places of burial were provided in localities outside the walls, corresponding somewhat to the potter's fields of modern cities. The well-to-do who wanted impressive burial places built them along the great highways. For miles roads near Rome were lined on each side with a row of elaborate and expensive tombs. The

For miles outside Rome, ancient tombs once lined the Appian Way

Tombs outside Pompeii

builders hoped that the inscriptions on the monuments would keep alive the names and virtues of their dead, and perhaps they also had the idea that the dead might still have some part in the busy life around them. The monuments and tombs of Rome's oldest aristocratic families lined the Appian Way, the most ancient highway. Many of them were still standing as late as the sixteenth century, and a few still remain. An idea of the nature of such monuments is given by the "Street of Tombs" outside Pompeii.

There were other burial places near

cities, less conspicuous and less expensive, and on farms and country estates provision was made for the burial of poor persons.

KINDS OF TOMBS

Tombs—for bodies, ashes, or both—differed in size and construction according to the purpose for which they were built. In some only one person was buried, but usually such tombs were public memorials. Most of those lining the Roman roads were family tombs—

Tombstone set up by Antonia Ionis for her husband, M. Antonius Chrysogonus, a freedman, and Alexandria, a verna

Two Roman sarcophagi of white marble in Algeria

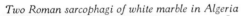

Funerary portraits of mother and son, with allegorical and mythological background

big enough to receive generations of descendants, retainers, freedmen, and even of hospites who had died away from their own homes.

MIDDLE- AND LOWER-CLASS BURIALS

Roman citizens not rich enough to erect their own tombs and without any claim on a family or clan burying-place could buy space for a few urns in tombs built by speculators. Many industrious poor belonged to coöperative burial societies which erected similar structures on the same plan. Some of these tombs were maintained by philanthropists, just as baths and libraries were often erected by generous men for the public good. Faithful freedmen were buried by their patrons, and very poor citizens were in general cared for by clansmen, patrons, or the benevolence of individuals.

POTTER'S FIELD

During the Republic all the refuse of Rome that the sewers could not carry away was carted to the eastern part of the Esquiline Hill. Here were grave pits for the pauper class. They were merely holes in the ground, about twelve feet square, without any lining. Into them were thrown the bodies of friendless poor, together with carcasses of dead animals and filth and scrapings of the streets. In time of plague the bodies of known citizens might be cast into these pits, just as infected bodies have sometimes been burned in piles in modern cities. The uncounted thousands buried in the potter's field of Rome were riffraff from foreign lands, abandoned slaves, victims that perished in the arena, criminal outcasts, and "unidentified" dead, who would now be buried at public expense.

Apparently these pits were kept open, even when filled, and the stench and disease-breeding pollution made the hill uninhabitable. So great was the danger to the health of the city that under Augustus new dumping grounds were provided at a distance. This part of the Esquiline, covered over—pits and all—with fresh soil to the depth of twenty-five feet, was made a park by Maecenas, known as the *Horti Maecenatis*.

Criminals executed by the authorities were not buried at all; their bodies were left to birds and beasts of prey at the place of execution near the Esquiline Gate.

TOMBS AND THEIR GROUNDS

Great variety is seen in the form and construction of Roman tombs, but those of the classical period seem to have been planned with the thought that a tomb was a home for the dead, in which they were not altogether cut off from the living. An effort was therefore made to give an air of life to the chamber of rest. A tomb—whether intended for one person or for many—was usually a building enclosing a room (*sepulcrum*), which was the most important part of the structure. Even the burial urns of ancient times were the shape of the early one-room house.

The floor of the sepulcrum was commonly below the level of the surrounding grounds and was reached by a short flight of steps. Around the base of the walls ran a slightly elevated platform on which coffins were placed, while urns were set either on the platform or in niches in the wall. There is often an altar or shrine at which offerings were made to the *manes* (spirits of the dead). Many lamps, as well as other simple articles of furniture have been found, and walls, floors, and ceilings were decorated in the

Interior of the tomb of the Scipios

Funerary urns shaped like an early Roman house

A funeral chest with a lead pipe for pouring in a libation

Receptacle for libation in the tomb

same style as those in houses. Articles that the living had liked to have around them—especially those used in their ordinary occupations—were placed in the tomb with the dead at the time of burial, or burned with them on the funeral pyre.

The tomb itself was always built on a plot of ground as large as the owners could afford—sometimes several acres in extent. There provision was made for the comfort of surviving members of the family, when they visited the resting place of their dead on annual festival days. If the grounds were small, there was a seat or a bench. On larger grounds there were shelters, arbors, or summerhouses. Dining rooms, too, in which were celebrated anniversary feasts, and private *ustrinae* (places for burning bodies) are frequently mentioned. Often

grounds were laid out as gardens or parks, with trees, flowers, and fountains. Sometimes there were also wells and cisterns and perhaps even a house and other buildings to accommodate the slaves or freedmen in charge.

There were many types of tombs. Monuments shaped like altars and temples were common; there were also memorial arches and niches. At Pompeii there are several of the semicircular benches —both covered and uncovered—that were used for conversation out of doors. Not all tombs have a sepulchral chamber; the remains were sometimes buried in the earth beneath the monument. In such cases a tube or pipe of lead ran from the surface to an underground receptacle, through which offerings of wine and milk could be poured.

Mausoleum of Augustus today

THE MAUSOLEUM OF AUGUSTUS

In the northern part of the Campus Martius stood the mausoleum which Augustus built for himself and his family in 28 B.C. On a great circular structure of concrete with marble or stucco facing, was a mound of earth planted with trees and flowers, and on its summit stood a statue of the emperor. At each side of the entrance were the famous bronze tablets inscribed with *Res Gestae*—a record of his achievements. The ashes of the young Marcellus were the first placed here, in 28 B.C., and those of the Emperor Nerva, the last, in A.D. 98. After being used as a fortress, hanging garden, bull ring, circus, and concert hall, it has been completely excavated in modern times.

Funeral inscription of Aurelius Hermia and his wife, a freedwoman

Funeral portrait of a Roman husband and his wife, whose dress indicates her foreign birth

COLUMBARIA

From the family tombs developed the immense structures intended to receive a great number of urns. From their resemblance to a pigeon house they were called *columbaria* (dovecotes). They first appeared in the time of Augustus, when the high price of land made the purchase of private burial grounds impossible for the poor people. Usually they were underground and rectangular in form, with a great number of niches in regular rows horizontally and vertically. A columbarium might hold a thousand urns.

Along the walls at the base extended a podium on which were placed *sarcophagi* for bodies which had not been burned; sometimes chambers were excavated under the floor for sarcophagi. If the building was high enough, wooden galleries ran around the walls. Under the stairway which led down into the room, there were also niches.

A columbarium in Ostia

Decorated urns for the ashes of the dead

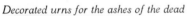

Tombstone of a soldier

Light was furnished by small windows near the ceiling, and the walls and floors were handsomely finished and decorated. On the outside over the door there was an inscription giving the names of the owners, the date of erection, and other particulars.

Some of the niches were rectangular; others were half round. In some of the columbaria the lower rows of niches were rectangular; those above, arched. These niches usually contained two urns each, placed side by side so that they could both be seen from the front. Occasionally niches were made deep enough for two sets of urns, the ones at the back being elevated a little above those in front. Over each niche or below it, there was a piece of marble (*titulus*), on which was cut the name of the owner. The titulus was fastened to the wall.

Relief on a tomb, showing the portrait of a young girl

If a family needed four or six niches, it was customary to mark them off from the others by wall decorations to show that they made a unit; also pillars were frequently erected at the sides, suggesting the front of a temple. The value of the niches depended on their position; those in the higher rows were less expensive than those near the floor; those under the stairway were least desirable. The urns, which were made of various materials, were usually cemented to the bottom of the niches. After the ashes had been placed in the urns, they were sealed, but small openings were left through which offerings of milk and wine could be poured. On each urn, or its cover, was painted the name of the dead person, with sometimes the day and month of death—rarely the year.

BURIAL SOCIETIES

Early in the Empire, associations were formed to meet the funeral expenses of their members or for the purpose of building columbaria, or for both. These coöperative burial associations were at first organized among members of the same guild or among persons with the same occupation. They were called by many names, but the objects and methods of all the associations were practically the same.

If a member of an association had already provided a place for the disposal of his dead, he could now arrange for necessary funeral expenses by paying weekly into a common fund a small fixed sum, easily within the reach of the poorest. When a member died, a stated sum was drawn from the treasury for his funeral, a committee saw that the rites were decently performed, and at the proper seasons the society made corporate offerings to the dead.

If the purpose of the society was just to build a columbarium, the cost was determined and the total sum divided into shares, each member taking as many as he could afford and paying their value into the treasury. Sometimes a benevolent person contributed generously toward the undertaking, and he was then made an honorary member of the society and called *patronus* (*patrona*). The erection of the building was entrusted to a board of *curatores* (trustees), chosen by ballot, naturally from the largest shareholders and most influential men. They let contracts and superintended construction, rendering account of all the money expended. The trustees considered their office an honorable one, especially as their names appeared in the inscription on the outside of the building. They often showed their appreciation by paying for the decoration of the interior, by furnishing all or part of the labels and urns, or by erecting on the grounds places of shelter and dining rooms for the use of members.

When the building was finished, the trustees allotted the niches, which were numbered, to individual members. Because the niches were not all equally desirable, the trustees divided them into sections as fairly as possible and then assigned the sections by lot to the shareholders. If a man held several shares of stock, he received a corresponding number of sections though they might be in different parts of the tomb. Members were allowed to dispose of their holdings by exchange, sale, or gift, and many of the larger stockholders probably engaged in the enterprise for the sake of the profits to be made in this way.

After the division was made, the owners had their names cut on the labels and sometimes put up columns or set up busts, to mark the sections. Besides the name of the owner, some of the tituli give the

M IAROVITIO F

TROSATVRNINO

PRAEFCOHORT SCVTATA

PRIMOPILO LEGXXII

TRIB MILIT LEG III

LEGXXII

CN CAESIVS ATTICTVS ADLECT

INTER CVIR STATVAM EX RVINA

TEMPLI MARTIS VEXATAM SVA INPENSA

REFECIT ET IN PVBLICVM RESTITVIT

number and position of his *loci* (sections) or urns.

One reads: *L. Abucius Hermes in hoc ordine ab imo ad summum columbaria IX ollae XVIII sibi posterisque suis,* "Lucius Abucius Hermes [has acquired] in this row, running from the lowest tier to the highest, nine niches with eighteen urns for [the ashes of] himself and his posterity."

Sometimes the titles record the purchase of *ollae*, giving the number bought and the name of the previous owner. Sometimes the name on an olla does not correspond with that over the niche, showing the owner had sold a part of his holdings, or that the purchaser had not replaced the titulus. The expenses of maintenance were probably paid from the weekly dues of members, as were the funeral benefits.

FUNERAL CEREMONIES

Almost all detailed accounts of funeral ceremonies that have come down to us concern persons of high position, and information from other sources is so scattered that there is danger of confusing usages of very different times. It is certain that no ceremonies marked the burial of a slave when conducted by his master (nothing is known of the forms used by burial societies), and that citizens of the lowest class were laid to rest without any formality. We know that burials took place by night except during the last century of the Republic and the first two centuries of the Empire. Probably even persons of high position were often buried with less pomp than that displayed on the occasions that Roman writers thought it worth while to describe.

(Left) *Inscription on the tomb of a military tribune*

Relief on a tomb

RITES IN THE HOME

When a Roman died at home, surrounded by his family, it was the duty of his oldest son to bend over the body and call him by name, as if to recall him to life. The formal performance of this act (*conclamatio*) he announced immediately with the words *conclamatum est*. The eyes of the dead were then closed, the body washed with warm water and anointed, and the limbs straightened. If the deceased had held a curule office, a wax impression of his features was taken to be kept in a cabinet with others.

The body was then dressed in a toga with all the insignia of rank that the living man had been entitled to wear and placed on a funeral couch in the atrium, with the feet toward the door, to lie in state until the time of the funeral. Around the couch—surrounded with flowers—incense was burned. Before the door of the house were set branches of pine or cypress as a warning that the house was polluted by death. In humble life these simple preparations were performed by relatives and slaves; with the rich they were made by a professional undertaker (*designator*), who also embalmed the body and superintended the rest of the ceremonies, at the house and on the way to the grave.

There are occasional references to the nearest of kin kissing the dying person as he breathed his last, as if his final breath was to be caught in the mouth of the living. In very early and very late times it was the custom to place a small coin between the teeth of the dead man to pay his passage across the Styx in Charon's boat. Neither of these formalities seems to have been usual in classical times.

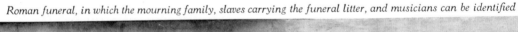

Roman funeral, in which the mourning family, slaves carrying the funeral litter, and musicians can be identified

THE FUNERAL PROCESSION

The funeral procession of an ordinary citizen was simple. Notice of the event was given to neighbors and friends. Surrounded by them and by members of the family and carried on the shoulders of sons or other near relatives, with perhaps a band of musicians in the lead, the body was borne to the tomb.

But the funeral procession of a great man was marshaled with all possible display. It occurred as soon after death as the necessary preparations could be made; there was no fixed intervening time. Notice was given by a public crier in the old formula: *Ollus Quiris leto datus. Exsequias, quibus est commodum, ire jam tempus est, Ollus ex aedibus effertur.* "This citizen has been surrendered to death. For those who find it convenient, it is now time to attend the funeral. He is being brought from his house."

Questions of order and precedence were settled by the undertaker. At the head of the procession went a band of musicians, sometimes followed by persons singing dirges in praise of the dead, and by bands of buffoons and jesters, who made merry with bystanders and imitated even the dead man himself. Then came an imposing part of the procession —actors wearing the wax masks of the dead man's ancestors, which had been taken from their place in the alae. These actors were dressed appropriately to the time and rank of the men they represented. It must have seemed as if the ancient dead had returned to earth to guide their descendant to his place among them. Servius, the Latin grammarian, tells us that six hundred masks were displayed at the funeral of young Marcellus, nephew of Augustus.

If the deceased had been a general,

According to some interpreters, this Roman is holding wax masks of two ancestors

memorials of the great deeds of the deceased came after the actors, as in a triumphal procession. Next the body of the dead was borne aloft on a couch with uncovered face. His family followed. The procession included his freedmen (especially those freed by the will of their master) and slaves, and then friends, all in mourning garb, and all freely expressing their grief. Torchbearers attended the funeral train, even by day, as a reminder of the older custom of burial by night.

THE FUNERAL ORATION

A funeral procession made its way from the house directly to the burial place, unless the deceased was important enough to be honored by public authority with a funeral oration delivered in the Forum. Then the funeral couch was placed before the rostra, with the masked men sitting on curule chairs around it, and the general crowd standing in a semicircle behind. Usually a son or other near relative delivered the eulogy, which recited the virtues and achievements of the dead and recounted the history of the family to which he belonged. Like such addresses in more recent times it often contained much that was false and more that was exaggerated. The honor of the eulogy was freely granted in later times, especially to members of the imperial family, including women. Under the Republic it was a less common honor and thus more highly prized; as far as we know the only women so honored belonged to the Julian gens. Caesar's address at the funeral of his aunt, the widow of Marius, marked him out to the opponents of Sulla as a future leader. When a eulogy in the Forum was not authorized, one was sometimes given privately at the house or at the grave.

Tomb of Gaius Cestius—the shape must have been influenced by Egyptian pyramid tombs

AT THE TOMB

When the procession reached the burial place, the proceedings, which varied according to the period, always provided for three rites ceremonially necessary: the consecration of the resting place, the casting of earth on the remains, and the purification of all polluted by the death. In ancient times a body which was to be buried was lowered into the grave either on the couch on which it had been borne, or in a coffin of burnt clay or stone. If a body was to be burned, couch and body were placed in a shallow grave filled with dry wood. The pile was then fired, and when everything had been consumed, earth was heaped over the ashes to form a mound. Such a grave was consecrated as a regular sepulcrum by the proper ceremonies.

In later times, in case of burial, the body was placed in a sarcophagus already in the tomb. If the remains were to be burned, they were taken to an ustrina—which was not regarded as a part of the sepulcrum—and placed on a pile of wood. Spices and perfumes were thrown on them, together with gifts and tokens from the persons present. The pyre was then lighted with a torch by a relative, who kept his face averted during the act.

After the fire had burned out, the embers were extinguished with water or wine, and those present called a last farewell to the dead. Water of purification was then sprinkled three times over those present, and all except the immediate family left. The ashes were collected in a cloth to be dried, and a ceremonial bone was buried. Next, a pig was sacrificed to make the place of burial sacred ground. Finally, after the mourners had eaten together, they returned to their home, which was purified by an offering to the lares—and the funeral rites were over.

SUBSEQUENT CEREMONIES

With the day of the burial or cremation of the remains began the "Nine Days of Sorrow," solemnly observed by the immediate family. At some time during this period, when the ashes of the deceased were thoroughly dry, members of the family went privately to the ustrina, and placed the ashes in a jar of earthenware, glass, alabaster, or bronze. Then with bare feet and loosened girdles, they carried the ashes into the sepulcrum.

At the end of nine days, the *sacrificium novendiale* (ninth-day sacrifice) was offered to the dead and the *cena novendialis* (ninth-day dinner) took place at the house. On this day, too, the heirs formally entered on their inheritance and the funeral games were originally given. The period of mourning, however, was not concluded on the ninth day. For husband or wife, parents and grandparents, and grown descendants, mourning was worn for ten months—the length of the ancient year; for other adult relatives, eight months; for children between the ages of three and ten, as many months as they were years old.

The memory of the dead was kept alive by annual "days of obligation," public or private. To the former belonged the *Parentalia*, or *dies parentales*, memorial days, lasting from the thirteenth to the twenty-first of February, the final day being especially distinguished as the *Feralia*, festival of the dead.

Privately observed was the annual celebration of the birthday (or burial day) of the person mourned, and of the festivals of violets and roses (*Violaria, Rosaria*), about the end of March and May respectively, when relatives laid violets and roses on the graves or heaped them over the urns. On these occasions offerings were also made in the temples to the gods and at the tombs to the manes, the spirits of the dead, and lamps were lighted in the tombs, where relatives dined together and offered food to their dead.

Our decoration of graves on Easter and Memorial Day occurs on dates nearly corresponding to these ancient celebrations.

By these recurring festivals the memory of the dead was kept alive among the descendants, and a Roman family, living and dead, remained in their own feeling, generation by generation, an unbroken line, a continuing unit. In this way, too, the peace of departed souls was secured, and the living expected that after death they, also, would rest happily and at peace.

AUXILIA

A lar

These lists include the most useful works in the field, but are not intended to be a complete bibliography of the subject. Books cited in chapter bibliographies are listed in full under "General Works of Reference" or "Books for Specific Reference and Additional Reading," along with other works valuable for historical background. Historical works are marked with ‡; those containing collections of interesting photographs, with *. Many works in foreign languages cite exhaustively those passages in Latin literature from which much of our knowledge of Roman life is derived. For this reason, and for their important illustrations and excellent bibliographies, they may be consulted with profit, even by those who have no knowledge of the languages. Archaeological discoveries continue to increase, and may be followed in publications relating to this field, including periodicals such as *American Journal of Archaeology* and *Archaeology* (published by the Archaeological Institute of America), *Memoirs* of the American Academy in Rome, and many others.

This brief chronology (from the founding of Rome in 753 B.C. to the death of the last emperor in 565 A.D.) is intended to help students to place developments and changes in the life of the Romans in their proper historical setting.

Latin words and phrases are defined in the sense in which they are used in *Roman Life.* Each Latin word is italicized in the text only when it first appears.

Information more complete than that given in the brief captions appears in the Descriptive List in page order. Sources for the illustrations are indicated, as are also the present locations of original art objects and remains, whenever that information is available. The Topical List indexes the pictures by subjects, some topics being extensions of those treated in the text. Museums mentioned in the Descriptive List are named, with an expansion of the key words used to identify institutions referred to several times. Key words influence the alphabetical order of Museums in this list.

This comprehensive list not only serves as an index to persons, places, and subjects discussed in *Roman Life,* but also eliminates the need for cross references in the text. Page numbers in italics refer to illustrations.

BIBLIOGRAPHY

Mosaic of ships

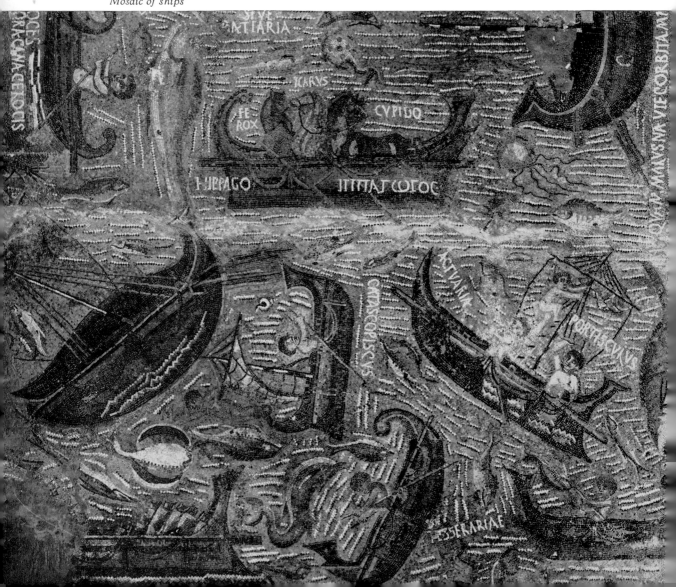

GENERAL WORKS OF REFERENCE

DAREMBERG, C. V., and SAGLIO, EDMOND. *Dictionnaire des antiquités grecques et romaines d'après les textes et les monuments.* Hachette, 1873–1919. A standard and authoritative work, with many illustrations.

Harper's Dictionary of Classical Literature and Antiquities. (H. T. Peck, ed.). American, 1923.

Oxford Classical Dictionary (M. Cary and others, eds.). Oxford, 1949.

PAULY-WISSOWA. *Real-Encyclopädie der classischen Altertumswissenschaft.* Metzler, 1894–1949. This monumental work, in process of revision, is the great authority on the life of the Romans.

PLATNER, S. B., and ASHBY, THOMAS. *A Topographical Dictionary of Ancient Rome.* Oxford, 1929.

SMITH, SIR WILLIAM; WAYTE, WILLIAM; and MARINDIN, G. E. *A Dictionary of Greek and Roman Antiquities.* Murray, 1890, 1891.

For maps and information on modern Rome see guidebooks.

BOOKS FOR SPECIFIC REFERENCE AND ADDITIONAL READING

ABBOTT, F. F. *The Common People of Ancient Rome.* Scribner, 1911.
_____. *A History and Description of Roman Political Institutions.* Harvard, 1911.
_____. *Roman Politics.* Longmans, 1923.
_____. *Society and Politics in Ancient Rome.* Princeton, 1909.

ABBOTT, F. F., and JOHNSON, A. C. *Municipal Administration in the Roman Empire.* Princeton, 1926.

ALLEN, J. T. *Stage Antiquities of the Greeks and Romans and Their Influence.* Longmans, 1927.

ASH, H. R. (trans.). Columella, *On Agriculture* (Loeb). Harvard.

ASHBY, THOMAS. *The Aqueducts of Ancient Rome.* Oxford, 1935.

BAILEY, CYRIL (ed.). *The Legacy of Rome.* Oxford, 1923.
_____. *The Religion of Ancient Rome.* Constable, 1907.

BENNETT, C. E. (trans.). Frontinus, *Stratagems and Aqueducts* (Loeb). Harvard.

*BITTNER, HERBERT, and NASH, ERNEST (eds.). *Rome.* Regnery, 1950.

BLÜMNER, HUGO. *Die römischen Privataltertümer* (3rd ed.). Part of the fourth volume of *Handbuch der klassischen Altertumswissenschaft* (Iwan von Müller, ed.). Beck, 1911. An elaborate work, rich in citation of authorities.
_____. *Technologie und Terminologie der Gewerbe und Künste bei Griechen und Römern.* Teubner, 1912. This work, in four volumes, is the most comprehensive description of the arts and industries of ancient Greece and Rome.

‡BOAK, A. E. R. *A History of Rome to A.D. 565.* Macmillan, 1955.

BOYD, C. E. *Public Libraries and Literary Culture in Ancient Rome.* Wisconsin, 1909.

BROGAN, OLWEN. *Roman Gaul.* Harvard, 1953.

BROUGHTON, T. R. S., and PATTERSON, M. L. *The Magistrates of the Roman Republic,* Volume I, *509 B.C.–100 B.C.*; Volume II, *99 B.C.–31 B.C.* (Philological Monograph 15). A.P.A., 1951, 1952.

CAGNAT, RENÉ, and CHAPOT, V. *Manuel d'archéologie romaine.* Picard, 1916–1920. A work of great value.

CARCOPINO, JEROME. *Daily Life in Ancient Rome.* Yale, 1940.

CARPENTER, RHYS. *The Humanistic Value of Archaeology.* Harvard, 1933.

CARRINGTON, R. C. *Pompeii.* Oxford, 1936.

CARTER, J. B. *The Religion of Numa and other Essays on the Religion of Ancient Rome.* Macmillan, 1906.

———. *The Religious Life of Ancient Rome.* Houghton, 1911.

‡CARY, MAX. *A History of Rome: Down to the Reign of Constantine.* St. Martin's, 1954.

CATO. *See* HARRISON.

CERAM, C. W. (pseud.). *Gods, Graves, and Scholars.* Knopf, 1951.

CHARLESWORTH, M. P. *Trade-Routes and Commerce of the Roman Empire.* Macmillan, 1926.

COLLINGWOOD, R. G. *Roman Britain.* Oxford, 1932.

COLUMELLA. *See* ASH.

DAVIS, W. S. *The Influence of Wealth in Imperial Rome.* Macmillan, 1910.

DILL, SAMUEL. *Roman Society from Nero to Marcus Aurelius.* Macmillan, 1904.

DUCKWORTH, G. E. *The Nature of Roman Comedy: A Study in Popular Entertainment.* Princeton, 1952.

DUFF, A. M. *Freedmen in the Early Roman Empire.* Oxford, 1925.

DUFF, J. W. *A Literary History of Rome, from the Origins to the Close of the Golden Age.* Barnes, 1953.

EGBERT, J. C., JR. *Introduction to the Study of Latin Inscriptions.* American, 1908.

FOWLER, W. W. *The Religious Experience of the Roman People from the Earliest Times to the Age of Augustus.* Macmillan, 1911.

———. *The Roman Festivals of the Period of the Republic.* Macmillan, 1899.

———. *Social Life at Rome in the Age of Cicero.* Macmillan, 1915.

FRANK, TENNEY. *Aspects of Social Behavior in Ancient Rome.* Harvard, 1932.

———. *An Economic History of Rome.* Johns Hopkins, 1927.

‡———. *A History of Rome.* Holt, 1931.

FRIEDLÄNDER, LUDWIG. *Roman Life and Manners under the Early Empire* (4 volumes). (L. A. Magnus, J. H. Freese, A. B. Gough, trans. 7th German ed.). Dutton, 1928.

———. *Town Life in Ancient Italy* (W. E. Waters, trans.). Sanborn, 1902.

FRONTINUS. *See* BENNETT and HERSCHEL.

‡GEER, R. M. *Rome.* Prentice, 1950. This work presents the culture of the Romans, with considerable historical background.

GEST, A. P. *Engineering.* Longmans, 1930. Modern science must pay tribute to the achievements of Roman engineers.

GRANRUD, J. E. *Roman Constitutional History.* Allyn, 1902.

GREENIDGE, A. H. J. *Roman Public Life.* Macmillan, 1901.

GWYNN, AUBREY. *Roman Education from Cicero to Quintilian.* Oxford, 1926.

HADAS, MOSES. *Ancilla to Classical Reading.* Columbia, 1954.

HALL, F. W. *A Companion to Classical Texts.* Oxford, 1913.

HARRISON, FAIRFAX ("Virginia Farmer"). *Roman Farm Management: The Treatises of Cato and Varro, Done into English with Notes of Modern Instances.* Macmillan, 1913.

HARSH, PHILIP. *Memoirs* (Volume XII): "Origins of the Insulae at Ostia." American Academy, 1935.

HEITLAND, W. E. *Agricola: A Study of Agriculture and Rustic Life in the Graeco-Roman World from the Point of View of Labour.* Macmillan, 1921.

HERSCHEL, CLEMENS (trans.). *The Two Books on the Water Supply of the City of Rome by Sextus Julius Frontinus, Water Commissioner of the City of Rome* A.D. *97*. Longmans, 1913. This valuable book contains text, translation, and illustrations, including a reproduction of the only Frontinus manuscript.

JERMYN, L. A. S. (trans.). *The Singing Farmer: A Translation of Vergil's Georgics*. Blackwell, 1947.

JOHNSON, A. C. *See* ABBOTT and JOHNSON.

JOHNSTON, H. W. *Latin Manuscripts*. Scott, 1897.

JOHNSTON, MARY. *Exits and Entrances in Roman Comedy*. Humphrey, 1933.

JONES, H. S. *A Companion to Roman History*. Oxford, 1912.

KELSEY, F. W. *See* MAU.

KENYON, SIR FREDERIC GEORGE. *Books and Readers in Ancient Greece and Rome*. Oxford, 1951.

*LaBANDE, Y. et E.-R. *Rome*. McGraw, 1952. Ancient, medieval, and modern Rome in text and photographs.

LANCIANI, RODOLFO. *Ancient and Modern Rome*. Longmans, 1925.

———. *The Ruins and Excavations of Ancient Rome: A Companion Book for Students and Travelers*. Houghton, 1897.

LEHMANN, P. W. *Roman Wall Paintings from Boscoreale in the Metropolitan Museum of Art*. (Monograph 5 on Archaeology and Fine Arts). A.I.A., 1953.

LOANE, H. J. *Industry and Commerce of the City of Rome (50* B.C.–A.D. *200)*. Johns Hopkins, 1938.

McDANIEL, W. B. *Roman Private Life and Its Survivals*. Longmans, 1924.

MAGOFFIN, R. V. D. *The Lure and Lore of Archaeology*. Williams, 1930.

*MAIURI, AMEDEO. *Pompeii*. Istituto Geografico de Agostini, 1929.

MARQUARDT, JOACHIM. *Das Privatleben der Römer* (August Mau, ed.). Hirzel, 1886. This seventh volume of the *Handbuch der Römischen Altertümer* by Marquardt and Theodor Mommsen supplies authoritative and detailed information on how Romans lived.

MAU, AUGUST. *Pompeii: Its Life and Art* (F. W. Kelsey, trans.). Macmillan, 1902.

MOORE, R. W. *The Roman Commonwealth*. English Universities Press, 1953.

*NASH, ERNEST. *Roman Towns*. Augustin, 1944. Photographic illustrations help in the understanding of Roman life.

———. *Rome*. *See* BITTNER and NASH.

*NORTON, LUCY (trans.). *Rome of the Caesars*. (Pierre Grimal, ed.). Phaidon 1953.

PETRIE, SIR W. M. FLINDERS. *Methods and Aims in Archaeology*. Macmillan, 1904.

PLATNER, S. B. *The Topography and Monuments of Ancient Rome* (2nd ed.). Allyn, 1911.

RANSOM, C. L. *Couches and Beds of the Greeks, Etruscans, and Romans*. Chicago, 1905.

REID, J. S. *The Municipalities of the Roman Empire*. Cambridge, 1913.

RICHTER, GISELA. *Ancient Furniture: A History of Greek, Etruscan, and Roman Furniture*. Oxford, 1926.

ROBATHAN, D. M. *The Monuments of Ancient Rome*. L'Erma di Bretschneider, 1950.

ROSE, H. J. *Ancient Roman Religion*. Longmans, 1950.

‡ROSTOVTZEFF, MIKHAIL. *A History of the Ancient World*, Volume II, *Rome*. Oxford, 1927.

———. *The Social and Economic History of the Roman Empire*. Oxford, 1926.

*SALVATORELLI, LUIGI. *Rome*. Istituto Geografico de Agostini, 1951.

SANDYS, SIR JOHN EDWIN. *A Companion to Latin Studies*. Macmillan, 1938.

Saunders, Catharine. *Costume in Roman Comedy*. Columbia, 1909.

Showerman, Grant. *Monuments and Men of Ancient Rome*. Appleton-Century, 1935.

———. *Rome and the Romans*. Macmillan, 1931.

Stannard, Harold. *Rome and Her Monuments*. Unwin, 1923.

Tanzer, H. H. *The Common People of Pompeii*. Johns Hopkins, 1939.

———. *The Villas of Pliny the Younger*. Columbia, 1924.

‡Trever, A. A. *History of Ancient Civilization*, Volume II, *The Roman World*. Harcourt, 1939.

Ullman, B. L. *Ancient Writing and Its Influence*. Longmans, 1932.

Van Buren, A. W. *Ancient Rome*. Dickson, 1936.

———. *A Companion to the Study of Pompeii and Herculaneum* (2nd ed.). American Academy, 1938.

Van Deman, E. B. *The Building of the Roman Aqueducts* (Pub. 423). Carnegie, 1934.

Varro. *See* Harrison.

Vergil. *See* Jermyn.

Waltzing, J. P. *Étude historique sur les corporations professionelles chez les Romains, depuis les origines jusqu'à la chute de l'empire d'occident* (4 volumes). Peeters, 1895.

Warsher, Tatiana. *Pompeii in Three Hours*. Industria Tipografica Imperia, 1930.

Wheeler, Sir Mortimer. *Archaeology from the Earth*. Oxford, 1954.

Wilson, L. M. *The Clothing of the Ancient Romans*. Johns Hopkins, 1938.

———. *The Roman Toga*. Johns Hopkins, 1924.

Woolley, Sir Charles Leonard. *Digging up the Past*. Scribner, 1931.

PUBLISHERS

Allyn and Bacon, Inc., 70 Fifth Ave., New York 11, N.Y.

American Academy in Rome, Via Angelo Masina 5, Rome 28, Italy

American Book Company, 55 Fifth Ave., New York 3, N.Y.

American Philological Association, Cornell University, Ithaca, N.Y.

Appleton-Century-Crofts, Inc., 35 W. 32nd St., New York 1, N.Y.

Archaeological Institute of America, 608 Library Bldg., University of Cincinnati, Cincinnati 21, Ohio

J. J. Augustin, Inc., Locust Valley, N.Y.

Barnes and Noble, Inc., 105 Fifth Ave., New York 3, N.Y.

Beck, Munich, Germany

Blackwell (Basil) & Mott, Ltd., 49 Broad St., Oxford, England

Cambridge University Press, 32 E. 57th St., New York 22, N.Y.

Carnegie Institution of Washington, 1530 P Street, N.E., Washington 5, D.C.

Columbia University Press, 2960 Broadway, New York 27, N.Y.

Constable & Company, Ltd., 10 Orange St., London W.C. 2, England

Dickson, 179 N. Michigan Ave., Chicago 1, Ill.

E. P. Dutton & Co., Inc., 300 Fourth Ave., New York 10, N.Y.

English Universities Press, Ltd., 102 Newgate St., London E.C. 1, England

L'Erma di Bretschneider, Via Cassiodoro 19, Rome, Italy

Librairie Hachette, 79 Boulevard St.-Germain, Paris 6, France

Harcourt, Brace and Company, 383 Madison Ave., New York 17, N.Y.

Harvard University Press, 79 Garden St., Cambridge 38, Mass.

Hirzel, Leipzig, Germany
Henry Holt and Company, 383 Madison Ave., New York 17, N.Y.
Houghton Mifflin Company, 2 Park St., Boston 7, Mass.
W. F. Humphrey, Geneva, N.Y.
Industria Tipografica Imperia, Rome, Italy
Istituto Geografico de Agostini, Novara, Italy
Johns Hopkins Press, Baltimore 18, Md.
Alfred A. Knopf, Inc., 501 Madison Ave., New York 22, N.Y.
Longmans, Green & Co., Inc., 55 Fifth Ave., New York 3, N.Y.
McGraw-Hill Book Company, Inc., 330 W. 42nd St., New York 36, N.Y.
The Macmillan Company, 60 Fifth Ave., New York 11, N.Y.
J. B. Metzler, Stuttgart, Germany
Murray (John), Ltd., 50 Albemarle St., London W. 1, England
Oxford University Press, Inc., 114 Fifth Ave., New York 11, N.Y.
V. Peeters, Libraire-éditeur, 20 Rue de Namur, Louvain, Belgium
Phaidon Publishers, Inc., 575 Madison Ave., New York 22, N.Y.
G. Picard et Cie., 25 r. Petit-Musc., Paris 4, France
Prentice-Hall, Inc., 70 Fifth Ave., New York 11, N.Y.
Princeton University Press, Princeton, N.J.
Henry Regnery Co., 20 W. Jackson Blvd., Chicago 4, Ill.
St. Martin's Press, Inc., 103 Park Ave., New York 17, N.Y.
Benj. H. Sanborn & Co., 5559 Northwest Highway, Chicago 30, Ill.
Scott, Foresman and Company, 433 E. Erie St., Chicago 11, Ill.
Charles Scribner's Sons, 597 Fifth Ave., New York 17, N.Y.
Teubner, Leipzig, Germany
University of Chicago Press, 5750 Ellis Ave., Chicago 37, Ill.
University of Wisconsin Press, 811 State St., Madison 5, Wis.
Allen (George) & Unwin Ltd., 40 Museum St., London W.C. 1, England
The Williams and Wilkins Company, Mt. Royal Ave., Baltimore 2, Md.
Yale University Press, 143 Elm St., New Haven 7, Conn.

A lantern

GIFTS OF ARCHAEOLOGY

CARPENTER.
CERAM, 3–17.
MAGOFFIN.
MAU-KELSEY, 25–30.
PETRIE.
ROBATHAN.
SHOWERMAN, *Monuments*, 1–73.
VAN BUREN, *Ancient Rome*.
WHEELER.
WOOLLEY.

DAYS IN ANCIENT ROME

FOWLER, *Social Life*, 24–134; 263–284.
McDANIEL, 106–115, 179–185.
SHOWERMAN, *Rome*, 137–147.

THE ROMAN WAY OF LIFE

ABBOTT, *The Common People*, 205–234; *Roman Political Institutions; Roman Politics*, 24–245.
BLÜMNER, *Die römischen Privataltertümer*, 372–385, 589–656.
CHARLESWORTH.
DAREMBERG-SAGLIO, *see "Collegium," "Mercatura."*
DILL, 100–195, 251–286.
FRANK, *An Economic History*, 219–345.
FRIEDLÄNDER, *Roman Life*, I, 98–206.
HARPER'S, *see "Commerce," "Collegium."*
JONES, 316–337.
LOANE.
McDANIEL, 106–115.
MARQUARDT, 607–634.
MAU-KELSEY, 383–399.
MOORE, 35–55.
PAULY-WISSOWA, *see "Collegium."*
ROSTOVTZEFF, *The Social and Economic History*, 38–124.
SANDYS, 202–208, 358–362.
SHOWERMAN, *Rome*, 137–147, 225–266.
SMITH, *see "Collegium," "Mercatura," and other Latin words in this chapter.*
WALTZING.

This stylus is handsomely decorated

LIFE IN ROMAN TOWNS

ABBOTT, *The Common People*, 145–204; *Society and Politics*, 3–21.
ABBOTT and JOHNSON, 56–68, 138–151, 197–231.
CARRINGTON, 39–61.
DILL, 196–250.
FRIEDLÄNDER, *Town Life*.
MAU-KELSEY, 485–508.
NASH, *Roman Towns*.
REID, 436–522.
TANZER, *The Common People of Pompeii*.
VAN BUREN, *Ancient Rome*, 83–106.

LIFE IN THE COUNTRY

BLÜMNER, *Die römischen Privataltertümer*, 67–89, 533–589.
CAGNAT-CHAPOT, II, 295–308.
CARRINGTON, 80–99.
COLUMELLA, *see* ASH.
DAREMBERG-SAGLIO, *see* "*Hortus,*" "*Rustica Res,*" "*Villa.*"
FOWLER, *Social Life*, 243–262.
FRANK, *An Economic History*, 1–15, 55–68, 96–107, 219–274.
FRIEDLÄNDER, *Roman Life*, II, 193–202.
HARPER'S; SMITH, *see* "*Agricultura,*" "*Hortus,*" "*Villa.*"
HARRISON, *Roman Farm Management*.
HARRISON, "The Crooked Plow," *The Classical Journal*, Nov. 11, 1916, 323–332.
HEITLAND, 131–335.
JONES, 170–184, 304–315.
MAU-KELSEY, 355–366.
PAULY-WISSOWA, *see* "*Ackerbau,*" "*Gartenbau,*" "*Gemüsebau,*" "*Getreide.*'
ROSTOVTZEFF, *The Social and Economic History*, 180–194.
SANDYS, 66–84, 211–227.
SHOWERMAN, *Rome*, 251–266.
TANZER, *The Villas of Pliny*.

Roman agent collecting rents from settlers in Germany

ROMAN HOUSES

BLÜMNER, *Die römischen Privataltertümer*, 7–160.
CAGNAT-CHAPOT, I, 1–39, 275–299.
CARRINGTON, 62–79.
DAREMBERG-SAGLIO; HARPER'S; SMITH, *see* "*Domus*," "*Murus*," *and other Latin words in this chapter.*
FOWLER, *Social Life*, 237–243.
FRIEDLÄNDER, *Roman Life*, II, 135–210.
HARSH, 7–66; Plates I–III.
JONES, 159–184.
McDANIEL, 3–16.
MARQUARDT, 213–250.
MAU-KELSEY, 245–354.
MOORE, 83–90.
PAULY-WISSOWA, *see* "*Atrium*," "*Compluvium*," "*Impluvium*," "*Römisches Haus*."
SANDYS, 217–226.
SHOWERMAN, *Rome*, 76–88.
VAN BUREN, *Companion*.
WARSHER.

INTERIOR DECORATION

CARRINGTON, 130–156; Plates XV–XXIV.
LEHMANN.
McDANIEL, 17–22.
MAIURI.
MAU-KELSEY, 321–340, 367–382, 437–444, 456–484.
RANSOM
RICHTER.

ROMAN FAMILIES

BLÜMNER, *Die römischen Privataltertümer*, 301–302.
DAREMBERG-SAGLIO; PAULY-WISSOWA, *see* "*Adoptio*," "*Cognatio*," *and other Latin terms in this chapter.*
HARPER'S, *look up* "*Familia*" *and notice the range of meanings.*
McDANIEL, 23–26.
MARQUARDT, 1–6.
MOORE, 56–57.
SHOWERMAN, *Rome*, 66–68.

ROMAN NAMES

DAREMBERG-SAGLIO; HARPER'S; SMITH, *see* "*Nomen*."
EGBERT, 82–102.
MARQUARDT, 7–27.
PAULY-WISSOWA, *see* "*Cognomen*."
SANDYS, 174–175.
SHOWERMAN, *Rome*, 91–92.

MARRIAGE CUSTOMS AND ROMAN WOMEN

ABBOTT, *Society and Politics*, 41–99.
BLÜMNER, *Die römischen Privataltertümer*, 341–371.
DAREMBERG-SAGLIO, *see* "*Gynaeceum*," "*Manus*," "*Matrimonium*."
FOWLER, *Social Life*, 135–167.
FRIEDLÄNDER, *Roman Life*, I, 228–267.
HARPER'S, *see* "*Conubium*," "*Matrimonium*."
McDANIEL, 41–59.
MARQUARDT, 28–80.
MOORE, 57–64.
PAULY-WISSOWA, *see* "*Coemptio*," "*Confarreatio*," "*Conubium*."
SANDYS, 175–179, 184–190.
SHOWERMAN, *Rome*, 112–123.
SMITH, *see* "*Matrimonium*."

ROMAN CHILDREN

BLÜMNER, *Die römischen Privataltertümer*, 299–311.
McDANIEL, 60–80.
MARQUARDT, 81–91.
MOORE, 64–65.
SHOWERMAN, *Rome*, 89–91.

EDUCATION

BLÜMNER, *Die römischen Privataltertümer*, 312–340.
DAREMBERG-SAGLIO; HARPER'S, *see* "*Educatio*."
FRIEDLÄNDER, *Roman Life*, I, 156–161; III, 216–281.
FOWLER, *Social Life*, 168–203.
GWYNN, 11–40.
McDANIEL, 69–78.
MARQUARDT, 80–134.
MOORE, 66–73.
PAULY-WISSOWA, *see* "*Schulen*."
SANDYS, 228–236.
SHOWERMAN, *Rome*, 92–111, 194–202.
SMITH, *see* "*Ludus litterarius*."

*Apollo driving his chariot—
a cameo carved on a shell*

SLAVERY

Blümner, *Die römischen Privataltertümer*, 277–298.
Daremberg-Saglio; Harper's; Pauly-Wissowa, *see Latin terms used in this chapter.*
Fowler, *Social Life*, 204–236.
Frank, *An Economic History*, 326–334.
Friedländer, *Roman Life*, II, 218–221.
McDaniel, 26–40.
Marquardt, 135–212.
Moore, 73–75.
Sandys, 362–365.
Showerman, *Rome*, 71–73; *see other entries under "slaves" in index.*

CLIENTES AND HOSPITES

Daremberg-Saglio; Harper's; Pauly-Wissowa, *see Latin terms used in this chapter.*
Dill, 100–137.
Duff, A. M.
Marquardt, 195–212.
Moore, 76–77.
Showerman, *Rome*, 71, 73.

CLOTHING OF MEN AND BOYS

Marquardt, 475–549.
Wilson, *Clothing*, 1–132, 169–172.
Wilson, *The Roman Toga*.

CLOTHING OF WOMEN AND GIRLS

Marquardt, 573–586.
Wilson, *Clothing*, 1–35, 133–169.

ROMAN FOOD

Blümner, *Die römischen Privataltertümer*, 160–204.
Daremberg-Saglio, *see "Cibaria."*
Friedländer, *Roman Life*, II, 146–173.

Augustus

CIRCUSES AND RACES

AMPHITHEATERS AND GLADIATORS

TRAVEL AND CORRESPONDENCE

BOOKS AND LIBRARIES

ROADS, AQUEDUCTS, AND SEWERS

Ashby.

Bailey, *Legacy of Rome*, 465–472.

Blümner, *Die römischen Privataltertümer*, 442–474.

Daremberg-Saglio; Harper's; Smith, *see* "*Aquaeductus*," "*Via*," *and other Latin words in this chapter*.

Gest, 62–107, 185–189.

Herschel.

Jones, 40–51, 76–83, 141–154.

Marquardt, 469–474, 731–738.

Mau-Kelsey, 227–233.

Platner, 90–109, 270–273.

Showerman, *Rome*, 485–499.

Van Deman.

ROMAN RELIGION

Bailey, *Legacy of Rome*, 237–264; *Religion*, 4–95.

Cagnat-Chapot, I, 137–171; II, 161–203.

Carter, *Religion of Numa; Religious Life*.

Dill, 443–626.

Fowler, *Religious Experience; Roman Festivals; Social Life*, 315–352.

Frank, *Social Behavior*, 35–63.

Jones, 267–303.

McDaniel, 101–105.

Mau-Kelsey, 63–69, 80–90, 102–109, 124–132.

Sandys, 150–165.

Showerman, *Rome*, 280–298.

THE ROMANS AND THEIR DEAD

Daremberg-Saglio; Harper's; Smith, *see* "*Columbarium*," "*Funus*," "*Sepulcrum*."

Egbert, 230–242.

Friedländer, *Roman Life*, II, 210–218.

Jones, 184–194.

Lanciani, *Ancient Rome*, 64–67, 129–133.

McDaniel, 186–197.

Marquardt, 340–385.

Mau-Kelsey, 405–436.

Moore, 77–81.

Nash, *Roman Towns*.

Pauly-Wissowa, *see* "*Columbarium*."

Platner, *see* "*Sepulcra*," *and* "*Sepulcrum*" *in the index*.

Showerman, *Rome*, 418–433.

PERIODS OF HISTORY

Corbridge lion

View of Vesuvius

THE KINGDOM (753–510 B.C.)

753–717 ROMULUS • Rome founded, 753
715–673 NUMA POMPILIUS • Religious institutions established
673–642 TULLUS HOSTILIUS • Destruction of Alba Longa
642–617 ANCUS MARCIUS • Ostia founded
616–579 L. TARQUINIUS PRISCUS • Treaty with the Latins
578–535 SERVIUS TULLIUS • Creation of tribes
535–510 L. TARQUINIUS SUPERBUS • Expulsion of king • Creation of annual consuls

THE REPUBLIC (509–27 B.C.)

509–265 CONQUEST OF ITALY • First consuls • First dictator • Organization of government and law • Building of Appian Way and Aqua Appia • Full political rights gained by plebeians
265–133 TERRITORIAL EXPANSION • Punic Wars • Eastern Wars • Acquisition of provinces
133–27 CENTURY OF CONFLICT • Gracchan reforms • War with Africa • Social War • Civil War • Mithridatic War • Catilinarian conspiracy • First triumvirate • Gallic War • Civil War • Beginning of Golden Age of Latin Literature

THE EMPIRE (27 B.C.–A.D. 565)

27 B.C.–A.D. 14 AUGUSTAN AGE • Emperor—Augustus • Annexation of Egypt • Development of provinces • *Pax Romana* • Building of Roman roads
A.D. 14–69 JULIO-CLAUDIAN AGE • Emperors—Tiberius (14–37) • Caligula (37–41) • Claudius (41–54) • Nero (54–68) • Galba, Otho, Vitellius (68–69) • Acquisition of new provinces • Commercial prosperity • Beginning of Silver Age of Latin Literature • Luxurious buildings • Persecution of Christians
A.D. 69–180 AGE OF THE FLAVIANS AND THE ANTONINES • Emperors—Vespasian (69–79) • Titus (79–81) • Domitian (81–96) • Nerva (96–98) • Trajan (98–117) • Hadrian (117–138) • Antoninus Pius (138–161) • Lucius Verus (161–169) and Marcus Aurelius (161–180) • Expansion of Roman Empire • Greatest extent of Empire in A.D. 117
180–284 DECLINE OF EMPIRE • Outstanding emperors—Septimius Severus (193–211) • Caracalla (211–217) • Alexander Severus (222–235) • Valerian (253–258) • Aurelian (270–275) • Military domination • German invasions • Universal citizenship • Financial chaos • Oppressive taxation • Walling of Rome • Pagan religions • Oriental cults • Growth of Christian church
284–337 REORGANIZATION OF EMPIRE • Emperors—Diocletian (284–305) • Constantine I, the Great (306–337) • Division of administration • Reorganization of army • Reform of coinage and taxation • Removal of capital to Constantinople • Spread of Christianity
337–395 FURTHER DECLINE OF EMPIRE • Outstanding emperors—Constantine II (337–340) • Julian (360–363) • Theodosius I (378–395)
395–565 DIVISION OF EMPIRE (*East and West*) • First emperors of divided Empire—Arcadius (*East*) and Honorius (*West*) • Last western emperor—Romulus Augustulus (475–476) • Last eastern emperor—Justinian (527–565) • Barbarian invasions • Codification of laws • Abolishment of consulship

GLOSSARY

Roman works of art

A

A., Aulus

abacus, counting board; sideboard

abolla, heavy woolen cloak

ab ovo ad mala, from egg to apples; from appetizers to dessert—a complete dinner

acetum, vinegar

adfines, relatives by marriage

adfinitas, relationship by marriage

adoptio, adoption

adrogatio, adoption of head of a family

adrogatus, man adopted as head of a family

Aedes Vestae, temple of Vesta

Ager Falernus, Falernian region famous for wine

agitatores, chariot drivers

agnati, relatives by descent through male line

agnatio, relationship by descent through male line

agnomina, names added to the usual three

alae, alcoves off atrium

alieno juri subjectus, subject to another's authority; dependent

amanuenses, secretaries

amictus, wrapped around (as a toga or cloak)

amita, aunt, father's sister

amphitheatrum, amphitheater; *Amphitheatrum Flavium*, the Colosseum

amphora, large jar with two handles

amurca, first fluid pressed from olives

angusti clavi, with narrow stripe (said of a knight's tunic)

antecena, first course, appetizers

aper, wild boar; pig

apodyterium, dressing room in bath

App., Appius

aqua (pl., *aquae*), aqueduct

arbiter bibendi, master of the revels; toastmaster

arbustum, vineyard planted with trees

arca, chest

arena, sand; racecourse

atavus, father of a great-great-grandparent; ancestor

atrium (pl., *atria*), primitive house; main room of house; *atrium displuviatum*, room with roof sloping away from compluvium; *atrium testudinatum*, room with no compluvium; *atrium tetrastylon*, room with pillars at corners of compluvium; *Tuscan atrium*, room with roof supported by beams crossing at right angles

Atrium Libertatis, hall of the goddess Liberty; first public library in Rome

Atrium Vestae, House of the Vestals

auctorati, volunteer gladiators

augur (pl., *augures*), priest who interpreted omens

Augustales, priests in charge of emperor worship

auriga (pl., *aurigae*), racing charioteer

avunculus, uncle, mother's brother

avus, grandfather; ancestor

B

balneae, baths

balneum (pl., *balnea*), bath

basterna, litter carried by mules

bibliotheca, library; *Bibliotheca Ulpia*, Ulpian Library

bracae, breeches

bulla (pl., *bullae*), child's locket; amulet

C

C., Gaius

caepe, onion

calcei, high walking shoes

caldarium, warm room in bath

caligae, soldiers' boots

calx, chalkline marking the finish of a race

camillus, boy attendant in religious ceremony

candelabrum, tall stand for lamps

candidati, men running for office, who wore the whitened toga

cara cognatio, close relationship

carbasus, linen; cotton

carceres, prisons; at race track, starting stalls

carnifex, butcher; slave appointed to punish

carpentum, kind of carriage

carruca, kind of carriage

cathedra, armless chair with curved back; *cathedra supina*, easy chair

catillus, upper millstone

causia, felt traveling hat

cave canem, look out for the dog

cavea, banks of seats in a theater

cena, dinner; main course; *cena novendialis*, banquet held on the ninth day after a funeral

cenotaphium, empty tomb as memorial

censor, official in charge of the census and in control of public morals

centenarius, horse that had won one hundred races

cera, wax

charta, sheet of papyrus

cicer, chickpea

cinctus Gabinus, way of wearing toga

circus, race track

cisium (pl., *cisia*), traveling cart

clepsydra, water clock

cliens (pl., *clientes*), client; free dependent

cloaca, sewer; *Cloaca Maxima*, main sewer

Cn., Gnaeus

coemptio, form of marriage ceremony

cognati, blood relations

cognatio, relationship by blood

cognomen (pl., *cognomina*), third of the three Roman names; *cognomen ex virtute*, surname given as title of honor *columbarium* (pl., *columbaria*), tomb holding many funeral urns

comissatio, after-dinner drinking

comitia curiata, patrician assembly

compluvium, opening in roof of atrium, admitting light and rain

compotatio, drinking party

conclamatio, the calling of a dead person by name at the moment of death

confarreatio, patrician marriage ceremony

consobrina, consobrinus, first cousin on mother's side

contubernia, slave marriages

conubii jus, right of intermarriage, as between plebeians and patricians

convivia, dinners; *convivia tempestiva*, early dinners, i.e., long-lasting parties

cornua, knobs on ends of rod on which book was rolled

crepundia, necklace made of small toys or charms

crux, crucem, cross

cubicula, bedrooms; *cubicula diurna*, rooms for rest in daytime; *cubicula dormitoria* or *nocturna*, bedrooms for use at night

culina, kitchen

cunei, vertical sections of seats in theater or circus

curatores, commissioners; directors

curia, Senate-House; city council; ancient patrician division of the people

curriculum, lap in a race; racecourse

*Curia, the meeting place
of the Roman Senate*

D

D., Decimus

dator ludorum, giver of shows

decimus, tenth

decuriones, members of a town council

De Finibus [*Bonorum et Malorum*], "On the Greatest Good and the Greatest Evil"

designator, undertaker

desultores, riders changing horses during race by leaping from one horse to another

dextrarum junctio, joining of hands in marriage ceremony

dies lustricus, day of purification; *dies parentales*, memorial days honoring dead relatives

dimachaerus, gladiator with two swords

discobolus, discus-thrower

doctores, trainers of gladiators; teachers

dominica potestas, master's power over his property

dormitoria, sleeping quarters

dos, dowry

ducenarius, horse that had won two hundred races

E

ego, I

emancipare, to set free

endromis, bathrobe

equites, knights, a class of society

essedarius, fighter in a war chariot

ex cathedra, with authority

exedrae, rooms for lectures, readings, and other entertainments

F

f., *filius* or *filia*

faba, bean

faces, torches

factiones, associations; companies

familia, household; troop of gladiators; *familia rustica*, farm slaves; *familia urbana*, city slaves

far, spelt, a hardy kind of wheat

fascis, bundle; *fasces*, bundles of rods carried by lictors escorting magistrates

fax (pl., *faces*), torch

feliciter, good luck; happiness

Feralia, festival of the dead, in February

Fescennini versus, rude verses sung during wedding procession

fibula, clasp; pin; brooch

filia, daughter

filius, son; *filius familias*, son in a household

flagellum, flagrum, lash

Flamen Dialis, priest of Jupiter

flamines, priests of special gods

fores, outer doors

fossa, ditch; the cut preliminary to road construction

frigidarium, cold room in bath

frumentum, grain, usually wheat

fugitivus, runaway slave

furcifer, man compelled to wear a forked log as punishment

G

gaudere, to rejoice

gemma, gem, jewel; seal

gener, son-in-law

genius, guardian spirit of a man

gens (pl., *gentes*), clan

gentiles, members of clan

gradus, row of seats in theater or circus

grammatica, study of literature and grammar

grammaticus, grammarian

graphium, tool for writing on waxed surface

gustus, appetizers

H

harena, sand; variant of *arena*

hoplomachi, heavy-armed (said of gladiators)

hortus (pl., *horti*), garden

hospes (pl., *hospites*), host or guest

hospitium, relationship between hosts and guests

hostis, stranger; enemy, public foe

hypocaustum, a kind of furnace

I

[*I*] *ad* [*malam*] *crucem*, [Go] to the [bad] cross (a curse)

Idus, Ides, a day in the middle of the month

imagines, wax busts or masks of ancestors

imperator, general, commander, emperor

impluvium, pool in atrium for rain water

indutus, put on (as a garment)

in manum viri, under a husband's authority

insula (pl., *insulae*), island; apartment house, tenement; city block

insularius, custodian of apartment house

ipse, ipsa, oneself; himself; herself; myself

J

janitor, doorman

janitrices, two women who married brothers

janua, door

jentaculum, breakfast

jugerum (pl., *jugera*), measure of land, about three-fifths of an acre

junctae, joined

Juno, a goddess; guardian spirit of a girl

jus, right; *jus conubii*, right of intermarriage; *jus osculi*, right to kiss

justa facere, to do the right things, especially to observe funeral rites correctly

justae nuptiae, legal marriages

K

K., Kaeso

Kalendae, Kalends, first day of the month

L

L., Lucius

l., libertus, freedman

lacerna, type of cloak

laconicum, sweat bath

laena, type of cloak

lar (pl., *lares*), a household god; *Lar Familiaris*, protector of the home

lati clavi, with wide stripe (said of a senator's tunic)

latrina, toilet

Animals in the circus (mosaic)

laudatio, funeral eulogy

lectus, couch

leges insanae, crazy laws; rules for drinking

Lemuria, festival of the dead, in May

Liber, god of wine, Bacchus

Liberalia, festival of *Liber*, March 17

libertinus (pl., *libertini*), freedman

libertus, freedman

librarii, copyists, secretaries

lictor, a public attendant escorting a magistrate

linum, flax; thread

loci, sections of a large tomb

ludi, games, shows; schools; *ludi circenses*, races; *ludi gladiatorii*, gladiatorial schools; *ludi scaenici*, dramatic performances

ludus Trojae, game of Troy, cavalry maneuvers

lux, light

M

M., Marcus

M'., Manius

Maecenatiana, Maecenatianus, of Maecenas

magister bibendi, toastmaster

magna, magnus, great

mala, apples

Mam., Mamercus

mane, in the morning

manes, spirits of the dead

manus, husband's authority over wife

mater, mother; nurse; *mater familias*, mother in a household; *Magna Mater*, goddess Cybele

matertita, aunt, mother's sister

Matronalia, Mother's Day, March 1

maxima, maximus, oldest; largest; chief, main

mensa delphica, three-legged table; *mensa secunda*, second table, dessert course of meal

merenda, refreshments; supper

meta (pl., *metae*), lower millstone; goal post on race track

mi, my (vocative)

minor, younger

missus, seven laps of race; spared (of gladiator)

monopodium, table with a single pedestal

Morituri te salutant, Those about to die salute you

mulleus, patrician's red shoe

mullus, mullet, a fish

mulsa, mead, fermented honey and water

mulsum, wine and honey

munera, shows; *munera gladiatoria*, gladiatorial shows

munire viam, build a road

munus gladiatorium, gladiatorial show

mustum, grape juice

mutare vestem, to change the costume, i.e., put on mourning

N

nasus, nose

nationes bracatae, nations who wore pants

naumachiae, mock naval battles for entertainment; artificial lakes for such battles

nepos, grandson

nihil intret mali, may no evil enter

nobiles, nobles

nomen (pl., *nomina*), name; *nomen gentile* or *gentilicium*, name of clan

nomenclator, slave who prompted master with names

Nonae, Nones, fifth day of the month (except March, May, July, when it was the seventh)

noverca, stepmother

novus homo, outsider; upstart

nubere, to marry (said of women)

numen (pl., *numina*), divine will; power of a deity

nuntius, messenger

nuptiae justae, regular marriage

nurus, daughter-in-law

nutrix, nurse; foster mother

O

oeci, large rooms in house

Oenotria, Land of the Vine, ancient Greek name for Italy

oleum olivum, olive oil

olla (pl., *ollae*), jar, urn

oppidum, town; in circus, row of stalls for chariots with towers at each end

opus, work; *opus caementicium*, cement work; *opus incertum*, irregular facing of walls; *opus reticulatum*, brickwork resembling netting; *opus Signinum*, waterproof lining for cisterns

orbis Romana, Roman world or civilization

orchestra, semicircle in front of stage in theater

ostium, door; entrance

ovum, ovo, (pl., *ova*), egg; egg-shaped marker used to count laps in race

ovis, sheep

P

P., Publius

paedagogus (pl., *paedagogi*), child's attendant

paenula (pl., *paenulae*), heavy cloak

palaestra, playground

palla, lady's shawl

paludamentum, general's cloak

palus, primus or *secundus*, first or second sword, i.e., first or second ranking gladiator

panis, bread; *panis castrensis*, army bread; *panis plebeius*, common bread; *panis rusticus*, country bread; *panis sordidus*, dark bread

papyrus, paper made from reed of same name

Parentalia, festival of the dead, in February

pater (pl., *patres*), father; senator; *pater familias*, head of a family

patria potestas, father's authority

patriae, home towns

patricii, patricians, highest class of citizens

patrona, patronus, patron; honorary member of a burial society

patruelis, first cousin on father's side

patruus, uncle, father's brother

pavimentum, floor

pecu, flock

peculium, money of one's own, as of a slave or child

pecunia, money

penates, household gods

periit, he was killed (said of a defeated gladiator)

peristylum, peristyle, interior court surrounded by columns

petasus, traveling hat

petoritum, open carriage; baggage wagon

pietas, devotion; family feeling; sense of duty

pilentum, carriage used in processions

pilleus, liberty cap

pinsitores; see *pistores*

pistores, millers; bakers

plagosus, thrasher; i.e., inclined to flog

plebeii, plebeians, the common people

plebeius, belonging to the common people

plebs, common people; body of regular members in a guild; men not entitled to serve in the council

podium (in circus), platform for box seats; (in columbarium), platform on which sarcophagi were placed

pollice verso, with thumb turned, signaling death

pompa circensis, circus procession

pontifex (pl., *pontifices*), priest of the state religion; *Pontifex Maximus*, chief priest

populus Romanus, Roman people, citizen body

por, boy, for *puer* in names of slaves

porca, sow

porcus, pig, hog

posticum, back or side door

postumus, last

potestas, power; *potestas dominica*, master's authority; *potestas patria*, father's authority

praecinctio (pl., *praecinctiones*), horizontal aisle in theater or circus

praenomen (pl., *praenomina*), first name

prandium, lunch

prima rudis, first or head fencer; fencing master

primus palus, first-ranking fighter in gladiatorial school

privigna, stepdaughter

privignus, stepson

promulsis, appetizer course of a meal

pronepos, great-grandson

pronuba, matron of honor at a wedding

proscaenium, back line of stage

publicanus, tax collector

puer, boy, child; slave

puls, porridge

pupus, baby

purpura, dye ranging in color from garnet to true purple

Q

Q., Quintus

quadrans, a small coin

quaestor, financial official of Roman government

Quando tu Gaius, ego Gaia, When—and where—you are Gaius, I—then and there—am Gaia

Quinquatria, festival of Minerva, in March

quintus, fifth

R

raeda (pl., *raedae*), cart, wagon

renuntiare, to renounce; to break an engagement

repudium renuntiare, to break an engagement

Res Gestae, deeds; history

rex bibendi, toastmaster

rex sacrorum, king of religious rites; high priest

rhombus, turbot

Rosaria, rose festival; a memorial day in May

rostra, speaker's platform in the Forum

rudis, wooden sword

A lion hunt (mosaic)

S

S., Spurius

sacra, religious rites

sacrarium, chapel; shrine

sacrificium novendiale, ninth-day sacrifice, offering made on the ninth day after a funeral

sacrum, holy thing, holy observance

sagum, military cloak

Salii, dancing priests of Mars; *Salii Collini*, priests directing the worship of Quirinus

salutatio, calling hour, round of calls

Salve, Good day, a greeting

sarcophagus (pl., *sarcophagi*), stone coffin

Saturnalia, festival of Saturn, in December

scaena, stage of theater

schedae, sheets of papyrus

schola grammatica, grammar school

scipio, staff

scribae, clerks in civil service

secunda or *secundus*, second; *secunda rudis*, second fencer; assistant fencing master; *secundus palus*, second-best gladiator in his class

secutores, heavy-armed gladiators

senes, old men

sepulcrum, grave, tomb

Ser., Servius

sermo patrius, native tongue

serva, female slave

servus (pl., *servi*), slave; *servi a manu*, secretaries; *servi ab epistulis*, secretaries for correspondence

Gold necklace

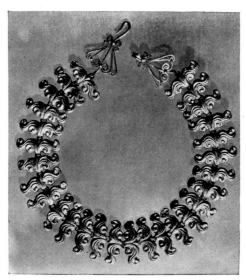

servire, to serve

sestertius, a small Roman coin

seviri, a board of six men; *seviri Augustales*, college of priests who had charge of emperor worship

Sex., Sextus

sextus, sixth

sigma, semicircular dining couch

signum, seal, signet

sinus, fold of a garment

sistrum, rattle used in worship of Isis

socer, father-in-law

socrus, mother-in-law

solarium, sundial; sun deck

soleae, slippers, sandals

soleas poscere, to ask for one's sandals; i.e., prepare to leave

solium, high-backed chair

sordidati, shabby, wearing the *toga pulla*

spatium, lap in a race

spina (pl., *spinae*), dividing wall in circus

spondeo, I promise; *spondes*, you promise

sponsa, engaged (said of a girl)

sportula, basket; dole of food or money

stilus (pl., *stili*), pointed tool for writing on wax, stylus

stirps, division of gens or clan

stola, long outer tunic worn by women; *stola matronalis*, matron's costume

strigilis, scraper used in bath

sub corona venire, to be sold at auction

sub hasta venire, to be sold at auction

subligaculum (pl., *subligacula*), shorts, trunks

sui juris, independent

suovetaurilia, sacrifice of a pig, a sheep, and a bull

sus, pig, swine

symposium, entertainment; banquet

synthesis, dinner costume for men

T

T., Titus

tabellae, writing tablets

tabellarii, messengers carrying letters

tablinum, master's room; office in house

tabulae, account books

Talassio, Talassius, customary cry at Roman wedding

tali, knucklebones

taurus, bull

tempestiva convivia, early dinners; i.e., long-lasting parties

tepidarium, warm room in bath

tertia, third

tessera (pl., *tesserae*), die, token

thermae, large public baths

Ti., Tiberius

tiro (pl., *tirones*), recruit in army; untrained gladiator

titulus, label; title of book; marble marker

toga, toga, Roman citizen's outer garment; *toga candida*, toga whitened with chalk; *toga libera*, free toga; *toga picta*, embroidered toga; *toga praetexta*, bordered toga; *toga pulla*, dark toga, for mourning; *toga pura*, plain toga; *toga virilis*, man's toga

topiarius, one who trims trees into fancy shapes; gardener

trabea, augur's cloak

triclinium, dining room

trigon, ball game

tritavus, grandfather of a great-great-grandparent; remote ancestor

triumvir, one of three officials acting together

tunica, tunic; *tunica angusti clavi*, knight's tunic; *tunica exterior*, outer tunic; *tunica interior*, under tunic; *tunica lati clavi*, senator's tunic; *tunica recta*, bride's tunic

U

umbilicus (pl., *umbilici*), rod on which scroll was rolled

umbrae, shadows; uninvited dinner guests

unctorium, room in bath for massage

ustrina, (pl., *ustrinae*) crematory

usus, plebeian marriage ceremony

uxor, wife

V

vela, curtains; awnings

venire, sub corona, sub hasta, to be sold at auction

vernae, slaves born in a household

versus Fescennini, rude verses sung during wedding procession

vesperna, supper

vestibulum, space between street and door of house

via, road, street; *Via Appia*, Appian Way

vicarius, slave's slave

vicit, he won (said of gladiator)

vilica, slave foreman's wife

vilicus, slave foreman on an estate

villa, farmhouse; *villa rustica*, country estate for profit; *villa urbana*, estate for pleasure

vinalia rustica, wine festival

vinum, wine

viola, violet, stock, wallflower

Violaria, violet festival; a memorial day in March

Virgo Vestalis (pl., *Virgines Vestales*), vestal virgin, priestess of Vesta

vitellus, calf

vitricus, stepfather

volumen, roll of papyrus, as a book

X

xystus, group of geometric flower beds; formal garden

Vestal virgin

Household shrine

ILLUSTRATIONS

DESCRIPTIVE LIST OF ILLUSTRATIONS

21 Excavation in Herculaneum. The deposit of hardened mud and ash is loosened with pickaxes, carried in baskets to cars, and moved away by rail to be examined for scraps of building material or artifacts.

21 Amateur archaeological excavation on Middle Brook Street, Winchester, England. Winchester City Museum.

22 Pompeii, with the two theaters and gladiators' barracks in the foreground. Stabian Street is on the right. E.P.T. Naples.

23 Arch in Timgad (*Thamugadi*), Algeria. W. Thompson.

23 A triumph (relief) from Leptis Magna, Libya. British S. Bronnero.

24 A mosaic (restoration). When almshouses in Exeter, England, were destroyed by bombing in 1946, a Roman courtyard of the second century A.D. came to light. Reuterphoto.

24 Roman Forum, with the Palatine in the background at right. Gertrude French.

25 Model of ancient Rome, built to scale. Press Association, Inc.

26 Gemma Augustea (sardonyx cameo of the time of Tiberius), one of the finest examples of ancient art. Stadtmuseum, Vienna. Alinari.

27 The seven hills of Rome (map).

27 Arch of Titus, Rome. On the inner faces, reliefs show part of a triumphal procession which took place in A.D. 71. Alinari.

28 Corinthian columns of the Temple of Venus Genetrix, in the Forum of Julius Caesar. This temple, dedicated by Julius Caesar in 46 B.C., as part of his celebration of four triumphs, was rebuilt by Trajan and rededicated in A.D. 113. These columns are from the reconstruction. Bromofoto, Milan.

28 Bronze statue, said to be of L. Mammius Maximus. Naples. Alinari.

29 The Curia, which has recently been cleared and restored in Rome. E.P.T. Rome.

29 A Roman shop where cloth was sold (relief). Shuttered windows and tiles of the roof can be seen. Uffizi. Alinari.

30 The Labors of Hercules (mosaic), from Liria, near Valencia, Spain. The center panel shows Hercules' punishment as slave to the Queen of Lydia. She compelled him to wear women's garments and spin, while she wore the lion's skin and held the club. Madrid.

31 Medallions on the north side of the Arch of Constantine, Rome (reliefs). These and six other medallions were taken from earlier monuments. Alinari.

32 Token used in distribution of bread. British M.

32 Augustus in an elaborately draped toga, holding a manuscript roll (statue). Uffizi. Alinari.

33 Comic actors, probably a money-lender and a slave (terra-cotta statuettes). British M.

33 Group called *Alimentariae Faustinianae*, orphan girls who received public assistance from a fund established by Antoninus Pius in honor of his wife Faustina and his daughter Faustina (relief). Villa Albani, Rome. Alinari.

34 Part of the grounds of Domitian's palace, Rome. This palace, once part of the imperial residence of Augustus, was rebuilt by Domitian. Cl. Trincano, Collection Arthaud, Grenoble, France.

35 Altar of travertine, Rome—a copy of one from remote antiquity. Anderson.

35 Silver denarius, the reverse of which shows a curule chair. The Museum of the American Numismatic Society, New York.

37 Roman corn ship, at the quay on the river below Colchester. In the background is the Roman city with a temple, and at the quayside are granaries, custom house, office of the harbor master, and tavern. Model made to scale by H. W. Poulter, Assistant Curator of the Colchester and Essex Museum, Colchester, England. Colchester.

37 Statue of a Roman magistrate in costume of the fourth century A.D. Conservatori. Alinari.

38 Julius Caesar as general (marble statue). Capitoline. Anderson.

39 Roman knights about to sacrifice a sheep (relief of the second century B.C.). British M.

41 Restoration of the Roman Treasury (modern painting by Giuseppe Sciuti). Galleria Nazionale d'Arte Moderna, Rome. Alinari.

42 Castor bowl with raised figures of a chariot race, found at Colchester. British M.

42 Covered bowl, part of the Mildenhall Treasure. The cover—which probably belonged to a different dish—has for a handle a Triton blowing on a conch. The relief frieze shows combats between centaurs and animals, separated by human masks. British M.

42   Banker's counter, after a relief (model).   Capitoline.

45   Religious festival, perhaps celebrating the opening of navigation in the spring (fresco from a public building in Ostia).   Two boys acting as priests and wearing garlands and fillets are pouring a libation. Vatican. Archivio Fotografico Gallerie e Musei Vaticani.

46   Procession of magistrates, each carrying a lar (relief from Pompeii).   Vatican. Archivio Fotografico Gallerie e Musei Vaticani.

47   Oculist's stamp, used to mark cakes of eye ointment.   The incised inscription gives the name T. Vindacus Ariovistus, and indicates that the ointment contained nard. British M.

47   A physician examining a patient (relief from a gravestone of Pentelic marble). British M.

48   Surgical instruments from Pompeii.   Naples.   Alinari.

49   Carpenters' tools.   British M.

50   Part of the Pont du Gard, Roman aqueduct at Nîmes (*Nemausus*).   Its three stories of arches, 160 feet high, were built late in the first century B.C. or early in the first century A.D.   Commissariat Général au Tourisme.   Denise Bellon.

51   Image of Mithras, found near Hadrian's Wall.   This Persian god of light was a favorite of Roman soldiers.   Behind the figure fire was placed, so that the god was seen against a background of flames.   King's College Museum, University of Durham, Newcastle upon Tyne.

51   Election notice painted on the wall of a Pompeian house.   It reads, "Q[VINTVM] POSTVMIVM MODESTVM QVIN[QVENNALEM], [Elect] Quintus Postumius Modestus quinquennal (magistrate with a five-year term)."   W. M. Seaman.

52   Tombstone of centurion, found near Colchester.   The inscription reads, "M[ARCVS] FAVON[IVS] M[ARCI] F[ILIVS] POL[LIAE] FACILIS>LEG[IONIS] XX VERECVNDVS ET NOVICIVS LIB[ERTI] POSVERVNT.   H[IC] S[EPVLTVS] E[ST], Marcus Favonius Facilis, son of Marcus, of the tribe Pollia, centurion of the twentieth legion.   Verecundus and Novicius, his freedmen, erected [this].   He is buried here."   Colchester.   Shell Photographic Unit, London.

53   Modern Arles before World War II.   Commissariat Général au Tourisme.   Photo Aérienne Greff, Pilote et Opérateur R. Henrard.

55   The traditional ceremony of plowing around the boundaries of a projected town (relief from a monument erected in honor of the founding of Aquileia).   Aquileia.

56 Mosaic from the floor of an atrium at Oudna (*Uthina*), Tunisia, showing activities of country life on an estate. At the top are plowing and a barn with domestic animals; in the middle, a well with a sweep, where animals are being watered, and cultivation of the ground; at the right, a pastoral scene; elsewhere, hunting scenes. Le Bardo.

56 Oxen yoked to a cart (bronze statuette). Metropolitan.

57 Farm tools of the first century A.D., from the Villa Rustica, Boscoreale, near Pompeii. Chicago.

58 Farm animals (bronze statuettes). Metropolitan.

59 Relief from a funeral monument near Trier, Germany, showing tenant farmers with contributions—a hare, two fish, a kid, probably an eel, a cock, and a basket of fruit —to the owner or manager of the estate, who stands at the curtained door of his atrium. Trier.

60 Relief from a sarcophagus, in which an estate owner supervises plowing and hoeing, reaping grain, transporting it, grinding it, and baking bread. The metrical inscription reads, "D[IS] M[ANIBVS] S[ACRVM] L[VCIVS] ANNIVS OCTAVIVS VALERIANVS ‖ EVASI EFFVGI SPES ET FORTVNA VALETE ‖ NIL MIHI VOVISCVM EST LVDIFICATE ALIOS, Sacred to the spirits of the dead. Lucius Annius Octavianus Valerianus. ‖ I've escaped; got clean away. Lady Luck and Hope, farewell. ‖ Naught have I to do with you; on others work your purpose fell." Lateran. Anderson.

61 On each side of the marble altar called the *Calendarium Pincianum* is inscribed a rural calendar for three months. Below the zodiacal signs for the month are given the number of days and their hours, the date of the nones, the farm work to be done, and the festivals. The inscriptions are translated thus: "Month [of] January, thirty-one days, the nones on the fifth. Day, nine and a half hours; night, fourteen [and a half] hours. The sun is in Capricorn. [Under] the guardianship of Juno. Swampy land is drained, the willow and the reed are cut. There are to be sacrifices to the penates.

"Month [of] February, twenty-eight days, the nones on the fifth. Day, ten and a half hours; night, thirteen [and a half] hours. The sun is in Aquarius. [Under] the guardianship of Neptune. Fields are hoed. The surface of the vineyards is cultivated, reeds are burned. [The festivals are] Parentalia, Lupercalia, cara cognat[i]o, and Terminalia.

"Month [of] March, thirty-one days, the nones on the seventh. Day, twelve hours; night, twelve hours. The equinox on the twenty-fifth. The sun is in Pisces. [Under] the guardianship of Minerva. Vine stakes are arranged in the ground which has been dug. Ninety-day [wheat] is sown. [Festivals are] ship of Isis, rites for Mamurius, Liberalia, Quinquatria, Laving." Naples.

62   Bronze statuette of a farmer with plow and oxen, found near Arezzo in Etruria. Though of Etruscan workmanship, it resembles a farmer of early Rome. Museo della Villa di Giulio, Rome.

63   Mosaic from a richly decorated Roman villa at Zliten, Tripolitania. Below the villa the vilicus is supervising farm labor. At the lower left, a woman, probably the mistress of the villa, looks on. Tripoli. Soprintendenza Monumenti e Scavi in Libia, Archivio Fotografico della Libia Occidentale.

64   Relief from a funeral monument found in Neumagen, Germany (restoration), showing barrels of wine being transported in a rowing barge. One of the two steersmen is marking time by clapping his hands. Trier.

65   Fragment of a relief from a child's marble sarcophagus, showing cupids picking grapes preparatory to making wine. Musée d'Art et d'Histoire, Geneva, Switzerland.

66   The pressbeam of a wine press (restored) in the Villa of the Mysteries, Pompeii. Excavation and restoration of this villa were completed in 1930. It was named from a series of handsome frescoes believed to portray the initiation of a young woman into the cult of Bacchus. Alinari.

66   Olive trees near Monte Carlo, planted in rows with wide spaces between to facilitate picking the fruit. W. Thompson.

67   Shop of an oil merchant at Ostia. Huge jars embedded in the earth were used to store oil until it was sold. Anderson.

Roman ships represented in mosaic

68 With this mosaic of cat, partridge, ducks, and fruit, compare the much finer mosaic on page 216.   Vatican.   Archivio Fotografico Gallerie e Musei Vaticani.

70 Roman houses of the first half of the first century B.C., seen from the street (fresco from a villa at Boscoreale).   More of the room decoration from this villa may be seen on page 96.   Metropolitan.

72 The House of Castor and Pollux, Pompeii, bears this name because there is a painting in the main entrance which shows the twins holding their horses by the bridles.   Anderson.

72 House of the Golden Cupids, Pompeii, named from cupids engraved on gold foil under glass discs, which decorated a bedroom.   The peristyle slopes up to the steps at the left.   Masks and carved marble discs suspended between the columns and theatrical masks on hermae around the grounds contrast with the planting, which has been restored.   Alinari.

72 Three simple houses from the Marble Plan, or *Forma Urbis*, made by Agrippa in the time of Augustus and probably set up in the Campus Martius.   New maps were made from time to time as the city grew, the last one in the time of Septimius Severus (A.D. 203–211).   More than a thousand fragments of this map have been found and assembled in the Palazzo Braschi, and there is a replica in the Palazzo dei Conservatori, Rome.

73 Plan of a simple Roman house.

74 This reconstruction of the interior of the House of Cornelius Rufus, Pompeii, gives a good idea of the home of a well-to-do Roman.   Lehmann's *Kulturgeschichtliche Bilder*.

75 The House of the Silver Wedding, Pompeii.   It is so called because, as part of the celebration of their silver-wedding anniversary (1893), the King and Queen of Italy were present when some of the excavating was done.   Alinari.

76 Atrium of a house in Herculaneum.   Wooden panels and curtain such as these may have been used in Roman times to secure privacy from the street entrance.   Carbone & Danno.

76 The House of the Menander, Pompeii, is named for the Greek poet, whose portrait is on one wall.   Bromofoto, Milan.

77 Relief from the tomb of a cutler, L. Cornelius Atimetus.   Vatican.   Archivio Fotografico Gallerie e Musei Vaticani.

78 Doorway of the House of Loreius Tiburtinus, Pompeii.   The door on the left, which fits into a pivot in the threshold, is ancient.   The other door is a restoration.   G. Vetti.

78 Mosaic pavement of the vestibule of the House of P. Paquius Proculus, Pompeii. Alinari.

79 Replanted and restored peristyle of the House of the Vettii, Pompeii. The columns were found in a fair state of preservation; most of the roof has been restored. In the foreground, twin fountains in the form of cupids holding ducks once had jets of water spurting from the ducks' bills. Brogi.

80 A corner of the kitchen in the House of the Vettii. The kettle rests on a shelf where fire once burned. Cooking pots are on the floor. Alinari.

81 Summer dining room in the House of Carus, Pompeii. Probably the original beams above were not covered by a roof, and vines may have been trained up the pillars and over the top to provide shade. The raised ridge at the end of each couch was to hold the cushions in place. Alinari.

82 Model of an elaborate villa, known as the House of Pansa, Pompeii—exterior and interior views. Metropolitan.

82 Plan of the House of Pansa. Based on the plat, *Pompeiorum Quae Effossa Sunt, Corpus Inscriptionum Latinarum IV, Suppl.*

83 Doorway of the House of Pansa. Generally called this because of an election notice, the house is now believed to have been owned by Gnaeus Alleius Nigidius Majus. Anderson.

84 Floor plan of the House of the Surgeon, Pompeii. This house, built of square slabs of stone, is the best remaining example of typical, early Roman dwellings of the fourth and third centuries B.C. The plan shows later additions which do not alter the basic character of the house. Based on the plat, *Pompeiorum Quae Effossa Sunt, Corpus Inscriptionum Latinarum IV, Suppl.*

84 House of the Surgeon today.

85 Plan of a typical provincial villa of the corridor-house type, at Newport, Isle of Wight. Based on a plan from *Antiquaries Journal IX*.

85 Excavation of the same house.

85 Hypocaust of a building in Roman Verulamium. It is about two and one half feet high. St. Albans, England.

86 Roman water pipes and joints. British M.

86 Large brazier, found in the Stabian Baths, Pompeii. Similar smaller ones were the usual heating equipment of houses in Italy. Naples. Anderson.

87 Ruins of the imperial palace at Ostia. Anderson.

89 Street in Herculaneum. At the right, opus incertum, from which the facing has disappeared, contrasts with brickwork in the restored house beside it, which retains some of its original stucco facing. Carbone & Danno.

90 Model of insula at Ostia, made on the scale of 1:50 by the Italian architect Gismondi. Ostia had many such apartment houses, as did Rome in the second century A.D. Capitoline. Alinari.

91 Here in Pompeii are the characteristic features of a Roman street—ruts made by cart wheels, sidewalk, stepping stones, and fountain with a water tower which acted as a primitive hydraulic ram to increase water pressure. Michigan.

92 Three of a group of decorative panels showing cupids engaged in activities of commercial life, perhaps occupations of the Vettii, owners of the house. In the first panel, cupid fullers are treading cloth in a vat of cleansing solution, carding the cloth, inspecting it, and folding it for delivery.

In the next panel, cupid engravers work on either side of a furnace which is surmounted by a figure of Hephaestus, patron saint of metal workers. A cupid before the furnace is blowing a bellows. Behind him another cupid works at a small anvil, and nearby is a counter for the sale of jewelry, with three drawers partly open, and with two pairs of scales on top. At the left, two figures are working at an anvil. A seated woman purchaser, in the form of a psyche, waits while a cupid weighs gold.

In the third panel, cupids act as perfumers. A press produces fine oil; then the oil is boiled and mixed with essences before being bottled. It is stored in a cabinet or cupboard, on the top shelf of which is a figure, perhaps a divinity. Finally, perfumed oil is sold to a woman attended by a slave. Alinari.

93 Mosaic of the Battle of Issus, in which Alexander the Great defeated Darius and the Persians. This mosaic—one of the most famous of antiquity—was damaged in ancient times by an earthquake, and repaired with cement. The figure of Alexander, at the left, is fragmentary. Darius is in the center. It was discovered in 1831 in the House of the Faun, Pompeii, so named from the statue of a dancing satyr found there. Naples. Anderson.

94 Mosaic from the House of the Faun, Pompeii. Naples. Anderson.

95 Couch (restoration). Walters.

96 Agrippina, granddaughter of Augustus and wife of Germanicus. Naples. Brogi.

96 This room, set up with restored Roman furniture, was at one time on exhibition in the Metropolitan Museum. The frescoed walls were from a villa at Boscoreale, near Pompeii. Metropolitan.

97 Roman silver goblet with the figure of a philosopher holding a scroll. Cabinet des Médailles, Bibliothèque Nationale, Paris.

98 (Top right) Table. Toronto.

98 (Top left) Bronze table of the first century A.D., from Boscoreale. Chicago.

98 (Middle) Pedestal of a table, carved with griffins, acanthus leaves, and grapes. Naples. Alinari.

98 (Bottom) Chest. Naples. Alinari.

99 Mosaic from Pompeii, of fish and other sea creatures. Naples. Alinari.

100 The pieces in this mosaic from Roma Vecchia, a villa on the Appian Way, are so tiny that they produce the effect of a painting. Vatican. Anderson.

101 The elaborately decorated and well-preserved wall of the tablinum in the House of M. Lucretius Fronto, Pompeii. Anderson.

102 Lamp of baked clay, the commonest kind. Verulamium Museum, St. Albans, England.

102 Lamp with three spouts. Since the light from a single wick in the oil chamber of a lamp was slight and flickering, some lamps had as many as ten or twelve wicks. Walters.

102 Ornamental candelabrum, providing an elevated spot for lamps. Walters.

102 A bronze tripod table to hold small objects or a lamp. Naples. Alinari.

102 Elaborate bronze lamp from Pompeii, with two spouts, on a diminutive bronze table. Naples. Anderson.

103 Marble table of the imperial period, with bronze fittings. Metropolitan.

103 Metal lamp stand from Pompeii, with four hanging lamps. Naples. Alinari.

104 One of the panels of *Ara Pacis Augusti*. Here priests, magistrates, and vestal virgins made an annual sacrifice. From ruins of the altar itself and many detached fragments the entire structure has been rebuilt on the bank of the Tiber. A frieze around the altar shows a religious procession, of which this is a part. On each side of the entrance were symbolical reliefs, one of which is shown on page 8.

105 Statue of Augustus, found in the Villa of Livia at Prima Porta. The little cupid at his feet symbolizes Augustus' descent through Aeneas from the goddess Venus. Vatican. Anderson.

106   (Left) Head of a Roman girl.   Walters.

106   (Right) Head of a Roman baby, found in Volubilis, Morocco.   French Embassy Press & Information Division.

107   Funeral monument of a husband and wife.   Louvre.   Alinari.

108   Funeral monument of a couple—sometimes called Cato and Porcia—with right hands clasped as a sign of marriage.   Vatican.   Alinari.

110   A Roman family (table illustrating the formation of new households).

111   Agnates (table showing relationship through a common male ancestor).

112   Cognates (a graphic representation of blood relationships).

113   Part of a relief, probably from the sarcophagus of a municipal magistrate, depicting his final journey.   Two attendants precede the litter, in which sits the magistrate with wife and child.   A small litter, possibly for the child or for a shrine, is carried by four men.   Aquileia.

115   Tomb relief of a husband and wife.   Metropolitan.

116   Relief on a family tomb.   Boston.

116   Part of a roll of names of army officers.   Lateran.   Archivio Fotografico Gallerie e Musei Vaticani.

117   Tomb of Cecilia Metella, on the Appian Way, a mile and three-quarters from the San Sebastiano Gate of Rome.   Sixty-five feet in diameter and set on a square base, this circular tomb was erected in the time of Augustus.   The crenelated top was added in the thirteenth century, to make the tomb a fortress.   A marble plate facing the road reads, "CAECILIAE Q[VINTI] CRETICI F[ILIAE] METELLAE CRASSI, To Cecilia Metella, daughter of Quintus Metellus Creticus, wife of Crassus."   Anderson.

117   Part of a list of generals who were awarded triumphs.   The name Metellus occurs three times, one mention of which reads, "Q[VINTVS] CAECILIUS Q[VINTI] F[ILIVS] Q[VINTI] N[EPOS] METELLVS A[NNO] DCX[XXI] BALIARIC[VS] PROCO[N]S[VL] DE BALIARIB[VS] PR[?], Quintus Caecilius Metellus, son of Quintus, grandson of Quintus, proconsul, [called] Baliaricus on account of [his conquest of] the Balearic Isles in the year 631, pr. . . ."   Some of the names include cognomina ex virtute, as Baliaricus was added to the name Q. Caecilius Metellus. Years (in Roman numerals) are counted from the founding of Rome (*Ab Urbe Condita*), 753 B.C.   Subtracting the number given from 754, results in the date as we write it.   For example, A.U.C. 631 is 123 B.C., the year Metellus suppressed piracy in the Balearic Isles.

118 Inscription in honor of Lucullus: "L[VCIVS] LICINIVS L[VCII] F[ILIVS] LVCVLLVS CO[N]S[VL] PR[AETOR] AED[ILIS] CVR[VLIS] Q[VE] TR[IBVNVS] MILITVM AVG[VR] [T]RIVMPHAVIT DE REGE PONTI MITHRIDATE ET DE REGE ARMENIAE TIGRANE MAGNIS VTRIVSQVE REGIS COPIIS CONPLVRIBVS PROELIIS TERRA MARIQVE SVPERATIS CONLEGAM SVVM PVLSVM A REGE MITHRIDA[TE] [C]VM SE IS CALCHADONA CONTVLISSET OBSIDIONE LIBERAVIT, Lucius Licinius Lucullus, son of Lucius, consul, praetor, and curule aedile, military tribune, augur, celebrated a triumph over Mithridates, king of Pontus, and over Tigranes, king of Armenia, having defeated large forces of both kings in numerous battles on land and sea. His colleague, who had been defeated by King Mithridates when he went to Calchedon, he freed from siege."

119 Inscription in honor of Appius Claudius: "APPIVS CLAVDIVS C[AII] F[ILIVS] CAECVS CENSOR CO[N]S[VL] BIS DICT[ATOR] INTERREX III, PR[AETOR] II AED[ILIS] CVR[VLIS] II Q[VE] TR[IBVNVS] MIL[ITVM] III COMPLVRA OPPIDA DE SAMNITIBVS CEPIT SABINORVM ET TUSCORVM EXERCITVM FVDIT PACEM FIERI CVM PYRRHO REGE PROHIBVIT IN CENSVRA VIAM APPIAM STRAVIT ET AQVAM IN VRBEM ADDVXIT AEDEM BELLONAE FECIT, Appius Claudius Caecus, son of Gaius, censor, consul twice, dictator, interrex three times, praetor twice, curule aedile twice, military tribune three times. He took many towns from the Samnites. He routed the army of the Sabines and Etruscans. He prevented making peace with King Pyrrhus. In his censorship he paved the Appian Way and brought water into the city. He built the temple of Bellona."

119 Freedman and freedwoman (relief). Lateran.

120 Tombstone of a lady, shown reclining at a sepulchral banquet. The inscription reads, "D[IS] M[ANIBVS] CVRATIA DI[O]NYSIA VIX[IT] AN[NOS] XXXX H[ERES] F[ACIENDVM] C[VRAVIT], To the spirits of the departed, Curatia Dionysia. She lived forty years. Her heir had this made." Grosvenor Museum, Chester, England.

121 Inscription in honor of Pompey the Great: "CN[AEO] POMPEIO CN[AEI] F[ILIO] MAGNO IMPER[ATORI] ITER[VM], To Gnaeus Pompeius Magnus, son of Gnaeus, [hailed as] imperator for the second time."

121 Bust of Lucius Caecilius Jucundus, a banker of Pompeii. One of a pair of identical portrait hermae found in his house. Naples. Anderson.

123 Portrait bust of Julia, daughter of Titus, son of Vespasian, and wife of Vespasian's nephew. Terme. Anderson.

123 Bust of Publius Cornelius Scipio Africanus Major, found in a suburban villa, House of the Papyri, at Herculaneum. Naples. Anderson.

123 Head of a Roman girl, probably Octavia. Walters.

124 Bust of Marciana. Naples. Anderson.

125 Sarcophagus of Lucius Scipio Barbatus. The epitaph, which is archaic, is in Saturnian verse. Translated, it reads, "Cornelius Lucius Scipio Barbatus, son of his father Gnaeus, a brave and wise gentleman. His appearance was equal to his merit. Consul, censor, aedile he was among you. Taurasia and Cisauna he took from Samnium; he conquered all Lucania and brought away hostages." Vatican. Alinari.

126 Statue of a Roman matron, sometimes called Juno Pronuba, goddess of marriage, who was always represented as a severe and majestic figure. Lateran. Anderson.

127 Bronze bust of a woman, possibly the daughter of the Jewish king, Agrippa I. Naples. Alinari.

128 Busts of Haterius and his wife, from the mausoleum of their family, which was erected outside Rome. Lateran. Alinari.

129 Wedding scene from a sarcophagus (relief). Gods stand at the left, looking on while a sacrifice is prepared. At the right the bride and groom join hands in the wedding ceremony. In front of them is the camillus; at the rear, the pronuba. Church of S. Lorenzo fuori le Mura, Rome.

130 Relief from a sarcophagus. British M.

131 Relief from a sarcophagus. The hands of bride and groom, now lost, must have been clasped. Naples.

132 A Roman lady in the garb of a priestess. Villa of the Mysteries, Pompeii. Alinari.

133 The bride's mother and perhaps a sister watch while a maid dresses her hair (fresco). Naples. Alinari.

134 Relief from a sarcophagus, showing bride, groom, pronuba, and a male attendant at a wedding ceremony. British M.

135 Camillus, dressed in belted tunic and sandals (bronze statue). Conservatori. Brogi.

136 Part of a famous fresco, formerly called the Aldobrandine Nuptials, now believed to represent a ceremony of one of the mysteries. Vatican. Anderson.

137 The Marlborough Cameo, carved in sard on a background of black onyx, about an inch and a half wide. The bride's veil, the torch, the basket of fruit or nuts, and the wedding couch at the left indicate that this represents bringing the bride to her new home. Boston.

138 Statue of a woman wearing a palla.   Naples.   Alinari.

139 Statue of Antonia, Mark Antony's daughter.   Naples.   Alinari.

140 Baby with pet lamb.   Conservatori.

140 Statue, called *Innocence*, of a girl with pet dove and snake.   Capitoline.   Anderson.

140 Boy with pet dove.   Galleria Borghese, Rome.   Anderson.

141 Children's game (relief from a sarcophagus).   Vatican.   Archivio Fotografico Gallerie e Musei Vaticani.

142 Wax tablet, part of the birth certificate of Herennia Gemella, a girl born March 11, A.D. 128, in Roman Egypt.   Michigan.

142 Such charms were strung on a cord to form the crepundia.   Metropolitan.

143 Bulla.   Toronto.

143 Terra-cotta statuette of nurse and child.   Metropolitan.

143 Statuette of baby in a cradle, of Gallo-Roman workmanship.   Musée des Beaux-Arts, Beaune, France.

143 Baby's bottle.   Colchester.

144 Doll of terra cotta, horseman, woven rush fan, and dog.   Toronto.

145 Statue of mother and child who wears a bulla and holds a scroll.   Capitoline.   Anderson.

145 Activities in a little boy's life: as a baby, being fed while his father watches, and being carried in the arms of his father; as a child, playing with a goat and cart, and declaiming to his father (relief from a sarcophagus).   The inscription is "M[ARCO] CORNELIO M[ARCI] F[ILIO] PAL[ATINAE] STATIO P[ARENTES] FECER[VNT], To Marcus Cornelius Statius, son of Marcus, of the Palatine tribe, his parents built [this]."   Louvre.   Alinari.

146 Statue found on the Esquiline Hill.   Capitoline.   Anderson.

147 Bronze statue of a youth of the Julio-Claudian family, said to have been found at Rhodes.   Metropolitan.

148 Terra-cotta statuette of the first century A.D.   Soprintendenza alle Antichità, Taranto.   Carrano Gennaio.

Mosaic of a circus with an unusual spina

149 Paedagogus with children (terra-cotta group from Tanagra). Louvre.

150 Marble bust, probably Lucius, grandson of Augustus. Vatican. Alinari.

150 Head of a Roman girl. Terme. Anderson.

150 Roman school (relief found at Neumagen, Germany). Probably it represents a teacher instructing the sons of wealthy Romans who lived in Belgian Gaul. Trier. The Bettmann Archive.

151 Terra-cotta groups of children and attendants. British M.

152 The so-called cursive writing was used in correspondence and business. The Latin of formal inscriptions is the source of our capital letters. Michigan.

153 Writing instruments. British M.

154 Wax tablet with Greek characters. Roman boys learned to read and write Greek as well as Latin. British M.

155 Drawing instruments. W. Thompson.

155 Girl, formerly called Sappho, the Greek poetess (fresco from Herculaneum). Naples. Alinari.

155 Bronze bust of a famous philosopher and mathematician. Naples. Alinari.

156 The Temple of Athena, of which this is a model, was one of the most conspicuous sights on the Acropolis of ancient Athens. Metropolitan.

157 Tile found at Silchester, England, on which was scratched a bit of verse from Vergil, at the end of a complaint, perhaps about a fellow student or worker. It reads, "PERTACVS PERFIDVS CAMPESTER LVCILIANVS CAMPANVS CON-TICVERE OMNES," which probably means something like, "That rascally Pertacus has run away to the fields and Lucilianus went with him. All fell silent." The final words are the beginning of Dido's invitation to Aeneas to tell his story. Reading Museum and Art Gallery, Reading, England.

157 Boy wearing toga and bulla. Louvre. Caisse Nationale des Monuments Historiques.

158 The knife-grinder, Roman copy of a Greek statue. Uffizi. Alinari.

159 Terra-cotta relief from a columbarium at Isola Sacra, near Ostia. The smith is represented both as working and as selling something; above, products are displayed. Naples.

160 Relief from tomb of Lucius Vibius, with smith, tools used by locksmiths, and lock. Aquileia.

161 Barbarian prisoners (polychrome statues). Louvre.

162 Statuary group showing Orestes and his sister Electra, believed to be by Menelaus, a Hellenistic sculptor, freedman of M. Cossutius, who worked in Rome in the first century B.C. Terme. Alinari.

163 This statuette may have been the base of a lamp stand. British M.

163 Sleeping child, dressed in tunic and paenula, with lantern. Terme. Anderson.

164 Two reliefs from the tomb of a merchant of Moguntiacum (Mainz) showing slaves loading barrels of wine and sifting grain. Mainz.

164 Tombstone of a grain merchant(?) with relief of a grain measure and scoop. The doggerel inscription reads, "EXTERNIS NATVS TERRIS MONIMENTA LOCAVI ‖ ET ARVO NOBIS QUOD LABOR ARTE DEDIT ‖ PATRONO ET VNA CONIVGI FECI MEAE, I, born in foreign lands, erected this monument to my patron and also to my wife on the land which labor yielded from my trade." Museo Civico, Bologna. A. Stanzani.

165 Relief, on which the emperor's face has been restored with the features of Trajan. The error of this restoration is proved by the upper part of the relief (Terme), which shows the Temple of Venus and Roma, built by Hadrian, Trajan's successor. Lateran. Anderson.

166 Relief of breadmaking, from the tomb of the Secundinii at Igel, Germany. This is an elaborate funeral monument showing life in the home as well as the business (wholesale clothing) of the builders. Erected in the early third century A.D. Trier.

167 Relief from the tomb of Marcus Vergilius Eurysaces, outside the Porta Maggiore of Rome, uncovered in 1838, when a tower into which it had been built was torn down. Eurysaces was the owner of a large public bakery. Alinari.

168 Relief from a funeral monument at Neumagen, Germany. One maid combs the lady's hair, another presents a mirror, a third has a flask of perfume, and a fourth, of which only the lower part of the figure remains, holds a pitcher. Trier.

169 Grave relief of Greek workmanship. National Museum, Athens.

169 Leather tunic. Toronto.

169 Reconstructed litter. Only the metal parts—of bronze inlaid with silver and copper —are ancient. Capitoline.

169 Slave collar. The inscription reads, "SERVVS SVM DOM[I]NI MEI SCHO-LASTICI V[IRI] SP[ECTABILIS]. TENE ME NE FVGIAM DE DOMO PVL-VERATA, I am the slave of my master Scholasticus, *Vir Spectabilis* [an honorary title given to an officeholder of senatorial rank]. Restrain me so that I may not escape from Pulverata House."

171 Part of a mosaic of a circus, from a Roman villa at Nennig, near Trier, Germany. Trier.

173 Silver container for pepper, which the Romans imported from India. The container is said to have been found in France. British M.

174 Votive relief of priest of Cybele and of Attis, her lover, found in 1736 near Civita Lavinia (*Lanuvium*), Italy. His festival dress is Oriental and his diadem has me-dallions with two images of Attis and one of Sozon, the great god of Asia Minor. Around his neck hangs a small shrine with another image of Attis. In his right hand are a pomegranate and three twigs (symbols of fertility); in his left, a basket of fruit and a pine cone, sacred to Cybele. The flagellum symbolizes penance. Above and at the side are musical instruments—cymbals, tambourine, pipe, and flute—and a chest, probably containing mystic symbols of Cybele. Capitoline.

176 Mosaic floor of a Roman villa at Oudna (*Uthina*), Tunisia. Le Bardo.

177   Relief of a slave who is probably being freed. The figure in a toga holding fasces is a lictor, who accompanied the presiding magistrate. Collection Warocqué. Musée de Mariemont, Belgium.

178   Statue known as the Verospi Jupiter, from the name of a previous owner. Vatican. Anderson.

179   Bridge over the Tiber, north of Rome. Its four central arches belong to the ancient Mulvian Bridge, first built of stone in 109 B.C. Alinari.

180   The Palatine Hill today, with the Via Sacra in the foreground. Cl. Trincano, Collection Arthaud, Grenoble, France.

181   Part of an elegant Roman house (reconstruction).

182   Four bronze dupondii, worth perhaps two cents each. On the upper one is a portrait of Faustina the Younger, wife of Marcus Aurelius. The inscription reads, "FAVSTINAE AVG[VSTAE] P[IAE] F[EMINAE] AVG[VSTI] FIL[IAE], To Faustina Augusta, an upright woman, daughter of Augustus [Antoninus Pius]."

   The next coin probably dates from A.D. 84. On the obverse is a head of Domitian and the words, "IMP[ERATOR] CAES[AR] DOMIT[IANVS] AVG[VSTVS] GERM[ANICVS] CO[N]S[VL] X CENS[ORIA] POT[ESTATE] P[ATER] P[ATRIAE], Emperor Caesar Domitianus Augustus Germanicus, consul for the tenth time, with the power of a censor, father of his country." Reverse, a priest offering sacrifice to Minerva, with the legend, "S[ENATVS] C[ONSVLTO], By a decree of the senate."

   On the obverse of the third coin is a head of Claudius' father, Drusus, with his name, "NERO CLAVDIVS DRVSVS GERMANICVS IMP[ERATOR]." Reverse, Claudius seated on a curule chair with the olive branch of peace, but with warlike symbols below, and the legend, "TI[BERIVS] CLAVDIVS CAESAR AVG[VSTVS] P[ONTIFEX] M[AXIMVS] TR[IBVNVS] P[LEBIS] IMP[ERATOR] P[ATER] P[ATRIAE] S[ENATVS] C[ONSVLTO], Tiberius Claudius Caesar Augustus, Pontifex Maximus, tribune of the people, emperor, father of his country, by a decree of the senate."

   The date of the fourth coin is about A.D. 47. It bears a head of Claudius and the words, "TI[BERIVS] CLAVDIVS CAESAR AVG[VSTVS] P[ONTIFEX] M[AXIMVS] TR[IBVNVS] PL[EBIS] IMP[ERATOR], Tiberius Claudius Caesar Augustus, Pontifex Maximus, tribune of the people, emperor." Reverse, figure of the goddess of freedom with the legend, "LIBERTAS AVGVSTA S[ENATVS] C[ONSVLTO], Freedom under the imperial regime, by a decree of the senate." Library of the University of Edinburgh.

183   Painting of a Roman street near the Forum, showing the entrance of a Roman house and a glimpse of the atrium.

184 Athens today, seen from the modern stadium, with the Acropolis in the distance.

185 Two sides of a token of hospitality in the form of a ram's head. It identified a person entitled to be treated as a guest in a certain household.

185 Caryatids of the Porch of the Maidens, the Erechtheum, Athens. Royal Greek Embassy. V. Papaïoanou.

186 Procession of senators whose dress shows three different styles of wearing the toga (relief from *Ara Pacis Augusti*). Uffizi. Brogi.

187 Roman soldiers in dress uniform (relief). Behind them is a standard with an eagle. Louvre. Historical Pictures Service.

188 Statue of a Dacian king, apparently as a prisoner of war. Naples. Anderson.

188 Statue of a camillus. Metropolitan.

189 (Top) Relief of Roman officials before the temple of Jupiter Capitolinus. Louvre. Alinari.

189 (Bottom) Part of a relief made near the end of Domitian's reign to honor him. On his death, an attempt was made to alter it to honor his successor, Nerva. It appears not to have been set up publicly. Vatican. Archivio Fotografico Gallerie e Musei Vaticani.

190 Statue of Augustus as Pontifex Maximus. The hollow in which the missing hand was inserted is visible. Terme. Anderson.

191 Diagrams of togas.

Pieces of carved ivory used in a game

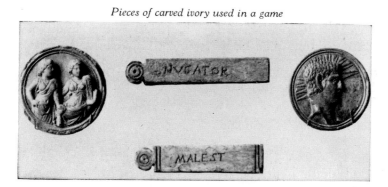

191 Bronze statue (called Arringatore) of an orator named Aulus Metilius. It was found at Sanguineto, near Lake Trasimeno, and is regarded as a masterpiece of Etruscan-Roman art. It probably dates from the second century B.C. Museo Archeologico, Florence. Alinari.

192 Drawing to illustrate the arrangement of the toga called *cinctus Gabinus*.

192 Statue, allegedly of Marcellus, conqueror of Syracuse. Capitoline. Alinari.

193 Statuette of genius dressed in a toga. Walters.

194 Bronze statuette about twelve inches high. Trier.

195 Relief from the Arch of Constantine in Rome. One of eight medallions taken from earlier monuments, each showing a hunting scene. Although the original sculpture is the work of artists of the Flavian period, the emperor's head has been replaced by a head of Constantine, with a halo.

196 (Top) Another portion of the relief at the bottom of page 189. The three figures to the left—probably a genius, Mars, and Roma—lead the emperor, while Minerva supports his arm. The bearded figure may represent the genius of the Roman Senate, followed by the genius of the Roman people. Soldiers and lictors are in attendance. Vatican. Archivio Fotografico Gallerie e Musei Vaticani.

196 (Center left) Three leather shoes found in London. British M.

196 (Center right) Wooden shoe sole. Vindonissa Museum, Brugg, Switzerland. Dr. R. Fellman.

196 (Bottom) Ivory foot wearing a sandal of the imperial period. Metropolitan.

197 Coin showing liberty cap and two daggers. The inscription reads, "EID[IBVS] MAR[TIIS], The Ides of March."

198 Traveler resting by the way (relief). Uffizi. Alinari.

199 Busts of eminent Romans: (Top left) L. Junius Brutus, leader of the revolution which substituted consuls for kings (bronze). Capitoline. Anderson.

199 (Top right) Lucius Verus, who shared the imperial power with Marcus Aurelius. Louvre. Alinari.

199 (Center left) Hadrian. Capitoline.

199 (Center right) Lepidus, who with Antony and Augustus formed the first triumvirate after Caesar's death. Vatican. Alinari.

199 (Bottom) Caracalla, eldest son of Septimius Severus, and his successor as emperor. Naples. Alinari.

200 Religious procession (relief from *Ara Pacis Augusti*). Uffizi. Brogi.

201 The central part of a relief from the altar of a temple of Neptune. A bull and sheep are led to sacrifice, and in the part not shown, there is a pig, making this a suove-taurilia. The presence of Mars and the attendant with palms indicate the celebration of a military victory. Louvre. Caisse Nationale des Monuments Historiques.

202 (Left) Statue of Ceres, with features sometimes attributed to Caesar's daughter, Julia. Vatican. Anderson.

202 Silver mirror from the House of the Menander, Pompeii. It was found in 1930, along with silverware, coins, and jewelry which apparently had been stored in the basement by the owner, while the house was being redecorated. Naples. Alinari.

202 (Right) Statue of a lady, perhaps the Empress Agrippina, dressed in tunic, stola, palla, and sandals, and seated in a cathedra. Capitoline. Anderson.

203 Brooches from Roman Britain. Colchester.

204 Family of Augustus (relief from *Ara Pacis Augusti*). Uffizi. Brogi.

205 (Top) Heads of Roman women with varied hairdresses. Terme.

205 (Center left) Bust, woman of the third century A.D. Toronto. Pringle & Booth.

205 (Center right) Bust of the Empress Messalina, wife of Claudius. Capitoline.

205 (Bottom) Bust of a woman of the first century A.D. Terme.

206 Hairpins of bone. Similar pins were made of gold, silver, or ivory.

206 Ivory combs, a comb case, and a hairpin. The lettering gives the name Modestina, and perhaps initial letters "V[IRGO] H[ONESTA] E[T] E[GREGIA], A fine, worthy girl." British M.

207 Ring of the second century A.D., made of dark-green glass, with a gold medallion showing a seated girl spinning, and a lamp on a table. Smithsonian.

207 Jewelry, mostly from Pompeii. Naples. Alinari.

208 Bronze shuttle, used in weaving. British M.

208 Scrap of Roman cloth. British M.

208   Model of a loom.   Capitoline.

209   Restoration of a relief from a temple of Minerva in the Forum of Nerva, Rome, of which only this relief and two Corinthian columns survive.   The relief honored Minerva as patroness of the arts and weaving.

209   Metal needles, similar to modern ones.   British M.

209   Iron scissors (found at Priene), needles in a bronze case, and a bronze thimble. British M.

210   Bakery at Pompeii.   Anderson.

211   Carbonized food of various kinds found in shops and houses of Pompeii.   Alinari.

212   Relief showing the abduction of Proserpina.   Below is a garland of fruits, probably symbolic of her mother, Ceres.

213   Relief of a shop.   While the butcher cuts the meat, his wife may be working on his accounts.   Staatliche Kunstsammlungen, Dresden.   Ministerium f. Volksbildung, Dresden.

214   Relief of a religious procession and ritual sacrifice of a pig, a sheep, and a bull.   Louvre.

214   Bronze statuette of pig and driver.   British M.

215   Mosaic of ducks and ducklings.   Metropolitan.

215   Mosaic of rabbit, mushrooms, and lizard.   Metropolitan.

215   Bronze statuette of little pig, from Pompeii.   Naples.   Alinari.

216   Mosaic picture in two panels from the House of the Faun, Pompeii.   Naples. Anderson.

217   Mosaic of goats.   Vatican.   Anderson.

218   Bread from Pompeii.   An oven full of bread, which had been put in to bake just before the bakers fled, was found in Pompeii.   Antiquarium, Pompeii.

218   Relief of mill turned by a horse and tended by a slave.   On one such mill in Pompeii, the wooden framework has been restored so that the mill can grind grain.   Vatican. Archivio Fotografico Gallerie e Musei Vaticani.

219   Hand mill for grinding grain in small quantities, from Pompeii (reconstruction). Kaufmann-Fabry.

219   Part of a bakery in Pompeii, showing the meta of one mill without the catillus and another mill with both upper and lower stones in position.   W. M. Seaman.

220   Samples of food found in Pompeii.   Naples.   Alinari.

221   Remains of a factory for preparing olive oil, in Madaure, Algeria.   W. Thompson.

221   Such an olive crusher, found in the Villa Rustica, Boscoreale, was designed to remove the pulp gently from the pits, which gave the oil a bad flavor if bruised.   Antiquarium, Pompeii.

222   Arbor of the House of Loreius Tiburtinus in Pompeii, with grapevines replanted. Below is a channel for water.   Avina P. Pompei.

223   Olive grove near Ariccia, Italy.   De Cou from Ewing Galloway, N.Y.

224   Mosaic floor, which shows remains of Roman food.   A cock's head, a wishbone, pieces of leafy vegetables, berries, cherries, nuts, fish bones, a snail's shell, a shrimp, and a lobster claw can be recognized.   Lateran.   Archivio Fotografico Gallerie e Musei Vaticani.   Anderson.

225   Relief from a tombstone at Neumagen, showing a family seated around a dining table.   Such variations from Roman custom in furniture, method of serving food, and costume were characteristic of life in Germany.   Trier.

226   Portable stove with a low iron frame supporting a hearth of cement, movable bars for broiling, and two circular frames to hold pans over a bed of charcoal.   Naples.

226   Bowls and jugs.   Toronto.

227   The large dish has a scroll border, with a figure of Minerva in high relief; it belongs to the Hildesheim hoard, comprising seventy articles of silver, which may have belonged to the Emperor Germanicus.   Berlin.

227   The smaller plate belongs to the Mildenhall Treasure, found in Britain in 1943. This silver was probably buried before a threatened invasion by the Picts and Scots in the fourth century A.D.   British M.

228   A tray, frying pans (one with a long, fixed handle, and one with a folding handle), a knife, and a cooking fork.   Toronto.

228   Utensils for serving wine—ladles, spoon, and strainers.   All the handles have ornamental details, and the perforations of each strainer are arranged in a pattern. British M.

229   Jug with a design of storks and leaves.   Walters.

229 Silver mug and shallow dish, dated about A.D. 100, from Tivoli (*Tibur*). Chicago.

230 Diagrams of arrangements of triclinium.

231 Bowls and plates from Pompeii—some repaired, some in the condition in which they were found. Naples. Anderson.

232 Glass from Pompeii. Most of it was originally fairly clear glass of uniform color. Time and burial have clouded it and changed its color; some pieces are now iridescent. Naples. Anderson.

232 Bowl from the Hildesheim hoard, with design of laurel branches with berries. Berlin.

233 Kitchen ware from Pompeii. Naples. Anderson.

233 Silver urn from the Hildesheim hoard, for mixing wine. Two griffins are at the base, and an acanthus design covers the entire surface. Little cupids in the vines are using tridents or lines to catch marine creatures. Berlin.

234 Silver dish, for serving eggs, or perhaps for molding pastries.

235 (Top) Bronze jug of the first century A.D. Walters.

235 (Bottom left) Shallow glass bowl with mottled colors. Metropolitan.

235 (Bottom right) Bowl of dark mottled glass. The Romans knew how to make beautiful glass. Smithsonian.

236 Bowl of pottery made at Arezzo, Italy. Boston.

236 Amphora of heavy glass from Cologne. The design is similar to that used in some of the finest modern glass. Mainz.

237 Two bowls and a jug of elaborately patterned colored glass found near the Rhine in the first century A.D. Bonn.

238 (Top) Handled cup. Metropolitan.

238 (Center) Bronze pitcher of the first century A.D. Walters.

238 (Bottom) This bronze pitcher is a cast of one in the Museo Nazionale, Naples. The handle is the figure of a young satyr, and its lower attachment is a female mask on a palmette. Chicago.

239 At the end of a banquet Romans are helped by their slaves. Naples. Anderson.

240 Bronze statue, the Discobolus, poised after having thrown the discus. Naples. Alinari.

241 (Top) Relief of fighters. Lateran.

241 (Bottom) Two wrestlers (statuary). This is probably Greek work. Uffizi.

242 Grounds of the palace of Septimius Severus, Rome. Anderson.

243 Part of a mosaic floor from the Baths of Caracalla, Rome. Lateran. Archivio Fotografico Gallerie e Musei Vaticani.

244 Dice and knucklebones used in games, and tesserae used for admission to the theater, from Pompeii. Naples. Anderson.

245 Bronze bathtub of the first century A.D. found at Boscoreale. Chicago.

246 Partial reconstruction of the elaborate baths at Bath, England. Until World War II this pool was still in use. British Information Services.

247 Dressing room of the Stabian Baths, so called because they are on "Stabian Street." These were the largest and oldest of the public baths in Pompeii.

Remains of buildings in Ostia, with theater portico at lower left

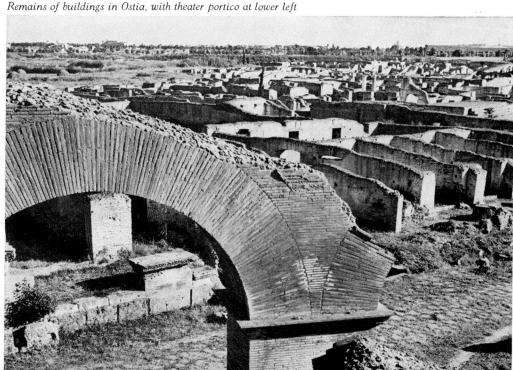

248 A view of the massive Baths of Caracalla in Rome. In recent years the remains of these baths have been used as a background for the staging of opera. Alinari.

250 Air heated by a furnace circulated under a mosaic floor. St. Albans (*Verulamium*), England.

251 Romans anointed their skins with oil after exercise, and slaves used strigils to scrape the oil from their masters' bodies. British M.

252 Plan of the Stabian Baths. Based on the plat, *Pompeiorum Quae Effossa Sunt, Corpus Inscriptionum Latinarum IV, Suppl.*

253 The cold plunge of the Stabian Baths. Alinari.

254 Plan of a small private bath at Caerwent (*Venta Silurum*), near Monmouth, England.

255 Arches of the Baths of Caracalla. Alinari.

255 Opera as recently presented at the Baths of Caracalla. The opera is *Poliuto*, by Donizetti. Compare the picture on page 248. Metropolitan Opera Guild.

256 (Middle) Representation of triangular tragic mask in ivory. British M.

256 (Lower right) Large satyr mask. British M.

256 (Remaining) Theatrical masks. Naples. Alinari.

257 Marble relief of the Hellenistic period, representing a writer contemplating comedy masks, while a woman looks on. The background is a temple wall decorated with garlands and discs. Lateran. Anderson.

258 Scene from a comedy (drawing of a fresco from Herculaneum). The actor at left center may be the Miles Gloriosus of Plautus' play and the man talking to him the slave Palestrio. The seated figures probably represent authors.

259 Mosaic of comic actors, from Pompeii. Naples. Alinari.

260 (Top) Theater at Sabratha, Libya. Semidetached columns of various colors form the back wall of the stage, which is broken by the three traditional entrances of Greek and Roman drama. Two stairways lead to the orchestra from the stage. The theater was built in the period of Augustus and repaired and restored in the third century. Arab Information Center, New York.

260 (Bottom) Model of the Sabratha theater, on the scale of 1:20, made by Giacomo Guidi. Capitoline.

261 Statuette of comic actor—probably portraying a runaway slave seated on an altar, where he has found sanctuary.   British M.

262 Fresco of a scene from a tragedy.   Lateran.   Anderson.

263 Mosaic of theatrical masks.   Capitoline.

263 Gigantic tragic mask of marble, from Rome.   Metropolitan.

264 Theater of Marcellus in Rome, begun by Julius Caesar, finished by Augustus, 13–11 B.C.   Enough of the building remains to give an idea of its original massiveness and magnificence.   Alinari.

265 Plan of a theater described by the Roman architect Vitruvius.

266 The large theater at Pompeii, built in the second century B.C. on the Greek plan, and remodeled in the time of Augustus.   It is at least a century older than any theater in Rome.   Alinari.

267 (Top) The small theater at Pompeii, built about 80 B.C. near the large theater.   The small one was roofed, to be used for entertainments with music.   Brunner & Co., Como.

267 (Bottom) This theater and a temple of Bacchus are all that remain at Sagunto (formerly Murviedro) in that part of Spain taken by the Romans from Carthage. Albert H. Travis.

268 Two reliefs from sarcophagi showing cupids in a chariot race, in which the spina with ova, dolphins, and metae are evident.   Vatican.   Anderson.

269 Scene of mythological chariot race (relief from a sarcophagus).   Oenomaüs, a king in Greece, did not wish his daughter Hippodamia to marry; so he required each of her suitors to compete with him in a chariot race.   Vatican.   Anderson.

269 Life-size statue of a charioteer.   The protective thongs worn around the body are clearly evident.   Vatican.   Anderson.

270 Restoration by Comm. G. Ripostelli of the Circus of Maxentius, on the Appian Way, built by Emperor Maxentius in the early fourth century A.D., in honor of his young son Romulus.   G. Mori.

271 An artist's conception of the Circus Maximus.

271 Mosaic, picturing a chariot race in the circus.   Museo Arqueológico, Barcelona, Spain.

272   Remains of the Circus of Maxentius.   Alinari.

273   Relief from a sarcophagus, depicting a chariot race of cupids.   Metae, ova, dolphins, and representation of a shrine on the spina are evident.   A ladder is placed against the platform which supports the dolphins, to facilitate turning them.   Vatican. Anderson.

274   Terra-cotta plaque showing a four-horse chariot race.   The protection for the body and legs of the charioteer is clearly distinguishable.   A charioteer in the lead has just rounded the spina.   British M.

276   A Roman chariot.   Capitoline.

277   Mosaic illustrating the uniforms of four syndicates (companies) of the circus.   Drivers of each company wore a different color.   Terme.   Anderson.

278   Racing chariot, called *biga*, because two horses drew it (marble sculpture).   Vatican. Anderson.

278   Ivory statuette of a charioteer.   Protection for the leg is distinct.   British M.

278   Model of a chariot.   Capitoline.

280   Terra-cotta plaque showing men fighting animals in the circus.   The box of the dator ludorum, the ova, and the statue on a pillar can be seen.   Terme.   Alinari.

281   (Top) Lion's head from a building.   Metropolitan.

281   (Bottom) Fresco from the House of the Vettii, Pompeii.   Anderson.

282   View of the Colosseum at night.   ENIT.

283   Bronze statuettes of gladiators.   British M.

284   (Top) A gallery of the Colosseum.   Anderson.

284   (Bottom) A gallery of the amphitheater at Pozzuoli (*Puteoli*).

285   Two views of the amphitheater at Pozzuoli.   Brogi.

286   Two sections of a mosaic of gladiators from a villa at Zliten, Tripolitania.   Soprintendenza Monumenti e Scavi in Libia, Archivio Fotografico della Libia Occidentale.

287   Tombstone from Ephesus of a gladiator, with protective equipment.   The wreaths indicate his many victories.   Berlin.

288 Exercise ground and barracks for gladiators, Pompeii.   Compare the same area in the aerial view on page 22.   Anderson.

289 Plan of the gladiators' barracks.   Based on the plat, *Pompeiorum Quae Effossa Sunt, Corpus Inscriptionum Latinarum IV, Suppl.*

290 The amphitheater in Verona, Italy.   V. Tosi, Verona.

291 (Top) The amphitheater at Italica, Spain.   Albert H. Travis.

291 (Bottom) Interior and underground galleries of the amphitheater at Capua, Italy. Alinari.

292 An ancient amphitheater in France has been repaired for modern use.   For a view of the exterior of the amphitheater and its surroundings in modern Arles, see page 53.

293 This amphitheater at Pompeii (the oldest one known) seated about 20,000 people. It was partially excavated before 1750.   When excavation was resumed in modern times, frescoes of gladiators were found on the outside wall, but these have since disappeared, and are known only from copies.   Brunner & Co., Como.

294 Reconstruction of part of the interior of the Colosseum by Duc, a French architect, in 1829.   *Fragments Antiques.*   J. E. Bulloz, Éditeur, Paris.

295 Interior of the Colosseum.   James Sawders—Combine.

295 Exterior of the Colosseum.   ENIT.

296 Reconstructions of the Colosseum—exterior and interior—made by Duc in 1829. *Fragments Antiques.*   J. E. Bulloz, Éditeur, Paris.

297 Elaborately decorated gladiator's helmet of bronze.   The holes around the ear flaps and the base of the crown were to permit sewing in a cloth lining.   Toronto.

298 Mosaic of net-fighters and opponents.   In the top panel the inscription, translated, reads, "Astyanax has conquered Kalendio."   Madrid.

299 Gladiator, from a villa at Zliten, Tripolitania (coarse mosaic).   Others from the same mosaic are shown on page 286.   Tripoli.   Soprintendenza Monumenti e Scavi in Libia, Archivio Fotografico della Libia Occidentale.

299 The famous Colchester vase, of pottery with barbotine decoration.   Someone scratched the names of gladiators on the vase after it was completed.   It was probably made in Colchester, where it was found in 1853.   Colchester.

301   Amphitheater at Verona.   The seats have been restored.   Brogi.

303   Amphitheater at El Djem, Tunisia.   W. Thompson.

304   The Roman Empire (map).

305   Fresco from Pompeii, picturing villas similar to some which have been excavated. Naples.   Alinari.

306   Tombstone of a shipbuilder and two freedmen.   The inscription reads, "P[VBLIVS] LONGIDIENVS P[ATRONO] L[IBERTVS] RVFIO P[VBLIVS] LONGIDIENVS P[ATRONO] L[IBERTVS] PILADES POSV[ERVNT] INPENSAM PATRONO DEDERVNT, Publius Longidienus and Publius Longidienus Pilades, freedmen, placed this in honor of their patron Rufius, and paid for it."   In the panel, the words read, "P[VBLIVS] LONGIDIENVS P[VBLII] F[ILIVS] AD ONVS PROPERAT, Publius Longidienus, son of Publius, is hurrying to his task."   Museo, Ravenna, Italy.   E.P.T. Ravenna.

307   Relief of a Roman vehicle drawn by two horses, probably a carruca dormitoria, since a passenger rides inside.   Maria Saal Dom, near Klagenfurt, Austria.

308   Relief of cart with one horse and one passenger, perhaps a cisium.   Trier.

308   Four-wheeled cart, passenger, and driver, from the tombstone of M. Viriatius Zosimus. Museo Lapidario, Verona, Italy.

308   Model of cart.   Capitoline.

309   Relief from a sarcophagus.   Apparently this gives two views of a vehicle and passengers.   The child playing is probably the same baby shown in the carriages. Museo Kircheriano, Rome.   Alinari.

310   Model of a carruca dormitoria, after various reliefs, including the one shown on page 307.   Capitoline.

311   Relief from a marble sarcophagus of the third century, representing a two-wheeled cart, probably a carpentum, used to convey images of the gods to and from the circus and for religious occasions.   The gods in relief on the sides are Jupiter and the twins, Castor and Pollux.   British M.

312   Plan of an inn in Pompeii.   Based on the plat, *Pompeiorum Quae Effossa Sunt, Corpus Inscriptionum Latinarum IV, Suppl.*

312   Remains of the shop of a seller of beverages in Ostia.   Traces of decorations can be seen on the wall over the stepped-back shelves.   Alinari.

313 Milestone. To show the distance from the golden milestone in the Forum of Rome, roads were marked with milestones, which have been found in large numbers throughout the Empire. This one is on the Appian Way, near Lanuvium, about twenty Roman miles from Rome. R. S. Rogers.

314 A business street of Ostia. Alinari.

315 The vault above the Stabian Gate of Pompeii has been restored. Anderson.

316 Writing materials. Toronto.

316 Two letters, one written on a wax tablet, the other on papyrus.

316 Manuscript in cursive Latin found in Egypt in 1922. The holes on the edge were for cords to seal the tablet of which this is one leaf. It is over six inches high, about five inches wide, and one-eighth inch thick. The text, translated, reads, "In the consulship of Marcus Claudius Squilla Gallicanus and Titus Atilius Rufus Titianus" [A.D. 127], "in the twelfth year of the Emperor Caesar Trajan Hadrian Augustus, when Titus Flavius Titianus was prefect of Egypt, acknowledgments of the births of children were received for record without judicial cognizance. Wherein there was written on tablet 8, page 2, in larger letters, when Lucius Nonius Torquatus Asprenas was consul for the second time with Marcus Annius Libo, and after other entries on page 9, under the date of March 27: 'Gaius Herennius Geminianus, whose census rating is 375 [thousand] sesterces, [declared] that a daughter, Herennia Gemella, was born to him on March 11, the mother being Diogenis Thermutharion, daughter of Marcus.' " Michigan.

317 (Left) Head, probably of Mark Antony—the imprint of an intaglio garnet gem; and the seal ring (found in Syria) which made the impression. The Oriental Institute of The University of Chicago.

317 (Right) Gold seal ring with a woman's head carved in sard, and an imprint of the seal. Metropolitan.

318 This statue of the Muse Erato, inspirer of love poetry, which was found near Tivoli, is probably a Roman copy of a statue by the Greek sculptor Praxiteles or his school. Vatican. Alinari.

319 Papyrus on the River Anapo near Syracuse, Sicily. Alinari.

320 This relief is from a temple altar or pedestal. The temple, believed from inscriptions to have been in the Circus Flaminius at Rome, was dedicated to Neptune by Domitius Ahenobarbus. Louvre. Caisse Nationale des Monuments Historiques.

321 Statue, possibly of Emperor Titus. Vatican. Alinari.

322   Marble statue of Polyhymnia.   Louvre.   Alinari.

322   Reconstruction of a relief, showing how a roll of manuscript was held as it was being read.   The young man has rolled up with his left hand the portion he has finished reading.

323   (Left) Bust called Vergil (perhaps erroneously).   It may be an Eleusinian deity. Capitoline.   Alinari.

323   (Right) Bust of Homer—an imaginative composition.   Naples.   Anderson.

324   (Left) Head of Julius Caesar.   British M.

324   (Right) Head of Cicero.   Vatican.   Archivio Fotografico Gallerie e Musei Vaticani.

325   Portion of a manuscript of Sallust's Histories.

326   (Left) Mosaic of Vergil, attended by the Muses Clio and Melpomene, supposed to be an actual likeness of the poet.   Found near Sousse, Tunisia.   Le Bardo.

326   (Right) Marble bust of Augustus as a young man.   Uffizi.   Brogi.

327   (Left) Model of a library, made by the architect Italo Gismondi, patterned after the library of Hadrian's villa at Tivoli, with architectural details from the library in Trajan's Forum.   The table rests on two pedestals similar to the supports of a sarcophagus in the Vatican.   The figure is the goddess Minerva, patroness of study and of libraries.   Cabinets at the sides of the room are for books.   Capitoline.

327   (Right) Marble bust of the Emperor Trajan, found in the Roman Campagna. British M.

328   Roads of the Roman Empire (map).

329   Hadrian's Wall near Housesteads, Northumberland—the longest section still standing.   The wall extended seventy-three miles from Solway Firth to Newcastle upon Tyne, forming a rampart against the barbarians on the north.   It is said to have been eight feet thick and as much as twenty feet high in some places.   Donald McLeish, London.

330   (Left) Mattock, which might have been used in making a roadbed.   Toronto.

330   (Right) Milestone which marked a boundary.   The inscription reads, "TERM[INVS] XV MILLIAR[IVS] A CONFINIBVS CIVIT[ATIS] VERONAE, Boundary fifteen miles from the limits of the city of Verona."   Toronto.

331   Roman bridge near Cori (ancient Cora) southeast of Rome.   Alinari.

Cart drawn by a donkey

331　Model of Roman wagon.　Capitoline.

332　Model, building the Appian Way.　Museum of Science and Industry, Chicago. U. S. Bureau of Public Roads, Department of Commerce.

333　Detail (roller) of the model on page 332.　U. S. Bureau of Public Roads, Department of Commerce.

333　Detail (stone carriers) of the model on page 332.　U. S. Bureau of Public Roads, Department of Commerce.

334　(Top) Roman road near Vienne, France.　Commissariat Général au Tourisme, Service de Documentation et de Propagande.　Goursat.

334　(Bottom) The broken line of the Aqua Claudia stretches across the Campagna outside Rome.　A fragment of a villa is in the central foreground.　Anderson.

335　The Acqua Paola in Rome, erected by Pope Paul V in 1612, drew water from the Aqua Trajana to supply Rome in his day.　Marble decorations came from the Temple of Minerva in the Forum of Nerva, and granite columns from the old church of St. Peter.　The inscription erroneously names as the fountain's source the ducts of Aqua Alsietina, whose waters—unfit for drinking—supplied the Naumachia Augusti. Anderson.

336　(Left) Public fountain, Pompeii.　W. M. Seaman.

336　(Top right) The pillar was a hydraulic ram to build up water pressure for the fountain below.　W. M. Seaman.

336　(Bottom right) Metal pipe joints.　Much Roman pipe was made of sheet lead rolled, with a folded joint, and was oval, rather than round like these pieces.　British M.

337　(Top) Called El Puente del Diablo, the Roman aqueduct at Segovia was in use from Trajan's time until recently.　The bridge portion is about half a mile long.　The rough-hewn granite blocks are laid without cement.

337　(Bottom) Arches of a Roman aqueduct at Maktar (*Mactaris*) in Tunisia.　Direction des Antiquités et Arts, Tunis.

338   A cistern, one of several on the Palatine, used for storing water in early times. R. Moscioni.

339   The mouth of the Cloaca Maxima can be seen from the Ponte Palatino, built in modern times not far from the ancient Pons Aemilius, now called Ponte Rotto.

340   The original Pantheon erected by Agrippa about 25 B.C. was burned in A.D. 80. Rebuilt by Domitian, it was destroyed by lightning during the reign of Trajan. The existing building dates from Hadrian's completely new construction, with later repairs and restorations. Its doors are the original bronze ones, repaired in the sixteenth century. The interior has seven niches for statues of the gods of the seven planets. The coffered ceiling of the dome reaches a height of 144 feet. Many eminent and famous people of modern times are buried in the Pantheon. ENIT.

341   Venus, from a Roman copy of the Venus of Cnidus by Praxiteles. Vatican.

341   Colossal marble head, from the Ludovisi Juno. Terme.

342   Altar to the lares of Augustus, with a carving in relief representing a sacrifice of a bull and pig. The participants have their togas drawn over their heads in the ritual manner. Capitoline. R. Moscioni.

343   Ludovisi Mars, part of a Greek marble group of the fourth century B.C. The cupid at Mars' feet is a Renaissance addition. In his hand Mars holds a sword with an animal's head on the hilt. Terme.

343   Statuette of a Roman goddess—called Fortuna, because of the cornucopia in her hand, or the Egyptian goddess Isis, because of her headdress. Walters.

344   Columns of the Temple of Artemis (Diana) in Jerash, Syria, once a Roman military outpost. The columns retain most of their ornate Corinthian capitals. Arab Information Center, New York.

345   (Top) Two temples in the Forum Boarium, the ancient cattle market, near the Tiber. The round temple was rebuilt in the early Empire, and again in the third century. The rectangular one, known as the Temple of Fortuna Virilis or Mater Matuta (a goddess of dawn), was built in the first century B.C. Alinari.

345   (Bottom) Marble relief representing the temple of Vesta, from the *Ara Pacis Augusti.* Uffizi.

346   (Left) Part of a statue of a vestal. Note the headdress and the veil. Terme. Anderson.

346   (Right) Base of a candelabrum, with the image of a goddess in Greek costume. Museo Nazionale, Naples. Alinari.

347 Relief from the Arch of Trajan at Beneventum, erected A.D. 115. Alinari.

348 (Left) Part of the marble statue of Venus Anadyomene, in which the goddess is represented as rising from the sea. Vatican. Alinari.

348 (Right) Marble statue of Diana, goddess of hunting, with a quiver of arrows on her shoulder, and a captured deer beside her. Louvre. Alinari.

349 Head of the marble statue known as Apollo Belvedere. Like his twin sister Diana (p. 348), Apollo carries a quiver of arrows. Vatican. Alinari.

350 Statue of Cybele, worshiped by the Romans as Magna Mater, in her classic pose, seated between two lions. Found at Rome. Naples. Alinari.

351 Roman copy of statue of Athena (Minerva) found at Velletri. The original was of Greek workmanship belonging to the period of Phidias. Capitoline. Alinari.

352 Marble statue of Apollo Musagetes (leader of the Muses), crowned with laurel and playing the lyre. Vatican. Alinari.

353 Statue of the Egyptian goddess Isis, bearing the rattle used in her worship. Naples. Alinari.

353 Six columns of the Temple of Jupiter, Baalbek, Lebanon, sixty-five feet high—said to be the tallest in the world. Individual blocks of stone in the columns weigh a thousand tons. Arab Information Center, New York.

354 Relief from the tomb of the Haterii, found in 1848 near Rome. The funeral couch of a woman stands in the atrium, the tile roof of which is shown. Back of the couch are the undertaker with a garland, and two mourning women; at the head of the couch, three seated figures (perhaps slaves), and at the foot, a mourner and a woman playing the flute. In front of the couch between two censers for incense are the mourning family, who are shown beating their breasts in grief. At the far right a slave is approaching. Torches, oil lamps, and candelabra light up the scene. Lateran. Alinari.

355 Another relief from the tomb of the Haterii, which represents the building of their elaborate mausoleum. A crane is operated by a treadmill run by slaves. The upper story is a chapel, the lower, the mortuary chamber. Lateran. Alinari.

356 Tomb erected by Hadrian for himself and his successors at Rome, now called the Castel St. Angelo. In ancient times there was a statue of Hadrian on the roof, which was replaced in 1752 by one of the Archangel Michael. Down to Caracalla, who died in 217, all Roman emperors were buried here. By the fifth century, the building had become a fortress, and was so used during the Gothic invasion and later. The last act of the opera La Tosca is set in this building.

357 Ancient tombs outside Rome, some of which have been restored. U. S. Bureau of Public Roads, Department of Commerce.

358 Streets lined with tombs were found outside each gate of Pompeii. Anderson.

359 (Top) Sepulchral altar, ornately carved. The inscription bears testimony to the favored position of some Roman slaves, since a woman erected this monument not only to her husband, but also to a favorite slave born in the household. Capitoline. R. Moscioni.

359 (Bottom) Two sarcophagi of white marble. Parc Trémeaux, Tipasa, Algeria. L. C. Briggs.

360 Relief from a sarcophagus, with a portrait medallion of mother and son inset in a representation of mythological figures, including cupids, centaurs, and satyrs. Louvre. Giraudon.

361 (Top) The tomb of the Scipios, on the Via di Porta San Sebastiano in Rome, was excavated in 1780. Perhaps originally a quarry, it consists of passages—formerly quite regular—carved in the rock. Sarcophagi of members of the family were placed here in the third to the first century B.C. In the first century A.D. a brick-walled tomb chamber was added for freedmen of the Cornelian gens.

361 (Bottom) Hut urns, in the shape of the original one-roomed houses of Italy.

362 A Roman burial chest for ashes of cremated bodies, with a pipe extending to the surface of the ground to permit the pouring of libations, and the same chest in place in grave. *Archaeologia*, Journal of the London Society of Antiquaries, Vol. XXXVI.

363 The Mausoleum of Augustus was built by that emperor in 28 B.C. for himself and his family. Most of his successors until the time of Nerva were buried there. Below the two-storied circular building containing the mortuary chambers was a square basement. Augustus was buried in a large central chamber, from which radiated fourteen smaller chambers. Above was a terraced mound of earth planted with cypresses and surmounted by a statue of Augustus. Via dei Pontefici, Rome. Alinari.

364 (Top) Relief from the tomb of a butcher from the Viminal Hill, Aurelius Hermia, and his wife Aurelia Philematio, who are shown with clasped hands. In the inscription each praises the other in glowing terms. British M.

364 (Bottom) Funeral portrait of a husband and wife, found at Flavia Solvia, Austria. The man, dressed in a toga, holds a scroll—probably the marriage contract. The scroll and the handclasp indicate a legal Roman marriage, even though the woman was evidently a foreigner. She wears the characteristic dress of Noricum (Austria). Landesmuseum Johanneum, Graz, Austria.

365   (Top) The niches of this columbarium at Ostia retain a few broken funerary urns. Alinari.

365   (Bottom) Burial urns of pottery, found in Britain.   Colchester.

366   (Top) Tombstone of a Roman soldier.   The inscription reads, "C[AIO] TITIENO C[AII] F[ILIO] LEM[ONIAE] FLACCO SEVIRO EQVO PVBLICO AEDILI, To Gaius Titienus Flaccus, son of Gaius, of the tribe Lemonia, member of the commission of six, knight, aedile."

366   (Bottom) Relief from a tomb.   Toronto.

368   Memorial inscription of a military tribune, which, translated, reads, "To Marcus Tarquitius Saturninus, son of Titus, of the tribe Tromentana, prefect of a shield-armed cohort, first centurion of the Twenty-second Legion, tribune of the Third Legion.   The Twenty-second Legion [set this up]."   Below is the added inscription of an official who repaired the stone a hundred years or more later: "Gnaeus Caesius Athictus, appointed to the centumviri, at his own expense repaired the statue damaged by the collapse of the Temple of Mars, and restored it to the public."   Lateran. Archivio Fotografico Gallerie e Musei Vaticani.

369   Relief from the tomb of C. Julius Maternus, in which the deceased is pictured as living, but larger than life, half reclining beside a table spread with food.   He holds a goblet in his hand.   His wife sits beside the table in an easy chair, holding a basket or dish.   Two servants are waiting on the table.   Museum Wollraff-Richartz, Cologne, Germany.

370   Relief from a sarcophagus, showing the funeral of a woman.   Musicians lead the cortege, followed on the upper level by two mourners with hair unbound, who make gestures of grief.   The husband and two sons follow the bier, where the dead woman lies on an elaborately decorated couch.   Professional mourners follow at the rear. Museo Aquilano, Abruzzi, Italy.   Alinari.

371   Statue, sometimes thought to represent Junius Brutus, holding the wax masks of two deceased family members.   Palazzo Barberini, Rome.   Alinari.

372   The tomb of Gaius Cestius Epulo, near the Porta San Paolo (ancient Porta Ostiensis), is in the form of an Egyptian pyramid, though much smaller.   It is built of concrete, faced with marble slabs.   Inscriptions on the sides identify the builders, and mention that Cestius, who died before 12 B.C., was praetor, tribune of the people, and one of the Septemviri Epulones, priests who had charge of solemn sacrificial banquets.   Anderson.

374   A lar, dressed in girdled tunic and high boots, holding aloft in one hand a drinking horn, and in the other a libation saucer.   Metropolitan.

376 Mosaic of a variety of Roman ships, from Medeina (*Altiburos*) in Algeria. Le Bardo.

381 Bronze lantern, with hemispherical cover that can be raised and lowered. The sides were originally enclosed with transparent material such as horn, bladder, or linen. British M.

382 Stylus of carved ivory, found in an early tomb at Eretria, on the island of Euboea. British M.

383 Roman settlers in Germany, perhaps veteran soldiers, paying rents to a Roman agent, or perhaps paying money to a banker (relief found at Neumagen). Trier. The Bettmann Archive.

385 Cameo of modern Italian workmanship, still in the shell from which it was carved. Apollo and the chariot of the sun was a favorite theme of classical art. American Museum of Natural History, New York.

386 Bronze head of Augustus, found at Meroë in the Sudan. Egyptian influence is evident, especially in the eyes. Charles Skilton Ltd., London. British M.

390 (Top) Statuary group found near Hadrian's wall, known as the Corbridge lion, with a sheep the lion has killed. Corstopitum Museum, Corbridge, England.

390 (Bottom) The Civil Forum of Pompeii, seen from the south. Just inside the arch the pedestal of a statue can be seen. There was probably also a statue of Tiberius on top of the arch. ENIT.

392 (Top) Medallion with laurel-crowned heads of members of the Roman imperial family, above the imperial eagle and two cornucopias.

392 (Bottom) Famous mosaic of doves perched on the basin of a fountain, from Hadrian's Villa near Tivoli. This copy of a work by Sosos of Pergamum was mentioned by Pliny in his *Natural History*. As a result, the work is often called "Pliny's Doves." Capitoline. Alinari.

394 Side view of the restored curia in the Roman Forum. Compare with the front view on page 29. W. M. Seaman.

395 Animals fighting in the circus (mosaic). At the left, a rider on an elephant provokes a fight between his mount and a bull tethered to a ring. At the right, another rider on a camel leads a lion on a leash. Vatican. Archivio Fotografico Gallerie e Musei Vaticani.

397 Mosaic of lion hunt, from a building in Leptis Magna. Soprintendenza Monumenti e Scavi in Eritria, Archivio Fotografico della Libia Occidentale.

398 Roman jewelry was often very beautiful and made with great skill.   Close inspection reveals highly developed craftsmanship in metalworking.   Toronto.

399 Marble statue of a vestal virgin holding a vessel for libations.   She stands by the flame symbolic of Vesta as goddess of the hearth.   Uffizi.

400 Shrine in the House of the Vettii, Pompeii.   The middle figure is a genius with face resembling Nero's.   He is holding a libation saucer and an incense box.   On either side are lares with drinking horns.   Many shrines were decorated with two serpents, representing the genii of the master and mistress of the household.   The single-crested serpent in this painting probably indicates that the head of the household was unmarried.

406 Mosaic floor of a commercial building, probably a shipping warehouse, Ostia.   The square-rigged sails and the rudder of Roman ships are evident.   Le Bardo.

415 A canal filled with water is the spina of the racecourse in this mosaic of a circus.   There is an obelisk in the center, and the goal posts are clearly discernible.   Lack of perspective makes the carceres at the left seem to lie on the ground.   Musée des Beaux-Arts, Lyons, France.

419 Ivory discs and pieces shaped like labels, for use in a game played by the Romans.   Although this game is now understood only imperfectly, it was probably somewhat like backgammon.   The pieces shown are numbered on the reverse.   Those inscribed *Nugator* (trifler) and *Malest* (bad luck) bear low numbers.   Higher-numbered pieces with complimentary inscriptions have also been found.   British M.

425 Ostia, seen from the theater; an arch of the portico is visible in the left foreground.   Paul M. Rietsch from Black Star.

433 A small portion of mosaic floor of baths near Porta Romana, Ostia.   Anderson.

440 Mosaic showing dancing girls and musicians performing in an inn.   Respectable travelers avoided staying at such places whenever possible. Vatican.   Archivio Fotografico Gallerie e Musei Vaticani.

444 Reconstructed oil press on the Via degli Augustali, Pompeii.

445 A fibula, perhaps of the sixth century B.C., found in Praeneste.   It is important because the inscription engraved on it is probably the earliest Latin extant in any form.   The lettering runs from right to left, and means "Manius made me for Numerius."

447 Even utilitarian objects such as this lock were often beautifully decorated by the Romans.   British M.

450   Replicas of four bronze scale weights from a set of six, from Pompeii.   Representing weights of one to ten pounds, they may have been used for weighing goats' milk.   Naples.   Chicago.

452   Head of a man sometimes thought to be Marcus Agrippa, Augustus' son-in-law, who was given extraordinary powers by the emperor.   Capitoline.   Anderson.

454   (Top) The large Tuscan atrium of the House of the Faun, Pompeii, is in the foreground.   The statue from which the house took its name has been set up in the impluvium.   In the background are the pillars of the first of two peristyles.   Anderson.

454   (Bottom left) Marble head of a little Roman boy, dating from the first century A.D.   Boston.

454   (Bottom center) Bronze statuette of a baby holding a bunch of grapes.   Metropolitan.

454   (Bottom right) Polychrome statue of a boy thought to be Annius Verus, child of Marcus Aurelius and his empress, Faustina the Younger.   Uffizi.   Alinari.

464   Decoration from the tombstone of a shoemaker, found in Rome near Porta Fontinale.   Two lasts for shoes are pictured, one inside a boot.   The regular beginning of a tomb inscription, D M for DIS MANIBUS, "to the spirits," appears on both sides of the monument.   Conservatori.

466   Head of Pompey the Great, found in Pompeii.   Naples.   Anderson.

468   Model of a Roman ship.

470   Clay figurine of a domestic cat with collar and bell.   Rome.   Chicago.

471   Tomb of the Haterii, near Rome.   For other views of this elaborate mausoleum, see pages 128, 354, and 355.   Alinari.

472   Marble bust, probably of Marcus Agrippa (63–12 B.C.).   Uffizi.

473   Vestal virgin.   Naples.

A scene at an inn

TOPICAL LIST OF ILLUSTRATIONS

An oil press

Fibula from Praeneste

Lock from an ancient door

450

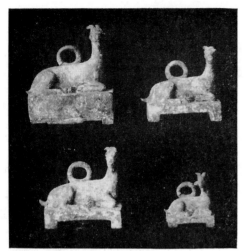
Scale weights in graduated sizes

Portrait of a Roman

MUSEUMS

American Museum of Natural History, New York

Antiquarium, Pompeii

Aquileia. Museo Archeologico, Aquileia, Italy

Berlin. Staatliche Museen, Berlin

Bonn. Rheinisches Landesmuseum, Bonn, Germany

Boston. The Museum of Fine Arts, Boston

British M. The British Museum, London

British S. British School at Rome

Cabinet des Médailles, Bibliothèque Nationale, Paris

Capitoline. Museo Capitolino, Rome

Chicago. Chicago Natural History Museum

Colchester. The Colchester and Essex Museum, Colchester, England

Conservatori. Palazzo dei Conservatori, Rome

Corstopitum Museum, Corbridge, England

Galleria Borghese, Rome

Galleria Nazionale d'Arte Moderna, Rome

Grosvenor Museum, Chester, England

King's College Museum, University of Durham, Newcastle upon Tyne, England

Landesmuseum Johanneum, Graz, Austria

Lateran. Museo Laterano, Rome

Le Bardo. Musée Alaoui, Le Bardo, Tunisia

The Library of the University of Edinburgh, Edinburgh, Scotland

Louvre. Musée National du Louvre, Paris

Madrid. Museo Arqueológico Nacional, Madrid, Spain

Mainz. Römisch-Germanisches Zentralmuseum, Mainz, Germany

Maria Saal Dom, Klagenfurt, Austria

Metropolitan. The Metropolitan Museum of Art, New York

Michigan. Kelsey Museum of Archaeology, University of Michigan, Ann Arbor

Musée d'Art et d'Histoire, Geneva, Switzerland

Musée de Mariemont, Belgium

Musée des Beaux-Arts, Beaune, France

Musée des Beaux-Arts, Lyons, France

Museo, Ravenna, Italy

Museo Aquilano, Abruzzi, Italy

Museo Archeologico, Florence, Italy

Museo Arqueológico, Barcelona, Spain

Museo Civico, Bologna, Italy

Museo Civico, Foligno, Italy

Museo della Villa di Giulio, Rome

Museo Kircheriano, Rome

Museo Lapidario, Verona, Italy

The Museum of the American Numismatic Society, New York

Museum of Science and Industry, Chicago

Museum Wollraff-Richartz, Cologne, Germany

Naples. Museo Nazionale, Naples

National Museum, Athens, Greece

The Oriental Institute of The University of Chicago

Palazzo Barberini, Rome

Reading Museum and Art Gallery, Reading, England

Smithsonian. The Smithsonian Institution, Washington, D.C., National Collection of Fine Arts

Staatliche Kunstsammlungen, Dresden, Germany

Stadtmuseum, Vienna

Terme. Museo Nazionale delle Terme, Rome

Toronto. The Royal Ontario Museum of Archaeology, Toronto, Canada

Trier. Rheinisches Landesmuseum, Trier, Germany

Tripoli. Museo, Tripoli, Libya

Uffizi. Galleria Uffizi, Florence, Italy

Vatican. Musei Vaticani, Rome

Verulamium Museum, St. Albans, England

Villa Albani, Rome

Vindonissa Museum, Brugg, Switzerland

Walters. Walters Art Gallery, Baltimore

Winchester City Museum, Winchester, England

A view of the House of the Faun, Pompeii, is shown above; below are portrait statues of Roman children

INDEX

Shoemaker's lasts

Pompey

468

Model of a Roman ship

470

Image of a cat

Tomb of the Haterii family

Probably M. Agrippa

Priestess of Vesta

ACKNOWLEDGMENTS

To all who have contributed to the illustration of *Roman Life* cordial thanks are given. For the courtesy which permits reproduction of the pictures on the pages cited, grateful acknowledgment is made to the following, to whom credit is also given in the Descriptive List of Illustrations, on pages 400–440.

The Colchester and Essex Museum, Colchester, England, and Shell Photographic Unit, London, 52

The Colchester and Essex Museum, 37 top, 143 lower right, 203, 299 right, 365 bottom

Commissariat Général au Tourisme, Service de Documentation et de Propagande, 50, 53, 334 top

Corstopitum Museum, Corbridge, England, 390 top

De Cou from Ewing Galloway, N.Y., 223

Direction des Antiquités et Arts, Tunis, 337 bottom

ENIT (Italian State Tourist Office), Chicago, 282, 295 bottom, 340, 390 bottom

E. P. T. (Ente Provinciale per il Turismo), Naples, 22

E. P. T. (Ente Provinciale per il Turismo), Ravenna, 306

E. P. T. (Ente Provinciale per il Turismo), Rome, 29 top

Dr. R. Fellman, 196 middle right

French Embassy Press & Information Division, 106 right

Historical Pictures Service, 187

Kaufmann-Fabry, 219 top

Kelsey Museum of Archaeology, University of Michigan, 91, 142 top, 152, 316 bottom right

King's College Museum, University of Durham, Newcastle upon Tyne, 51 top

The Library of the University of Edinburgh, 182

Donald McLeish, London, 329

The Metropolitan Museum of Art, 56 bottom, 58, 70, 82 top, 82 center, 96 bottom, 103 top, 115, 142 bottom, 143 top center, 147, 156, 188 right, 196 bottom, 215 top right, 215 bottom left, 235 left, 238 top, 263 bottom, 281 top, 317 center right, 317 right, 374, 454 bottom center

The Metropolitan Opera Guild, 255 bottom

Ministerium f. Volksbildung, Dresden, 213

Musée Alaoui, Le Bardo, Tunisia, 56 top, 176, 326 left, 406

Musée d'Art et d'Histoire, Geneva, Switzerland, 65

Musée des Beaux-Arts, Beaune, France, 143 top right

Musée des Beaux-Arts, Lyons, France, 415

Musée de Mariemont, Belgium, 177

Museo Archeologico, Aquileia, 55, 113, 160

Museo Arqueológico, Barcelona, 271

Museo Arqueológico Nacional, Madrid, 30, 298

Museo Capitolino, 42 right, 90, 169 top right, 174, 208 right, 260 bottom, 263 top, 276, 278 bottom right, 308 bottom, 310, 327 top, 331 bottom

Museo Civico, Bologna, 164 right

Museo Nazionale, Naples, 61

The Museum of the American Numismatic Society, New York, 35 right

The Museum of Fine Arts, Boston, 116 top, 137, 236 top, 454 bottom left

The Oriental Institute of the University of Chicago, 317 left, 317 center left

Press Association, Inc., 25

Reading Museum and Art Gallery, Reading, England, 157 left

Reuter-photo, P. A.—Reuter Features, Ltd., London, 24 top

Rheinisches Landesmuseum, Bonn, Germany, 237

Rheinisches Landesmuseum, Trier, Germany, 59, 64, 166, 168, 171, 194, 225, 308 top

Paul M. Rietsch and Black Star, 425

Römisch-Germanisches Zentralmuseum, Mainz, Germany, 164 top left, 164 bottom left, 236 bottom

The Royal Ontario Museum of Archaeology, 98 top right, 143 top left, 144, 169 bottom left, 205 lower left, 226 bottom, 228 top, 297, 316 top left, 316 top right, 330 right, 330 left, 366 bottom, 398

James Sawders—Combine, 295 top

W. M. Seaman, 17 bottom, 51 bottom, 219 bottom, 336 top left, 336 top right, 394

The Smithsonian Institution, National Collection of Fine Arts, John Gellatly Collection, 207 top, 235 bottom right

Soprintendenza alle Antichità, Taranto, Italy, 148

Soprintendenza Monumenti e Scavi in Eritria, Archivio Fotografico della Libia Occidentale, 397

Soprintendenza, Monumenti e Scavi in Libia, Archivio Fotografico della Libia Occidentale, 63, 286 left, 286 right, 299 left

Staatliche Museen, Berlin, 227 left, 232 bottom, 233 bottom

Albert H. Travis, 267 bottom, 291 top

U.S. Bureau of Public Roads, Department of Commerce, 332, 333 left, 333 right, 357

Walters Art Gallery, Baltimore, 95, 102 bottom left, 102 center, 106 left, 123 bottom, 193, 229 top, 235 top right, 238 middle, 343 right

Winchester City Museum, Winchester, England, 21 bottom

Special thanks are extended to the following, who helped in securing photographs not available commercially.

J. S. P. Bradford, Pitts River Museum, Oxford, England

British, French, and Italian Consulates

F. E. Brown, Jonathan Edwards College, Yale University (formerly professor in charge of School of Classical Studies, American Academy in Rome)

École des Beaux-Arts, Paris

Gertrude French, Chicago

Dorothy K. Hill, The Walters Art Gallery

Italian State Tourist Office, Chicago

The London Society of Antiquaries

Paul L. MacKendrick, University of Wisconsin, to whom thanks are also due for his critical reading of the text

H. W. Poulter, The Colchester and Essex Museum, Colchester, England

The Royal Greek Embassy

W. M. Seaman, Michigan State University

The Society of Antiquaries of Newcastle upon Tyne

Edith Swanson, Chicago